£4

This publication is licensed to A.KRST, a company registered in the United Kingdom under company number 14799105. The contents of this book are protected under international copyright laws and other intellectual property rights.

No part of this publication may be reproduced, distributed, or transmitted in any form or by any means, including photocopying, recording, or other electronic or mechanical methods, without the prior written permission of the publisher, except in the case of brief quotations embodied in critical reviews and certain other non-commercial uses permitted by copyright law.

Requests for permission to reproduce any part of this book should be sent to info@a-krst.com.
The views and opinions expressed in this book are those of the authors and do not necessarily reflect the official policy or position of A.KRST Limited.

Every effort has been made to ensure that the information contained in this book is accurate and up to date at the time of publication. However, the publisher and authors do not accept any responsibility or liability for any errors or omissions, or for any consequences arising from the use of the information contained in this book.

ISBN 978-1-7394903-0-0

Cover design by Ricardo Sorzano and Kieran Trestain
Interior design by Ricardo Sorzano and Kieran Trestain

Copyright © 2023 A.KRST Limited. All rights reserved.
Produced in the United Kingdom

WELCOME TO THE MUSIC BUSINESS BLUEPRINT

Your ultimate guide to achieving success in the vibrant and ever-evolving world of music. Whether you're a budding musician, aspiring producer, or seasoned industry professional, this comprehensive resource is your go-to companion for navigating the intricacies of the music business.

Inside these pages, you'll find a wealth of knowledge and insights from our team of industry experts and seasoned business consultants. We've carefully crafted this guide to provide you with a practical roadmap for excelling in the music industry, regardless of your level of experience.

From the foundational principles of the music business to the latest innovations shaping the industry, we leave no stone unturned. Dive into essential topics such as music publishing, distribution, branding, and legal considerations, and discover the strategies and tactics used by successful artists and industry veterans.

Our goal is simple: to empower you with the knowledge, tools, and strategies you need to thrive in this competitive landscape. We've distilled our collective expertise and years of experience into this guide, ensuring that it serves as an indispensable resource for anyone looking to make their mark in the music industry.

So, whether you're just starting out and seeking guidance on building your career from the ground up or a seasoned professional aiming to stay ahead of the curve, the Music Business Blueprint is here to support you every step of the way.

Table Of Contents:

VII - Acknowledgement

VIII - Preface

IX - How To Use This Book

X - The Music Business Blueprint Resource Guide

CHAPTER 1: MUSIC INDUSTRY INTRODUCTION

2 - History Of The UK Music Industry

3 - International Impact Of UK Music

4 - Setting Trends With International Collaborations

5 - Digital Transformation

6 - Case Study: Dave & Central Cee

7 - Entertainment's Impact On Creative Professionals

8 - Careers and Networking

10 - Becoming A Business

11 - The Role Of A Music Manager

12 - Industry Insight: Thor Sutherland

15 - Case Study: G Frsh

16 - Artist & Repertoire (A&R)

17 - Industry Insight: Hannah Edmonds

19 - Case Study: Glyn Aikins and Riki Bleau - Shaping the UK Music Industry

21 - Navigating A Competitive Industry

22 - Building Relationships

23 - Pro Tip: Finding Opportunities

25 - Utilizing Linkedin To Network

27 - Job Search Strategies

28 - Pro Tip: After The Spotlight

CHAPTER 2: PILLARS OF THE INDUSTRY, ARTIST, PRODUCERS & ENGINEERS

30 - What Is A Music Artist

31 - Case Study: Kano

32 - Case Study: J. Cole And The Artist Way

33 - The Role Of A Record Producer

34 - Industry Insight: Sphero

36 - Case Study: Steel Banglez

37 - Case Study: Fumez The Engineer

38 - Industry Insights: Lotes, Executive Producer And Founder Of Bl@ckbox

40 - Music Production Software & Digital Audio Workstations

42 - Pro Tip: What Makes A Good Engineer
44 - Industry Insights: Mikey Joe

CHAPTER 3: PUBLISHING, DISTRIBUTION AND LABELS

48 - Introduction To Music Publishing
51 - Royalty Management And Distribution In The UK
53 - Types Of Income That Can Be Generated Through Music Publishing
54 - The Benefits And Challenges Of Self-Publishing
55 - Copyright Law And Music Publishing In The UK
56 - Exploiting Your Own Copyrights
57 - Case Study: Chance The Rapper
58 - The Role Of The Publisher In Exploiting And Promoting Your Compositions
59 - The Benefits And Challenges Of Working With A Publisher
60 - Types Of Publishing Agreements
61 - Pro Tip: Negotiating A Fair Publishing Agreement
62 - Case Study: Kamille
63 - Ownership Of Compositions And Masters
64 - Publishing Administration And Covers
65 - Samples And Clearing Rights
66 - Releasing A Remix Of A Song In The UK
68 - How to Legally Clear a Sample For A Song Or Beat In 2023
70 - Royalties And Sync Fees
71 - Factors That Can Affect The Amount Of Royalties And Sync Fees
73 - Music Distribution
74 - Types of Music Distribution Models
75 - Sound On
77 - Pro Tip: Distribution Strategy
78 - Distribution Deals
79 - Case Study: Aj Tracey Utilizing Distribution
80 - UPC Barcodes And ISRC Codes In The Music Industry
81 - Metadata
82 - Industry Insights: Craig Evans, Head Of Hip Hop At Believe
84 - The Major Labels vs Independent Label
86 - Industry Insights: Despa Robinson, Cultural Icon & BE83 Founder
88 - Types of Record Deals
90 - Key Record Deal Terms
93 - Case Study: The Inspiring Story Of Independent Artist Bugzy Malone
95 - Pro Tip: Deal Or No Deal?

CHAPTER 4: LEGAL SIDES OF THE INDUSTRY

98 - Lawyers

99 - Pro Tip: Choosing The Right Lawyer

100 - Contracts In The Music Industry

101 - Pro Tip: Reviewing And Negotiating Contracts

103 - Understanding Management Contracts

106 - Pro Tip: Other Types Of Industry Contracts

107 - Enforceability Of Contracts

108 - Case Study: Ivorian Doll

117 - Industry Insights: John Sorzano, Sports And Entertainment Lawyer

119 - Case Study: The Agreement Between Russ Millions And Pressplay Media

120 - Pro Tip: Audits

121 - Case Study: Chamillionaire And The Hidden Funds Introduction

122 - Case Study: Rihanna vs Accountant

CHAPTER 5: SYNC AND BRAND PARTNERSHIPS

124 - Sync Licensing

125 - Why Is Sync Licensing Important For Musicians And Visual Media Creators?

126 - Pro Tip: Key Terms And Concepts Related To Sync Licensing

127 - Case Study: Sync and Vince Staples' Success

128 - Brand Partnerships

128 - Case Study: Central Cee x Trapstar

129 - Industry Insights: Ephraim Yeboah, Head Of Partnerships At Ground Up Chale

131 - Pro Tip: Reach Decision makers Of Companies On LinkedIn

133 - Case Study: AJ Tracey And His Partnership With Tottenham Hotspur

134 - Case Study: Skepta x Havana Club

135 - Case Study: Krept & Konan x Puma

136 - Pro Tip: Be Brand Ready

137 - Navigating Brand Guidelines As An Industry Professional

138 - Financial management

139 - Financial Planning For Music Projects

140 - Accounting And Record-Keeping For Music Businesses

141 - Case Study: J2K - The Entrepreneurial Pioneer in the Music Industry

142 - Case study: Fredo and Kick Game

144 - Case Study: The Entrepreneurial Journey Of Krept A Musician's Success In Business

146 - Pro Tip: Negotiating And Managing Collaborations

CHAPTER 6: MARKETING, BRANDING AND PUBLICITY

148 - Introduction To Marketing And Branding

149 - Brand Identity

150 - Pro Tip: The Concept Of "Shop Windows"

151 - Case Study: Virgil Abloh And "Design Language"

153 - Pro Tip: Critical Thinking

154 - Industry Insights: Emma Rose, Multi Genre DJ

156 - Building A Social Media Presence

157 - The Dilemma Of Clout Chasing

158 - Marketing On TikTok

159 - Pro Tip: Growing Your Audience And Getting Your Music Shared

161 - Understanding And Utilizing The TikTok

163 - Tik Tok x Spotify integration

164 - Marketing On Instagram

165 - Understanding YouTube

167 - Pro Tip: The YouTube Algorithm

168 - Platforms vs Independence

169 - Music Promotion On Reddit

170 - Discord For Musicians

171 - Pro Tip: Content Calendar

172 - How To Create A Wikipedia Page For An Artist

173 - Creating A Professional Website

174 - Playlist On Spotify

175 - The Spotify Popularity Index

176 - Pro Tip: Understanding When To Release Music

178 - Crafting A Campaign

181 - Case Study: Stormzy's Marketing and Branding Strategies for 'Gang Signs & Prayer'

182 - Case Study: Central Cee's "Wild West"

184 - Case Study: Adele's Marketing and Branding Strategies for "25" Album

186 - Music Videos

187 - Pro Tip: Being Resourceful With Music Videos

188 - Content Outside Of Music Videos

189 - Videographers (In House Media)

190 - Industry Insights: J-Mal, Founder Of JFX Visuals

193 - Treatments

194 - EPKS

196 - Pro Tip: Be Ready - One Sheets & Assets

197 - Decks: Elevating the Artist's Business Arsenal

198 - Radio promotion in the UK

199 - Industry Insights: DJ Limelight, Radio Pioneer & National Icon

201 - Pro Tip: Create At Least 5 Version Of Your Releases

202 - Music Public Relations And Media Relations

203 - Pro Tip: How To Write A Music Press Release

204 - Pro Tip: Press Training

205 - Industry Insights: Millie May, Music publicist

CHAPTER 7: TOURING AND LIVE EVENTS

208 - How To Book And Promote Shows

209 - Touring And Live Events

210 - Touring Budgets And Financial Management

211 - Logistics For Tours

212 - Case Study: Big Narstie's Successful Independent Touring Strategy

213 - Navigating Legal And Insurance Issues For Live Music Events

214 - Case Study: Tragedy at Brixton academy

216 - Pro Tip: The Golden Rules For Ticket Sales

217 - Working with Marketing Agencies

219 - Pro Tip: Marketing Activations

221 Case Study: Fredo Unfinished Business Album Launch

223 - Pro Tip: The Marketing Plan For A Live Show/Tour

224 - Case Study: Lancey's Immersive Experience

CHAPTER 8: INNOVATION IN THE INDUSTRY

228 - Blockchain And The Music Business

230 - Case Study: Ard Adz & His NFT Release On Opulous

232 - AI For Musicians

234 - Pro Tip: Custom GPTS

235 - Pro Tip: Staying Up To Date On Industry Trends

236 - Case study: Tencent Music Entertainment's Ai- Generated Vocal Tracks

237 - Case Study: JME's Alternative Approach To Trends In The Music Industry

CHAPTER 9: SOCIAL AND POLITICAL AWARENESS

240 - Social And Political Awareness

241 - Ethics And Social Responsibility In The Global Music Industry

242 - Engaging With Social And Political Issues

243 - Representation
244 - Case Study: The Impact of Childish Gambino's "This Is America"
245 - Case Study: The Met Police And YouTube's Efforts To Monitor And Remove Music Videos Of London's Rap And Drill Artists
247 - Case Study: The Impact Of Drill Music On Youth Culture: Krept & Konan's Short Film
248 - Case Study: Lowkey And The Pro-Israel Campaign To Silence Him
249 - Mental Health And Music
250 - Pro Tip: Healthy Habits
251 - Maintaining Work-Life Balance And Avoiding Burnout
252 - Setting Boundaries
253 - Public Pressure / Calling Out
254 - Case Study: The Closure Of Radar Radio

AFTERWORD
256 - Conclusion
257 - References
261 - About the Authors

Acknowledgments:

We extend our heartfelt gratitude to our families for their unwavering support and encouragement during the writing process. We could not have completed this book without their constant love and understanding. We would like to thank the following individuals who helped with the read-throughs of the early material, providing us with invaluable feedback and perspective that greatly improved the book. We would also like to express our sincere appreciation to the individuals in the music industry for generously sharing their valuable insights and contributions, which allowed us to elevate this book to new heights:

- Despa Robinson
- Dj Limelight
- Kaiden
- Kaila
- Thor Sutherland
- Emma Rose
- Millie May
- Jmal
- Tony Weeks
- Ephraim Yeboah
- John Sorzano
- Hannah Edmonds
- Sphero
- Lotes
- Mikey Joe
- Kyle
- Liban

Preface:

The music industry has long been an enigmatic and ever-changing landscape. With the advent of technology and digital platforms, it has become increasingly difficult for artists and industry professionals to remain up to date, navigate the complex terrain of music production, promotion, and distribution. However, with the right guidance and expertise, anyone can thrive in this dynamic field.

In this comprehensive guide to the music business, Kieran Trestain and Ricardo Sorzano share their collective knowledge and experience to provide invaluable insights into the inner workings of the music business. Drawing on their diverse backgrounds and unique perspectives, they offer practical advice on everything from securing recording deals and building a brand, to navigating legal issues and developing a sustainable career in music. What sets this book apart from others is its emphasis on all roles played within the industry. Kieran and Ricardo recognize the importance of creating opportunities for individuals from all walks of life, regardless of their background or credentials.

They offer practical strategies for breaking down barriers and promoting greater inclusivity and opportunities within the industry. Whether you're an aspiring artist, producer, manager, or industry professional, this book is an essential resource for anyone looking to succeed, with transferable principles to all areas of work life.

At its core, this book is a testament to the power of perseverance and determination. Kieran and Ricardo's personal stories serve as powerful reminders that anyone can achieve success in music, regardless of their background or level of formal education. They demonstrate that with the right mindset, the right knowledge, and the right support, anything is possible.
So whether you're a seasoned industry veteran or a newcomer to the world of music, we hope that this book will serve as a valuable resource and source of inspiration for you. We believe that by sharing our knowledge and experience, we can help to create a more innovative music industry that truly benefits everyone involved.

How To Use This Book.

This book is designed to provide a comprehensive guide for all those involved in the music business, whether you are an aspiring artist, a music industry professional, or simply someone interested in learning more about the industry.

Made up of five categories, the book is designed to provide you with specific information and insights.

1. **General information:** These pages provides an overview of the industry, including its history, structure, and key players. It also covers the latest trends and technologies in the industry. If you are new to the industry or have little experience, we recommend reading these sections thoroughly. However, if you are already familiar with the industry, you can skip this section.
2. **Strategies:** These pages breaks down the strategies for success in music, taking an action oriented approach to the education. It covers everything from artist development to marketing and promotion. The strategies outlined in this section are essential for anyone looking to thrive in the industry.
3. **Case studies:** Provides real-life examples of success stories and references to drive home the facts we are teaching. The case studies cover different aspects of the industry, including artist management, record labels, and music publishing.
4. **Pro Tips:** These pages features opinion-based tips from the authors, Kieran Trestain and Ricardo Sorzano. The tips are based on their experiences and insights into the industry.
5. **Industry insights:** The pages titled industry insight includes conversations with industry experts from around the world. These experts share their valuable insights and years of knowledge gained from working in the industry. The insights provided in this section are invaluable and can only be gained through years of experience.

To get the most out of this book, we recommend reading it from cover to cover. However, if you are short on time, you can focus on the categories that are most relevant to you. The book is designed to be a reference guide that you can return to time and time again.

We hope that you find this book informative and valuable. Our goal is to provide you with the knowledge and strategies you need to succeed in the industry. Remember, success in the music business is not just about talent. It's about having the right information, strategies, and mindset. This book provides you with all of these things and more. Good luck on your journey to success in the music industry!

The Music Business Blueprint Resource Guide

Along with The Music Business Blueprint, we have developed a free resource guide that is designed to help you effectively apply the knowledge and insights gained from this book. The provided templates serve as practical tools to assist you in various aspects of the music sector.

Customizing The Templates

The templates provided are flexible and can be customized to suit your specific needs. Whether you're an independent artist, a label executive, a music producer, or involved in any other role within the industry, these templates can be adapted to match your goals and requirements. To personalize the templates, you can use a PDF editor or even import the document into design platforms like Canva, allowing you to add your unique touch.

It's important to remember that these templates are versatile tools meant to be applied within the context of your individual circumstances and objectives. As you navigate the dynamic landscape of the music industry, you may find that certain templates are more applicable to your current situation than others. Feel free to modify and adapt them as needed to align with your goals.

Ongoing Resources

This collection of templates is just the beginning. Our commitment to your success means that we will continue to provide updates and new resources to ensure that you have access to the latest tools and strategies in the ever evolving music business landscape. Use these templates as a foundation, but don't hesitate to explore additional strategies and tactics that align with your unique journey.

We're excited to support you as you navigate your path in the music business. Keep an eye out for new resources and updates, and let's work together to make your music career thrive.

ACCESS ALL THE AVAILABLE RESOURCES DIRECTLY AT WWW.A-KRST.COM

THESE TEMPLATES ARE INTENDED FOR CUSTOMIZATION AND GUIDANCE PURPOSES ONLY AND DO NOT CONSTITUTE LEGAL OR PROFESSIONAL ADVICE.

CHAPTER 1
INTRODUCTION TO THE UK MUSIC INDUSTRY

The History Of The UK Music Industry

The UK music industry has a long and rich history. The origins of music on the British isle can be traced back to the medieval period, when minstrels and troubadours performed for upper class in castles and town squares. In the 16th and 17th centuries, music became increasingly popular in the UK, with the rise of opera and classical music. The 18th and 19th centuries saw the development of popular music genres such as folk and jazz, and the emergence of the music publishing industry.

The 20th century brought significant changes including the rise of recorded music and the growth of the music publishing industry. The 1950s and 1960s saw the rise of popular music genres such as rock and roll, and the period defined as the British Invasion, with bands like the Beatles and the Rolling Stones storming the world and gaining international fame. The 1970s and 1980s saw the rise of more genres such as punk, new wave, electronic music, and the emergence of a DIY independent music scene.

In the 1990s and 2000s, the industry continued to evolve, with the rise of digital music and the growth of streaming services. Today, the music business is a major contributor to the UK economy, and is known for its diverse range of music genres and artists. The industry continues to face challenges, such as the impact of digital technology on revenue streams and the need to adapt to changing market conditions. Despite these challenges, the UK music business remains a vibrant and important part of the UK cultural landscape.

Uk Music Timeline

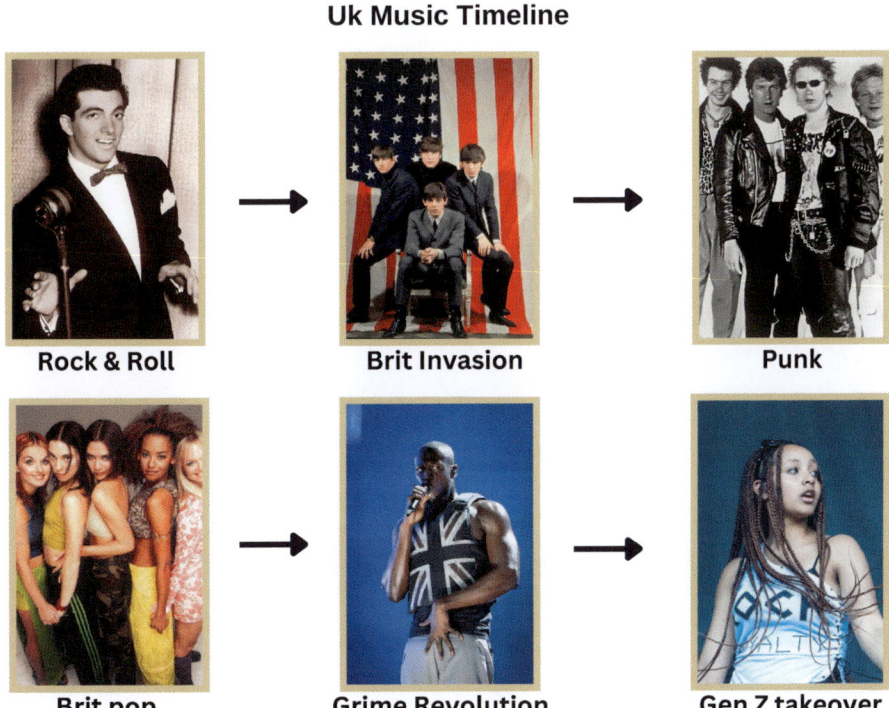

International Impact Of UK Music

As we delve into the world of music, it is important to acknowledge the impact of specific genres and their sub-genres on the industry as a whole. UK Rap and Grime, has had a significant influence on not only the UK's music scene, but on global music culture.

One of the key factors that set the genres apart in the beginning was the DIY nature and strong call to independence. This allowed artists to experiment with their sound outside of the mainstream and push the boundaries of what was considered popular music. It paved the way for the emergence of other independent genres, such as UK drill, trap, and Afroswing.

One of the most recognized names to emerge from the genre is Skepta. Winner of the Mercury Prize in 2016 for his album "Konnichiwa", Skepta is known for his reflective and socially conscious lyrics, which address issues such as race, inequality and police brutality. He also founded the independent record label Boy Better Know, which has artists such as Frisco, Shorty, Dj Maximum, Jammer and JME. Skepta was just one example of leading figures in the scene that took their success in music and the swing of the cultural pendulum towards new British music, and left their mark as independent entrepreneurs.

The grime scene and the sub-culture it has birthed, such as UK Drill, have continued to influence the sound of some of today's biggest stars, most notably New York native Pop Smoke, who played a pivotal role in shifting the landscape of drill internationally, staying connected with Uk producers and artist, and the roots of the sound he was developing. Central Cee, encapsulated the impact of Uk music perfectly, one of his recent international collaborative tracks, Eurovision, with saw artist such as Rondodasosa, Baby Gang, A2Anti, Morad, Beny Jr, Ashe 22, and Freeze Corleone all on the same track.

We have seen iconic hip-hop labels such as Def Jam Records, invest heavily into UK music with a new division, lead by respected artist Wretch 32 as the creative director. Stormzy's signing under this new venture underscores the global appeal of UK talent, and just how important they are the label's future success. Wretch's journey from artist to creative director mirrors the evolution of UK music, where artists become influential decision-makers.

Central Cee　　　　　　　　　　**Skepta**

Setting Trends With International Collaborations

With a history of being trendsetters and early adopters of new sounds, the UK continues to be a melting pot of diverse musical genres, attracting artists and audiences from all over the world. The scene has attracted attention from global artists seeking to collaborate with emerging British talent.

One such collaboration is between the Canadian rap superstar Drake and prolific UK artists such as Skepta, Giggs, Jorja Smith and Central Cee. These partnerships exemplify the growing recognition of British musicians on the international stage.

Jamaican dancehall artist Popcaan has found common ground around the world with some massive songs in his catalogue. His affinity with the UK can be seen across his collaboration with artists such as J Hus and Giggs. The cross-cultural collaborations that blend the distinct sounds of both regions have not only enriched the UK's music scene but have also broadened the appeal of British artists in the global market.

Nigerian Afrobeat sensation Burna Boy is another massive talent that has gained immense popularity in the UK, resulting in fruitful collaborations with British artists and producers. These partnerships have solidified the UK's position as a global music hub that welcomes diverse influences and facilitates cross-cultural exchanges.

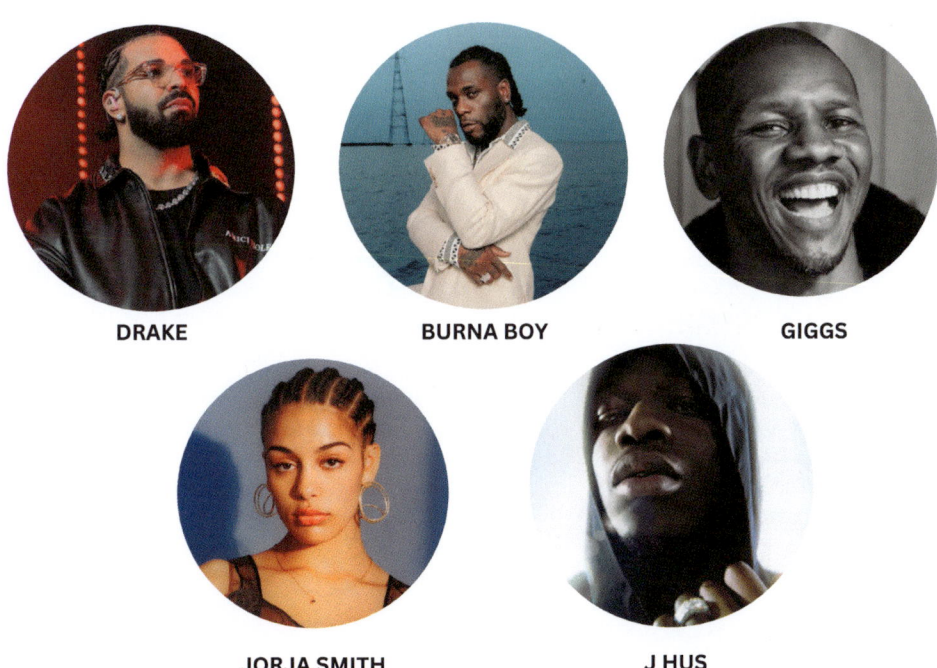

Digital Transformation

The emergence of digital platforms in the early 2000s transformed the music scene, enabling artists to reach a wider audience through platforms like YouTube. Today, modern platforms like TikTok and Instagram have revolutionized the discovery process for artists, with many labels and organizations now signing and collaborating with talent discovered on these platforms.

PinkPantheress is an artist from the UK who gained recognition for her unique sound and style. She first gained attention in 2021 with her single "Just for me," which quickly went viral on TikTok. This led to her signing with Parlophone Records, one of the UK's most prominent record labels, and a string of successful releases followed. PinkPantheress was recently named the winner of the BBC's Sound of 2022 poll, cementing her status as one of the most exciting new talents in the industry. Her success is a testament to the power of digital platforms like TikTok in shaping the industry and the opportunities they provide for emerging artists to be discovered.

The UK's music scene continues to be a melting pot of diverse musical genres and international collaborations. The emergence of new sounds such as Amapiano, Jersey Club, Drill, and Alternative Hip Hop music, allows more music boundaries and fusion to occur, cross pollinating an already diverse pot with more flavour. The UK's position as a powerhouse in the global music industry ensures that its influence on global music trends will remain enduring and significant.

Emerging New Sounds

The UK's music landscape has continually evolved with the emergence of new and exciting sounds. Various noteworthy music genres have gained traction in the UK and beyond.

Afrobeat: The rise of Afrobeat in the UK music scene has been a significant cultural shift. Influenced by traditional African rhythms and Western music styles, Afrobeat has captured the hearts of British audiences and has become a driving force in shaping contemporary popular music.

Drill: Drill, known for its gritty lyrical content and trap-influenced beats, has emerged as a raw expression of urban life in the UK. It has resonated with the younger generation and provided a platform for artists to share their experiences and perspectives on social issues. As recent as 2023, we have seen the fusion of Jersey Club music into trend setting new music from emerging UK artist such as Nemzzz, among many other new comers. The space within Drill has begun forming it's own lane and has gained momentum with the UK's youth culture.

Alternative Hip Hop: The UK's alternative Hip Hop music scene remains a hub for creative experimentation and innovation. Taking heavy inspiration from alt American artist and innovate pioneers. Often heavily involved in avant garde creative pursuits such as film and fashion, we see these artist connecting on online communities and developing the new mainstream sounds of the future. The UK has a long-standing tradition of producing alternative music, fusing together genres like indie rock, experimental pop, and drum and bass.

Case Study: Dave + Central Cee

Dave and Central Cee, joined forces for their first official collaboration, **"Split Decision."** The project between the British rap heavyweights resulted in a ground breaking achievement on the Official Singles Chart. With tracks showcasing the distinctive creative voice and vision of each artist, whilst simultaneously contributing to its widespread appeal among fans of British rap music.

Their unique styles, lyricism and instrumental selection resonated with audiences, with "Sprinter" making a tremendous impact in its opening week on the Official Singles Chart. It debuted at Number 1, marking Dave's third chart-topping single and Central Cee's first. The song amassed an impressive 108,200 chart units, including a ground breaking 13.4 million streams, setting a new record for a rap single.

Dave and Central Cee's collaboration benefited from its popularity on streaming services, making it the biggest week of streams for a UK rap single ever. "Sprinter" not only dominated the summer charts but also etched its name in the history books. It became the longest-running UK Rap track to hold the Number One spot, an impressive feat that showcased the enduring appeal of Dave and Central Cee's masterpiece. The icing on the cake came when the song spent an incredible 10 consecutive weeks at the top of the Official Singles Chart.

For Dave, "Sprinter" marked his third Number One track, solidifying his status as a British rap heavyweight and adding another gem to his crown of achievements, including Brit and Mercury Prize wins. Central Cee, on the other hand, celebrated his first chart-topper, a significant milestone in his burgeoning career. The song's monumental success extended to amassing a grand total of 812,000 UK chart units and an astounding 105 million UK streams, a testament to its enduring popularity.

Their live debut of the EP at Glastonbury in June was a standout moment, where they brought the magic of "Sprinter" to life for an eager audience. The success of "Sprinter" extends beyond the chart rankings, as it has also brought attention to the UK rap scene as a whole. The success of "Split Decision" has created a blueprint and drawn attention to the potential for future collaborations between established and emerging artists within the scene.

Entertainment's Impact On Creative Professionals

The success on the global stage has led to increased collaborations with brands. Stylists and designers have experienced a surge in demand as artists become influencers, shaping trends and expanding into new industries. The demand for captivating content and elevated fan experiences have diversified the roles of video and production teams, photographers, set designers, editors, animators and Ai prompt engineers are becoming indispensable team members.

The rise of UK music has also put the spotlight on talented music producers and engineers who work behind the scenes. More producers are taking to the charts and building personal brands that speak just as loudly as the artists. The demand for high-quality production has increased, providing more opportunities for these professionals to shine. Their expertise is essential in translating artists' visions into stunning visual experiences.

The Evolution Of Jobs In The Global Industry

The global music industry has undergone significant transformations over the years, following a massive shift in the pandemic and further fuelled by advancements in technology and changing consumer preferences. These changes have not only revolutionized the way music is created, distributed, and consumed but also led to the emergence of new job economies within the entertainment sector.

As artists and labels strive to connect with their fan base and build a strong online presence, the demand for content creators and social media managers has soared. These roles involve producing engaging multimedia content, managing social media channels, and implementing digital marketing strategies to promote artists and their music effectively.

The expansion of the music business has also led to increased demand for music licensing and sync professionals. These individuals work with filmmakers, advertisers, and content creators to secure rights for using music in commercials, TV shows, films, and other media. This role facilitates a mutually beneficial partnership between the music sector and other areas of entertainment.

In an era driven by data, the industry heavily relies on data analytics and insights to make informed decisions. Jobs in data analysis, market research, and consumer insights have become essential for understanding audience preferences, tracking trends, and optimizing music marketing strategies, with labels leaning on more external consultants and agencies to provide in-depth knowledge on these trends.

The expansion of the sector has not only brought forth a diverse range of musical styles but has also created new job economies to support and thrive within this dynamic landscape. As technology continues to shape the way we consume and engage with music, professionals in these emerging roles play a pivotal role in ensuring that artists and their work find their rightful place in the ever-evolving world of entertainment. The global music industry's ability to adapt to new technologies and changing consumer tastes will continue to drive job growth and opportunities for creative individuals seeking a career in this exciting and dynamic field.

Careers And Networking

From artists and musicians, to managers, producers, and executives, the industry supports a diverse range of roles and professions and one of the key aspects of building a successful career in this industry is networking.

Developing a strong network of contacts can provide valuable opportunities for career advancement and personal growth, majority of the networking can be done online, through social media and professional networking platforms such as LinkedIn, but we can never understate the importance of making a deeper and genuine connection in person, It can help to build trust and lead to collaborations on exciting new projects and opportunities. By building a strong online presence and engaging with other professionals in the industry, it is possible to connect with potential collaborators and industry contacts from anywhere in the world

There are many organizations and events that provide opportunities for networking in the music industry. For example, the Association of Independent Music (AIM) hosts regular events and workshops for its members, which provide a platform for networking and collaboration. Additionally, many music festivals and conferences offer networking opportunities, such as the annual Great Escape Festival in Brighton, which is dedicated to showcasing and supporting emerging talent in the music industry.

Example Roles In The Industry

Manager: The Manager plays a pivotal role in an artist's career, serving as a primary point of contact for all business-related matters. They are responsible for managing finances, negotiating deals, and coordinating with various industry professionals, such as agents, publicists, and record label representatives. Additionally, the Manager guides an artist's career trajectory, ensuring that they remain true to their artistic vision while also achieving commercial success. They possess valuable industry insights, which can aid in identifying opportunities for growth and mitigating potential risks. Good communication skills, organization, and industry connections are crucial to succeed in this role.

Videographers And Camera Operators: Across various levels of video production, the role of directors and videographers remain multifaceted. They are professionals who specialize in capturing and producing high-quality visuals. They work on a variety of projects, including music videos, commercials, documentaries, films, and more. Their responsibilities can include developing concepts, scouting locations, coordinating with talent, directing and filming scenes, and editing footage to create a finished product that meets their clients' needs and expectations. They have a deep understanding of camera techniques, lighting, sound, and post-production processes and use these skills to create compelling visual content

A&R (In A Label): A&R, an acronym for Artist & Repertoire, they work within a label and are responsible for locating and selecting musical talent and material for record production. They assist in procuring demos, vocalists, producers, songwriters, and remixes, in addition to providing advice on the ideal radio edit lengths and potential re-arrangements for radio play.

Marketing Manager: A marketing manager develops and executes marketing strategies to promote an artist music and brand. They conduct market research, create promotional materials, and collaborate with creative professionals to build a fanbase. They measure campaign success with data analytics and promote upcoming shows and products. The goal is to increase exposure and achieve commercial success.

Product Managers: Product managers oversee the development and release of an artist music and merchandise. They manage budgets and schedules, coordinate with creative professionals and marketing managers, and track sales and revenue streams. The goal is to ensure high-quality products that are successfully promoted and sold to fans.

Social Media Manager: A social media manager is responsible for promoting an artist music and brand on social media platforms. They create and execute a social media strategy, engage with fans, build a following, stay up-to-date on trends and best practices, and use data analytics to measure success. Overall, they play a vital role in building and maintaining a strong online presence for the artist or band, many of whom do not want to run their own social media pages.

Publicist: A publicist is responsible for creating and maintaining a positive public image for an artist. They develop and execute PR strategies, secure media coverage, coordinate events, and work with management and labels to ensure messaging is consistent. Their aim is to enhance the artist or band's career success and increase exposure.

Radio Dj's: Radio DJs are professionals who select and play music on radio shows, and often engage with listeners by providing commentary, conducting interviews, and announcing news and events. They may also be responsible for programming, scheduling, and promotions, and use their skills to create engaging and informative content for their listeners.

Radio Plugger: The Radio Plugger is the designated professional responsible for introducing an artist's music to radio networks. They are often equipped with established industry connections and have the authority to enlist the services of external experts if necessary. Additionally, they often collaborate with the Pr Manager to devise a strategy for determining which radio stations to approach and when.

Music Journalist: Music journalists and critics are professionals who specialize in reporting and critiquing the latest music news, releases, and trends. They write reviews and opinion pieces on various genres of music, conduct interviews with musicians, and provide expert analysis on the music industry. Their work appears in publications such as newspapers, magazines, and online media outlets.

Events Coordinator: Event coordinators are professionals who organize and oversee various types of events, such as festivals, gigs, fashion shows, and corporate activations. They are responsible for managing all aspects of an event, including logistics, budgeting, vendor coordination, and attendee experience, to ensure that the event runs smoothly and meets its objectives. Event coordinators must have strong organizational and communication skills, attention to detail, and the ability to manage multiple tasks simultaneously under time pressure.

Booking Agents: Music booking agents helps artists secure live performances by negotiating deals with event organizers, promoters, and venue owners. They serve as a bridge between musicians and the industry, providing guidance and support to advance the careers of their clients. Booking agents handle everything from logistics to contracts and fees, ensuring that artists have a well-planned and successful tour.

Fashion Stylist: A fashion stylist works with musicians and artists to create their personal style and image. They collaborate with designers, brands, and other creatives to curate looks that reflect the artist's music and personality. Fashion stylists are responsible for selecting clothing, accessories, hair, and makeup to create a cohesive and visually stunning image for the talent on and off stage. They often work with music video directors and photographers to ensure that the artist's image is consistent across all media. The role often walks a fine line between a creative or art director as the coordinating elements of shoots, mean the clothing must fit with the overall direction and world the artist is looking to represent with their image.

In addition to the careers listed above, there are many other roles and professions that support the music industry. For example, sound technicians and lighting engineers are essential to the live music scene, and are responsible for creating the audio and visual experience at concerts and events. Additionally, there are many careers in music technology and production, which involve working with software and hardware to create, record, and distribute music.

Becoming A Business

As a musician, choosing the right legal business structure is an important decision that can impact your financial liability and tax obligations. Whether you're a artist or part of a group, a DJ, or a videography, it's essential to understand the different options available to you and choose the one that best suits your needs and goals.

Sole Trader: One option is to register as a sole trader, which means that you are running a business on your own. This is a relatively easy and straightforward option to start with, but it also carries a significant risk. As a sole trader, you are 100 percent liable for the business when it comes to things like debts and agreements, so it's important to be careful with your investments and decision-making.

Business Partnership: Another option is to set up a business partnership, which is a good choice if you're starting a business with multiple people, such as a DJ duo or band. When setting up a business partnership, no minimum capital is required, and all entrepreneurs contribute something in the form of money, goods, or labour. However, with this form, you are fully responsible and liable for any debts. If, for example, a partner incurs a significant debt, the other partners will also be held personally liable unless otherwise agreed in the aforementioned agreements.

Before you start the business partnership, it's essential to make good arrangements with your partners and draw up a written contract. This way, you know what happens if, for example, someone wants to leave the band or if debts arise within the band.

Limited Company: The third option is to set up a limited company (Ltd.), which is an excellent choice if your musical career is going well and you want to establish a more significant business entity. An Ltd can be established alone or with various people, and when starting one, there is more work that goes into filling in required documents and setting up a company plan. However, the benefit of an Ltd is that you, as an individual, are not responsible for the company's debts since the company is a separate legal entity. If the company ever goes bankrupt, your private belongings won't be in danger. Additionally, Ltd companies also have benefits regarding taxes and expenses, which become more important when the profits and costs of your company grow.

It's important to carefully consider the pros and cons of each business structure before making a decision.

The business partnership is an easy structure to set up and is usually best suited for smaller bands or duos because everyone has the same rights, liability, and contributions.

Problems can occur when groups don't make proper agreements with each other and leave the band earlier than agreed. It's always advised to draw up a contract to avoid any misunderstandings. If you're a solo artist, becoming a sole trader is a logical business option since you're only working for yourself, and it could be too ambitious to start an Ltd straight off the bat. Choosing the right legal business structure can be a complex decision, but taking the time to consider your options and make informed choices can help set you up for success in your music career.

The Role Of A Music Manager

Artists are responsible for creating and performing music, but they also need someone who can take care of the business side of things. This is where a music manager comes in to help the artist navigate a complex and ever-changing landscape.

A music manager is essentially the representative of an artist or band on the business side of the industry. They take care of a wide range of tasks, including financial management, making and maintaining important connections, securing signings and placements, negotiating with touring agents, advising on all music business matters and many times they can even play the role of a therapist, keeping their artist level headed and motivated. By handling these tasks, managers allow artists to focus on what they do best - creating and performing music - while ensuring that their logistical and business goals are well taken care of.

For Artist: If you're an artist considering working with a manager, it's important to understand what their responsibilities are and whether or not you actually need one. While having a manager can be beneficial, it's not always necessary, especially if you're just starting out. If you can focus on your creative aspirations without the help of a manager, you might want to wait until you actually need one.

However, if you do decide to work with a manager, it's important to choose someone who you feel a strong connection with. This is someone who will be handling an important aspect of your life, so you want to make sure that you're on the same page and that you have a good understanding of what they can do for you.

For Managers: If you're interested in becoming a music manager, there are many advantages to supporting local creators in your community while building your own personal network of connections. To be an effective manager, you should form a business entity for each of your clients to assist with financial organization and taxes. You should also ensure that your clients are on top of distribution, society affiliation, music publishing, and additional revenue streams.

When considering a deal with a manager, it's essential to have a lawyer to ensure that the contract is fair and that both parties are happy with the agreement. Common parts of a contract include Sunset Agreements, Management Commissions, Expenses, and Length of Contract. By having a lawyer, both parties can ensure that their interests are protected and that the agreement is legally binding.

Whether you're just starting out or already established, having a good manager can help you reach your creative goals while ensuring that the logistical and business aspects of your career are well taken care of.

Industry Insight: Thor Sutherland, Co-Founder Of Way Out Music & Managing Director Of Catalyst Management

In this industry insight interview with Thor Sutherland, Managing Director of Catalyst Management & Co-Founder of Way Out Music, he shares his experiences and insights on a range of topics including his journey to his current position, the role of a manager, building relationships, release strategy, publishing, distribution, and the importance of managing an artist's mental health.

Journey To Position: Sutherland's journey to his current position is a testament to his passion for music and his entrepreneurial spirit. Starting as a DJ at 16 years old, he worked his way up by performing at festivals and events, saving money, and reinvesting it into founding Nu:Motion. A Drum and bass event company hosting day festivals, Raves & Club nights with a capacity of unto 1,500 people. He eventually worked his way up via Anglo Management, before establishing his own management company, Way Out Music, which represents artists such as King Kuda, Yxng Dave, Glowe, and Songer.

Role Of A Manager: Managers are also responsible for building relationships and navigating the industry on behalf of the artist. According to Sutherland, the actual role of a manager is multifaceted. It involves being an A&R, creative, accountant, running the artist's business, serving as a therapist, video director, and getting involved wherever necessary. He continued on to say that mangers should just roll up their sleeves and get involved, recounting his experience of carrying sofas up flights of stairs to assist in set design for music video. This shows the importance of a manager's ability to wear many hats and provide holistic support to their artists.

Building Relationships: During the interview great importance was placed on building relationships and networking in the industry. He advises managers to attend networking events, do research on potential contacts, and establish connections with those who can add the most value because If you have no one to take the good artist to, it's worthless! He also shared his experience of meeting Martin Elbourne, the head booker of Glastonbury:

> "I had the goal of booking Glasto. Scoped out a Glastonbury network event, Martin Elbourne, head booker, saw him at an event, walked up to him, invited him to the artist show, offered him a bottle of wine and he came to watch the artist".

The power of personal connections and networking in the industry cannot be understated, especially in a post Covid world where we have the ability to meet in person again. Always seek to establish a better connection with people organically and it is easier to do that when you meet them in person. Thor ended by saying, Don't be scared to hit people up, the most they're going to say is no.

Determining The Manager's Role: Sutherland emphasized the importance of having a release strategy that sets clear goals and targets for the desired outcome, such as streams or tastemaker support, and to target what you want and attack a plan for it. He advises managers to assess the artist's needs and determine where they can add the most value. Using the example of his artist, he said;

"Certain singles were aimed at radio, and some weren't. Every single can do a slightly different thing."

Sutherland believes that the key pillars of a release strategy are streaming, radio, social media, press and live events. This highlights the importance of a strategic approach to releasing music and the various factors that should be considered.

Managers And Mental Health: Sutherland spoke on the importance of keeping artists positive and supporting their mental health, something that is reiterated by managers and industry professional alike. He advises managers to be aware of what's going on in their lives and emphasized that If they need time to take a break, you just got to give them that time. Know your artist character and when they're stepping out of it, you can often spot the tell tail signs an artist might be going through a rough patch, i.e., if the artist is always in the studio, then they drop off.

"Growth isn't straight up, there's always going to be ups and downs in every campaign."

Dig deeper and see if there's anything you can do to provide them with the necessary support when needed. He stated that the reality is, artist don't make money for a while in the start, it can take a few years and with no basic guarantee you can eat at the end of the month, it is hard. If you're young, Most artist will need a need a job half the time and then find the balance with the artistry and managers will be the main touch point for artist, beyond the fan feedback or social circles, to feel connected to the continued progression of their careers whilst surviving through day to day necessities.

Distribution And Publishing: Sutherland stressed the importance of distribution and publishing in the music industry. He believes that distribution is the route for most people and advises artists to use a distro. All his artist are independently distributed, as he knows the team works hard and can do it because ultimately you keep your money and control. Distributors can build your artist reputation with DSP's and some will fund you as well.

When taking that next step to bigger Distros, Thor highlighted that you need to show that it's working. If they invest money in you, they're going to want to back. It can all start with your core sound, Image and the consistency, making the Distributor more likely to take a risk on you. He also believes that publishing is fundamental and emphasized its importance as a long- term investment, It's like a pension, that is not going to pay you something immediately but over 20 years, you can constantly earn royalties on them. Sutherland advised artists to focus on building a strong catalogue of works that can generate royalties over time, providing a source of income over the course of their career.

Release Strategy: Sutherland emphasizes the importance of a clear release strategy that targets specific goals and outcomes, such as streams or tastemaker support. He also highlights the importance of visuals in the release strategy, stating their importance in capturing audiences' attention and generating interest. Sutherland takes a overview, strategic and well-executed approach to releasing music to the masses, with his key pillars being: #

- Streaming strategy
- Press & Radio run
- Social media plan (Tik Tok, Instagram ect)
- Live plot
- Disruption / Noise making Moment / Activation / Visual (unique expression)

Insights On The Importance And Timing Of Record Labels: As an aspiring musician, it's crucial to understand the significance of record labels in the music business. Major record labels are like hit machines that have the resources and connections to take an artist's career to the next level. However, Thor highlights that timing is essential; Waiting for the boiling point of your career and keeping them at bay until you've got the best leverage, is a key strategic perspective on when is the right time to sign with a label. He goes on to say:

> *"Majors are best suited for artists who have reached a certain level of success and are ready to go global, with sold-out tours and plans for expansion into markets like Europe and America."*

Additionally, having the right team behind you is just as important. You need to know each member of your team and ensure they are invested in your success for the right reasons. It's also important not to rush into any deals without consulting a lawyer, as once you're in, it can be challenging to come back out.

Insights On Creative Financing: Creative financing is a critical aspect of the industry, especially for independent artists who are looking to fund their music projects. Brands can provide a valuable source of funding for music videos and other related projects. Additionally, there are multiple grants available from organizations like Help Musicians, BPI, and PRS, which can provide financial assistance to artists. It's also worth exploring small publishing deals, which can offer a steady source of income and a platform to showcase your music to a wider audience.

> *"In the music industry, following your instincts and trusting your gut is crucial. It's essential to stay true to yourself and your music, regardless of how others say you should be. In most cases, sticking to your vision and what works for you will lead to success. It's also important not to give in to the pressure to conform to industry norms or sign deals that don't align with your goals. Remember, if you continue to push forward and stay true to yourself, something great will eventually happen. Always think about your legacy."*

Thor Sutherland

Case Study: G FrSH's Career Evolution In The Music Industry

G FrSH, a prominent figure in the UK music scene, but what sets him apart is his ability to adapt and remain relevant while being innovative. He began his career as a rapper and member of the FrSH collective, releasing his first solo body of work, Mr Bigwillyflysh*t, in 2007.

G FrSH gained attention with his breakout project Legoman – Where's My Brick in 2010, which featured collaborations with Wretch 32, Scorcher, and Tinie Tempah.

Merchandising: At the same time, G FrSH was selling merchandise to go along with his music, which included a clothing line heavily tied to the FrSH collective. This fashion element played a part in the rollout of his Alfie project, which featured T-shirts and jumpers to go along with it. Though the quality of merchandise went up, the website that stocked all FrSH clothing closed down a few years after.

Musical Direction: G FrSH didn't rest on his laurels and continued pushing the boundaries of UK music, which led to mixed results. He followed up Legoman with a shorter release Purgatory, which stood out as sounding like nothing else produced in the UK scene. However, this didn't resonate well with fans who were not able to appreciate the change in sound. G then came back in 2013 with Legoman 2, which featured names like Cashh (Cashtastic), Krept & Konan, and Blade Brown, to name a few.

Conceptual Project: Then a year later, he dropped Alfie, a conceptual project based around the themes of the film of the same name. From start to finish, it is undoubtedly G FrSH's best project, but he chose not to go with the most popular sounds of the time and instead carved his own niche on the project. Though it was a huge success and was even nominated for a GRM award, it was his last project as an artist to date.

Career Evolution: G FrSH, has now joined UTA as an A&R Consultant, where he signs new talent and develop and maintain relationships between the company and other parts of the industry. Previously, he managed high-profile artists under his FrSH Entertainment banner and worked as a Senior A&R at Disturbing London, working with talent like Tinie Tempah, Wizkid, Yxng Bane, and Poundz. G FrSH has also had a hand in the culturally important Prince of Peckham pub.

G FrSH's career evolution is a testament to his contentment in the music business. He has been able to adapt and innovate while remaining relevant, and his knowledge as a music artist has helped him manage artists at the top level. His willingness to take risks has not always resulted in success, but it has led to a career that has remained dynamic and continues to grow.

Artist & Repertoire (A&R)

The A&R (Artists and Repertoire) role has changed and developed as the music business has shifted across time. Traditionally, they were responsible for discovering, nurturing, and guiding the careers of new and emerging artists. The success of an A&R executive can make or break a label, and their expertise and instincts can shape the sound of popular music for years to come.

A good A&R executive possesses key qualities that set them apart from others in the industry. First and foremost being their deep passion for music and the culture. This makes it easier for them to find the next big thing and keep their ear to the ground. They have a keen perception for new sounds and trends and are able to identify potential hits before they become mainstream. This requires a strong knowledge of the history of music, as well as an understanding of current popular culture and the ways in which they intersect.

In addition to a deep love of music, successful A&R executives are also skilled networkers and communicators. They are able to build strong relationships with artists, producers, managers, and other industry professionals, and are able to work collaboratively to create the best possible outcomes. They have a strong sense of what their artists need to succeed, and are able to provide the support and resources necessary to help them achieve their goals.

To foster the qualities necessary for a successful A&R career, aspiring executives should focus on developing their listening skills and expanding their knowledge of the music business. This can be accomplished by attending industry events, networking with professionals in the field, and seeking out mentorship from experienced A&R executives.

Another way to learn from successful A&R executives is to study their careers and strategies. For example, Clive Davis, the legendary music executive, has discovered and nurtured the careers of numerous music icons, including Whitney Houston, Alicia Keys, and Bruce Springsteen. His approach to A&R involves identifying unique and distinctive voices, as well as investing in artists with a strong work ethic and willingness to collaborate.

Similarly, Sylvia Rhone, the first black woman to lead a major record label, has been responsible for discovering and developing the careers of various major hip-hop and R&B artists, including Missy Elliott, Busta Rhymes, and Wu-Tang Clan. Her approach to A&R involves working closely with artists to understand their unique creative vision and developing a tailored strategy to help them achieve their goals.

A&R's require a deep passion for music, strong networking and communication skills, and an ability to identify and develop emerging talent. Aspiring A&R executives can learn from successful industry professionals by studying their strategies and approaches, and by seeking out mentorship and guidance from experienced executives. Keeping their finger to the pulse will allow them to stay on top of what it coming, guide their artist in the right direction and contribute to their labels success.

Industry Insights: Hannah Edmonds International Content Creator And A&R

Hannah Edmonds, a dynamic figure in the music industry, has carved a niche for herself as an International Content Creator, A&R, Artist Manager, and Music Journalist. Renowned for independently producing 'BL@CKBOX New Zealand' and currently working on the 'BL@CKBOX Australia' series, Hannah's journey is a testament to her versatility and passion for music.

From Journalism to Music Mastery
Beginning her career in journalism within education, Hannah quickly realized her true calling lay in music. This revelation led her down a path where her passion and skills became a powerful tool in the industry. While at university, Hannah embarked on a project that involved creating an extended play (EP) taking on the responsibility of managing various facets of this project, from marketing and branding to the selection of artists and the determination of the central themes for the songs. This experience was pivotal, as it provided her with hands-on experience in managing music projects and laid the groundwork for her future endeavours in the industry. Joining Blackbox in 2020, she played a pivotal role in the 'Hardest U18s Cypher' from 2020 to 2023, the 'Sheffield Cypher,' and the blackout series showcasing her adeptness in the A&R role.

Blackbox and Beyond
Hannah's involvement with Blackbox since 2020 marks a significant transition from journalism to a focused A&R role. Her initiatives include curating impactful cyphers and managing ambitious projects like the 'BL@CKBOX Australia' series, reflecting her keen eye for talent and market trends. Hannah's international experience offers unique perspectives on music scenes across New Zealand, Australia, and the UK.

She observes that The music scenes different, it's a bit like when grime was coming out of London, the rest of the county hasn't caught on just yet and while New Zealand is gradually embracing new music genres, Australia boasts a more robust scene, drawing inspiration from local artists. Hannah's UK background facilitated easier integration and understanding of these varied cultural dynamics.

Industry challenges and triumphs:
Hannah Edmonds' journey in the music industry is marked by a series of challenges and triumphs, particularly as a woman in a field that is often male-dominated. Her experiences reflect a nuanced understanding of the industry's dynamics and the resilience required to navigate them. Hannah has observed that reaching a certain level of success often brings additional scrutiny, especially for women, as their achievements can be surprising to some in the industry. This heightened attention underscores the gender biases that still exist within the music world. However, Hannah has not let this deter her; instead, she has used it as a motivation to push further in her career.

Hannah advises women in the industry to maintain self-assurance, even if it means adopting a 'fake it till you make it' attitude at times. Her experiences of often being the only woman in the room highlight the importance of having engaging conversations and expressing well-informed opinions. She emphasizes the significance of showing genuine interest and energy in professional settings. Being knowledgeable about the intricacies of music creation and avoiding participation merely for clout are crucial for earning respect and credibility. Hannah's stance against being undervalued or tested unjustly is a powerful message for women striving to make their mark in the music business.

How to A&R: Curating with Passion and Research

The role of an A&R (Artists and Repertoire) representative, as explained by Hannah, is deeply intertwined with personal taste and a profound love for music. She emphasizes that the music one chooses to promote should reflect one's personal playlist, advocating for the promotion of artists that resonate personally. This approach ensures authenticity in the selection process. Hannah's experience in Sheffield, where she spent three years for university, allowed her to carve out a unique niche.

Starting projects within one's network can build confidence and provide a foundation for more expansive work. She recommends a thorough digital investigation to understand artists and their communities, following a 'rabbit hole' approach to see who artists follow and who supports them. This deep dive into social media, hashtags, and online communities forms a crucial part of understanding current trends and identifying potential talent. Her method involves engaging with the community, understanding mutual connections, and exploring beyond the surface to grasp the full scope of an artist's influence and potential.

Artist Development: Adapting to an Ever-Changing Market

Hannah's perspective on artist development emphasizes the necessity of staying abreast with the constantly evolving music scene. She notes that audiences' preferences have shifted from platforms like GRM Daily to newer trends like TikTok, illustrating the dynamic nature of music consumption. Her advice underscores the importance of adapting to these changes, even if they don't align with personal preferences. The concept of 'news jacking' is mentioned as a strategy, but with caution, to avoid being perceived as inauthentic or 'cringe.' Developing a strong, identifiable theme for artists is crucial for building a loyal following. This approach ensures that the audience knows what to expect, fostering a deeper connection. Hannah also highlights the interconnectedness of music with other industries, like fashion, suggesting that artists provide multiple platforms for audiences to engage and connect with them. This multi-faceted approach to artist development is key to creating a lasting impact in the industry.

Working on Projects: Strategy and Identity

When working on projects, creating a buzz and anticipation is vital. Hannah points out that impactful projects often involve strategies that are not necessarily costly but are effective in building hype. She cites the example of Margs, who successfully built anticipation for his work. The importance of strategic planning is emphasized, particularly in timing releases and balancing trend engagement. Before launching major projects, an artist needs to establish their identity to ensure the audience is invested in their work. This investment is less about the project's length and more about the audience's trust in its quality. Hannah touches on the critical aspects of branding, finding the right sound and producers, and leveraging social media effectively. These elements are integral to shaping an artist's identity and ensuring their work resonates with their audience.

Hannah Edmonds' journey in the industry exemplifies the power of blending passion with versatility. Her transition from journalism to music highlights her adaptability and deep-rooted love for the craft. In navigating the challenges of the industry, especially as a woman, Hannah demonstrates resilience and a forward-thinking mindset. Her approach to artist development and project management, marked by authenticity and strategic insight, sets her apart as a true innovator in the music world.

"Enjoy the process. Get in and find your feet and see where you fit best"
Hannah Edmonds

Case Study: Glyn Aikins and Riki Bleau - Shaping the UK Music Industry

The names Glyn Aikins and Riki Bleau, are recognizable across the industry and resonate as influential figures who have significantly shaped the trajectory of the UK music.

This case study delves into the careers of these two stalwarts, exploring their individual journeys and the intertwined path that led to the establishment of Since93, a record label with a vision to redefine the UK music charts.

Early Influences

Glyn Aikins and Riki Bleau's upbringing in culturally diverse environments significantly influenced their understanding of the music market. This background provided them with unique insights into audience preferences and emerging trends, crucial for their future roles in the music industry. Their journey showcases remarkable resilience. Adaptability, vision, and psychological strength were evident as they navigated the challenges and transformations of the music industry. These traits were instrumental in maintaining their focus and creativity amidst industry pressures.
Their ability to cultivate influential networks, engage in strategic collaborations, and understand industry politics played a pivotal role in their success. This aspect of their journey highlights the importance of social intelligence and networking skills in achieving business success.
We now turn our attention to the strategic and business prowess that propelled their careers forward. Their ability to identify and nurture talent, alongside their adaptation to digital trends, set a new benchmark in the industry. Moreover, their nuanced approach to deal-making and artist development highlights a sophisticated blend of ethical and commercial sensibilities, crucial in their journey to redefine the UK music industry.

Key Strategies
- **Talent Identification:** Aikins and Bleau demonstrated exceptional skill in identifying and nurturing raw talent. Their ability to foresee which artists would resonate with both national and international audiences was instrumental in shaping the careers of many now-famous artists. This talent scouting went beyond just musical ability; it involved understanding an artist's potential to influence and shape cultural trends.
- **Adapting to Digital Trends:** Both Aikins and Bleau were early adopters of digital platforms and online marketing strategies. They leveraged social media and streaming services to promote their artists, understanding the shifting landscape from physical album sales to digital streams. This foresight allowed them to stay ahead in an industry increasingly dominated by online presence.
- **Innovative Marketing and Promotion:** Their marketing strategies were not just about broad exposure but also about creating a narrative around their artists that appealed to a specific audience. This approach helped in building a loyal fan base for their artists.

Business Acumen
- **Deal-making:** Their negotiation skills were pivotal. They crafted deals that balanced artist interests with commercial viability, often pioneering agreements that were ahead of industry norms. This included embracing new revenue streams and ensuring fair artist compensation in an era of changing music consumption patterns.

- **Artist Development:** They focused on long-term career building rather than short-term gains. This involved investing in artist branding, helping artists develop a unique identity, and guiding them through various stages of their career. Their approach wasn't just about selling records but creating sustainable, impactful careers in the music industry.

The story of Glyn Aikins and Riki Bleau in the music industry is a profound lesson in the synergy of cultural understanding, strategic innovation, and ethical practices. Their success, rooted in an acute awareness of diverse musical influences, highlights the necessity of cultural sensitivity in today's global music market. Their early adoption of digital technologies and emphasis on social media marketing are exemplary for modern digital engagement strategies. Equally important is their approach to artist development, emphasizing long-term career sustainability over short-term gains. Their practices, combining ethical business conduct with innovative marketing, set a standard for how to adapt traditional music industry models to contemporary challenges, providing a rich educational resource for the next generation of music professionals.

Navigating A Competitive Industry

With a rapidly evolving landscape influenced by technology, trends, and audience preferences, staying up-to-date with the latest developments is crucial. Artists and industry professionals alike must be adaptable and ready to integrate new technologies and strategies to remain relevant and competitive. Having access to abundant information alone does not guarantee success. The experience behind a perspective or analysis, can be the deciding factor on whether you will perform at your optimal level. We must connect with those that have these skills and knowledge, to make our journey through the business smoother and refined.

Networking is the pivotal aspect of building a successful career in any industry. Beyond merely collecting business cards and contacts, the focus should be on creating genuine connections with like-minded individuals. An essential element of effective networking is knowing where and how to present your best qualities. Whether it's showcasing your work through digital platforms, participating in online forums, or attending live events, finding the medium that best represents your strengths is vital. Engaging in person or online, the key is to highlight your unique qualities and leave a lasting impression on those you connect with.

Building a strong online presence and sources of reliable information is equally important in today's digital age. Leveraging social media to connect with relevant industry professionals can open doors to new opportunities and valuable insights. With platforms leaning further into discovery capabilities, creating valuable and authentic content tailored to your niche will attract the right audience and potential collaborators.

Finding your niche and community within the industry is another essential aspect of navigating the competitive landscape. Networking with peers who share similar interests and goals can provide a supportive community that fosters growth and collaboration. Before seeking to connect with higher-level industry professionals, tapping into your immediate community can provide valuable opportunities and support.

The infrastructure that goes into making successful music on a commercial scale, often requires starting from the position of an outsider and building the connection. Cold outreach to potential connections can seem daunting, but it is a valuable skill to master. Expressing genuine interest and showcasing the value you can bring will resonate more with industry professionals and potentially lead to fruitful collaborations. This is often a process of trial and error but indevoured to refine the language and approach for cold outreach to effectively establishing meaningful connections.

Persistence and resilience are qualities that can make or break a career in the music industry. Challenges and setbacks are inevitable, but maintaining focus and determination in the face of adversity will propel you forward. Learn from mistakes, continuously improve, and stay committed to your goals.

Staying informed about industry trends and developments, building genuine connections, and leveraging digital platforms are all essential components of success. By persistently pursuing your goals, remaining resilient in the face of challenges, and finding your niche within the industry, you can increase your chances of thriving in this competitive landscape.

Building Relationships

Industry professionals, including record label executives, music managers, and booking agents, possess extensive knowledge and resources to help you succeed in the industry. By building relationships with these professionals, you can gain new insights, opportunities for exposure or access to new collaborators. Similarly, fostering connections with other musicians can yield numerous benefits. Collaborating with fellow artists not only fosters creativity and innovation but also opens doors to new audiences and expands your artistic horizons. Connecting with fellow musicians can lead to joint performances and exciting collaborative projects.

To cultivate strong relationships with industry professionals and musicians, it is crucial to make a positive impression and exhibit professionalism and respect in your interactions. This includes being well-prepared and knowledgeable about your music, being receptive to feedback and advice, and following up diligently after initial introductions. Genuine and authentic interactions are key to building meaningful connections that are based on mutual benefit and support.

Networking etiquette plays a vital role in establishing a positive reputation within the business. Employing good networking etiquette ensures that your interactions are polite, respectful, and professional, leaving a lasting positive impression. Here are some essential tips for practicing good networking etiquette:

1. **Be Respectful And Polite:** Demonstrate punctuality, attentive listening, and refrain from interrupting others during conversations.
2. **Be Prepared:** Thoroughly research the individuals you will be meeting and have a clear understanding of your music and career goals to engage in meaningful discussions.
3. **Be Authentic:** Avoid coming across as overly aggressive or pushy. Instead, be genuine and sincere in your interactions, allowing others to see the real you.
4. **Follow Up:** After an initial introduction, express gratitude and send follow-up messages to maintain communication and nurture relationships.

Apart from etiquette, projecting confidence and professionalism is crucial in making a positive impression. Dressing appropriately for various industry events, maintaining a firm handshake, and maintaining eye contact demonstrate your professionalism and commitment to your music career. Being well-prepared to discuss your music and career goals, and confidently answering questions about your work, further reinforces your credibility.

Effective follow-up is an essential aspect of successful networking. Sending thoughtful thank-you notes or follow-up messages after initial meetings can leave a favourable impression. Additionally, maintaining regular contact with industry professionals and fellow musicians shows your commitment to the relationship and opens doors for future opportunities.

Networking is not a one-time event, it is an ongoing process that requires consistent effort and dedication. Engaging in meaningful conversations, sharing your knowledge, and actively participating in discussions can boost your visibility and reputation within the industry.

Pro Tip: Finding Opportunities

In this business, finding opportunities is a crucial step in advancing your career and achieving your goals. One of the most effective ways to uncover these opportunities is through your network! Regularly engaging with your community via social media, you will find more opportunities than a sporadic google search.

Live shows offer a platform for artists to showcase their talent and connect with audiences. Networking plays a vital role in securing performance opportunities, whether it's at local venues or larger festivals. Forge relationships with booking agents and venue managers, you increase your chances of being considered for gigs. Regularly keeping in touch with these professionals can lead to consistent performance opportunities, enhancing your exposure and reputation in the industry.

Collaborations with fellow musicians can be a transformative experience. Not only does it foster creativity and innovation, but it also exposes you to new audiences and expands your artistic horizons. Networking with other artists allows you to explore potential collaborations and discover like-minded individuals who share your passion for music. These partnerships can lead to ground-breaking projects and mutual growth as artists.

Industry events, such as conferences, festivals, and workshops, provide invaluable networking opportunities. Attending these events can give you insights into the latest trends and developments. Additionally, rubbing shoulders with industry insiders, music executives, and established artists can lead to potential partnerships, mentorship, and even career-changing encounters. The biggest gems are gained through conversation, putting yourself in bigger and better rooms is only going to strengthen your standing and knowledge base.

To effectively find opportunities through networking, it is essential to have a clear understanding of your goals. Identifying what you want to achieve in your music career will guide your networking efforts and enable you to focus on connections that align with your aspirations. Once you've established your goals, conduct research to identify potential contacts who can support you in reaching those objectives. This can include music managers, record label executives, booking agents, and fellow musicians.

Creating opportunities yourself, is also one of the fastest ways to attract new options. Everyone in the industry, plays at a different level, but by taking charge of your own direction, you can galvanize those in a similar position to yourself. Take time to deeply understand your brand, direction and position in the market, and connect with like minded individuals that can also create opportunities for you down the line.

Following up and maintaining contact with your network is vital in nurturing fruitful relationships. Express gratitude for any assistance or advice received, and keep your contacts informed about your progress and achievements. Consistently seeking opportunities and connections within your network demonstrates your commitment and dedication to your music career.

In addition to networking, there are other strategies you can employ to enhance your opportunity search in the music industry. Building a strong personal brand is essential in setting yourself apart from the competition. Create a professional online presence, such as a highly curated social page, a website or LinkedIn profile, that showcases your skills, accomplishments, and unique qualities as an artist. A well-crafted personal brand can capture the attention of potential employers and collaborators, leading to exciting opportunities.

Finding opportunities requires a multifaceted approach that includes networking, personal branding, staying informed, and engaging in collaborations. The main thing is to put yourself in the best possible position for success whether that be in the studio or at an event. By being proactive, open-minded, and committed to your goals, you can uncover a myriad of exciting possibilities and pave the way for a successful and fulfilling music career.

Utilizing LinkedIn To Network

As an artist or music professional, social media is a crucial tool for promoting your brand and connecting with fans. While platforms like TikTok, Twitter, and Instagram are the go-to for reaching audiences, LinkedIn is often overlooked. However, this professional-themed app can offer unique benefits for those in the music business.

Linked in is a major resource underused within the Independent side of music. A professional form of social media, LinkedIn allows your to lead source your own collection of contacts in any given industry, connect with and message them all from the push of a few buttons.

Some key factors to crafting a successful profile to network with are:
- Professional profile image
- Professional but personal bio that reflects the individual
- A clear work history
- Regular content in the form of written, media or other creative pieces
- Case studies attached to your profile, highlighting milestones in your career so far
- Relevant skills endorsed by your network
- Connections to relevant thinkers within your niche/industry

Adding your own personal branding elements, will help your profile standout; LinkedIn provide various assets and options, for improving your profiles rating on the platform.

LinkedIn provides a platform for making important contacts that can help develop your career and build your professional network. While it may not directly increase your fan base, the social platform offers the opportunity to appear on the radar of influential industry figures. Here are some reasons why you should consider using LinkedIn as an artist or music professional.

Finding Music Industry Connections

LinkedIn is full of potential connections in the music. However, this doesn't mean you should be spamming record label executives with links to your latest tracks. Rather, you should focus on reaching out to people who can help with tasks you might not have the technical ability or experience to do yourself. For instance, graphic designers, music promoters, music photographers, web developers, social media gurus, sound techs, promoters, and producers are all valuable connections to make on LinkedIn.

Building Relationships Through Groups

One of the most valuable features of LinkedIn is the ability to join groups relevant to your industry. These groups are great places to meet new industry contacts and put your profile in front of people who can make a difference to your career. Instead of joining groups of other musicians, it's important to look beyond this to all areas of music. For instance, you can join groups of promoters, music supervisors, bookers, or even find a music manager through LinkedIn.

Maintaining Professional Relationships

Once you've added someone to your LinkedIn network, you have a quick and easy way to reach out to them without relying on outdated email addresses or phone numbers. It's important to remember that the connections you make on LinkedIn should remain strictly professional. It's not a place to harvest fans, but rather a place to build mutually beneficial relationships within the music business.

Making A Great First Impression

A professional LinkedIn profile can give a great first impression to potential new contacts. Ensure that you're utilizing your profile's appearance to its full potential. Start by using a real photo of yourself. While you may be tempted to use your band's logo or an artsy shot of a live performance, using a simple headshot is recommended. Remember, LinkedIn is a platform designed for professionals to connect with each other.

Instead of filling up your page with an in-depth analysis of your sound and influences, focus on showcasing your real achievements in music. For example, if you've been featured by blogs, websites, or print publications, or if you've won any awards or competitions for your music, LinkedIn is the perfect place to show them off.

Job Search Strategies

Finding a job in the industry can be a challenging yet highly rewarding endeavour. To increase your chances of success in this competitive field, it is crucial to develop a well-defined job search strategy that aligns with the unique aspects of the industry.

One of the most effective job search strategies in the business is through your direct connection and reaching out to build new relationship with decision makers. As previously mentioned, networking plays a pivotal role in establishing a successful career in music. Actively participating in online discussions, attending events, joining professional organizations, and engaging with fellow professionals online, can forge valuable connections that may lead to exciting job opportunities and invaluable support during your job search.

Conducting extensive research and targeting specific companies and organizations that resonate with your interests and career aspirations can significantly enhance your job search. Thoroughly exploring active players in the industry and identifying those that align best with your skill set and experience will allow you to tailor your job applications and increase your likelihood of success.

Beyond networking and research, cultivating a compelling online presence and a strong personal brand is becoming increasingly crucial in the digital age. Your voice extends further than either through the medium of digital content, especially with the algorithmic nature of todays platforms. Creating and regularly updating a professional online profile, can effectively showcase your skills, experiences, and achievements to potential employers. Maintaining an impressive online presence not only allows you to exhibit your expertise but also enhances your visibility in the competitive job market.

When applying for jobs, it is essential to recognize that crafting a resume and cover letter tailored to this unique field can make a significant difference in the eyes of potential employers, especially in a market as saturated as music. While the fundamental principles of resume and cover letter writing remain the same, certain specific factors deserve special consideration.

Emphasizing any relevant experience and skills specific to the music business should take centre stage in your application. This might encompass your background as a musician or artist, as well as other experiences closely related to the music realm, such as music production, event management, or music retail.

Expressing your genuine passion and enthusiasm for music is of paramount importance. Employers within the business are keen to hire individuals who exhibit a deep-rooted passion for music and the industry itself. Therefore, it is crucial to convey your interest and commitment to music in a compelling manner through your resume and cover letter.

Personalization is key when crafting your application materials. Tailor your resume and cover letter to the specific job and company you are applying to. This entails conducting thorough research on the company and the position and effectively showcasing how your unique experiences and skills align with the job requirements.

Always ensure that your resume and cover letter are meticulously proofread before submitting them. A polished and error-free application reflects professionalism and attention to detail, which can impress potential employers and substantially increase your chances of securing an interview.

Pro Tip: After The Spotlight

Aspiring artists often dream of a successful and enduring career in music, basking in the glory of the spotlight. However, akin to industries such as sports, the harsh reality of the music business reveals that a career as a top tier performer is often short-lived, with many artists' careers ending before they reach the age of 35. The industry's rapid pace and ever-changing landscape demand that aspiring artists be prepared for what comes after the spotlight fades.

To thrive long term, it is crucial for aspiring artists to develop a diverse skill set and portfolio that extends beyond their prowess as performers. While musical talent is undoubtedly important, it is not sufficient to ensure a lasting career. The industry is vast and complex, offering numerous paths and opportunities for those who possess the necessary skills and knowledge.

Understanding the inner workings of this dynamic field is paramount. Ensure to take to time time to fully grasp the intricacies, so you can identify your unique opportunities and hidden areas for growth that might otherwise go unnoticed. The ability to see the bigger picture enables artists to recognize and nurture talent in themselves and others, opening doors to collaborations and partnerships that can take their careers to new heights.

Building a foundation of business skills is equally essential for long-term success in the music industry. Musicians must evolve their creativity into new realms, remaining savvy and entrepreneurial, to allow you to navigate the competitive and cutthroat nature of the business. Embracing core business principles that are universal across all industries and sectors allow creatives to establish themselves as more than just performers or artist, empowering them to pursue various avenues and explore diverse revenue streams.

The benefits of acquiring transferable skills cannot be overstated. By honing their talents and network in other fields, aspiring artists gain a competitive edge that extends far beyond music alone, often serving as new inspiration to their personal story and approach, making them more versatile and attractive to potential collaborators, brands or employers alike.

A cautionary tale of the music business reminds us that numerous talented individuals have stumbled and faltered due to a singular focus on their musical abilities. To avoid this fate, aspiring artists must recognize that the industry is not merely a platform for musical expression but a complex and multifaceted business. Acquiring business acumen and learning to operate the various verticals within the industry's structures are indispensable for building a lasting and impactful career, with a lot of skills being transferable to new spaces.

Aspiring artists must understand that the music business demands more than just musical talent. Building a sustainable career requires a holistic approach that encompasses business skills, strategic thinking, and adaptability. Cultivate these attributes to navigate the competitive landscape, and transcend the ephemeral nature of fame, leaving an enduring mark on the music sector and beyond.

CHAPTER 2
PILLARS OF THE INDUSTRY
ARTIST, PRODUCERS & ENGINEERS

What Is A Music Artist

A music artist steps beyond general understandings these days. Many of the most successful mainstream talents today didn't start in a traditional musical background. At its core, a music artist is a "alchemist" of sorts, who uses their skills with instruments, tech or their voice to transform raw emotions, experiences, and ideas into sound that can heal, inspire, and transform.

Artists come in many forms, often associated with a dreamer who dares to push boundaries and challenge the status quo, a sage who shares their wisdom through lyrics and performances, a healer who uses music to soothe and lift our spirits, a catalyst who ignites our passions and awakens our creativity, and a visionary who sees beyond the present moment and imagines a better future.

As an artist, you have the power to create something beautiful and meaningful. You are in charge of your creative spark, and your art can light up the path and guide communities towards a brighter tomorrow. Through music, artists connect us at a deep, soulful level, reminding us of our humanity, interconnectedness, and the beauty of being alive. They are poets who weave together words and notes to create stories that touch our souls and make us feel seen and understood.

The mindset of an artist who has built longevity into their brand is one of authenticity and staying true to themselves. These artists understand that trends come and go, and instead of chasing them, they focus on creating art that speaks to their unique vision and perspective. They are not afraid to take risks and push boundaries, but they do so in a way that is true to their own voice and style. They understand that their art is a reflection of who they are, who they are becoming and that they must stay true to themselves even in the face of criticism or changing tastes.

With the pervasive influence of social media and the homogenization of music pricing and distribution, being an artist today encompasses far more than just creating music. Artists must now embrace the role of content creator, engaging with their audience in a multifaceted digital landscape. This dual responsibility places a substantial burden on artists who primarily seek to focus on their creative process. Nevertheless, it is increasingly evident that success in this era hinges on an artist's ability to adapt and carve their unique path in navigating these new rules of audience engagement.

Those that take the time to engage with their fans in a real and authentic way, whether it's through social media or in person at shows, and listen to their feedback and incorporate it into their art will thrive in the new landscape. Whether their mediums are live streaming, innovative content formats, or strategic marketing campaigns, those who thrive in this evolving landscape are the ones poised for long-term success, regardless of the chosen format of expression.

Successful artists have a deep dedication to their craft. They are constantly honing their skills and pushing themselves to be better. They understand that success is not just about talent, but also about hard work and perseverance. They are always seeking to learn and grow, and they are not content to rest on their laurels.

Artists play a vital role in our lives by creating a universal language that transcends cultural and linguistic barriers, touching our souls, and inspiring us to create a better world. They are a gift to us all, and we must cherish and support them as they continue to elevate our collective culture through their art.

Case Study: Kano

British artist Kano, whose real name is Kane Robinson, is an excellent example of an artist who has built longevity into his brand by staying true to himself and evolving with the times. Kano began his music career in the early 2000s as a grime MC and quickly gained a reputation as one of the genre's most talented and lyrically adept performers.

One of the keys to Kano's longevity is his ability to stay relevant by adapting to changing trends while still maintaining his unique style and voice. He has collaborated with artists from a variety of genres, including Gorillaz, Chase & Status, and Damon Albarn, and has incorporated elements of Garage, R&B, and dance music into his own sound. In addition to his music career, Kano has also branched out into acting, appearing in the likes of "Tower Block" and "Top Boy,". His success in the acting world has only added to his versatility as an artist and expanded his reach to new audiences.

One of the main reasons Kano has been able to sustain his career over such a long period is his commitment to staying true to himself and his roots. He has always been vocal about his love for grime music and his desire to represent his community through his music and art. He has also used his platform to speak out on social and political issues affecting Black British communities, such as racism and police brutality.

Another key factor in Kano's longevity is his ability to constantly push himself creatively and take risks with his art. His most recent album, "Hoodies All Summer," was praised for its introspective lyrics and willingness to tackle complex issues like gentrification and the Grenfell Tower fire.

Kano's mindset as an artist with longevity is grounded in staying true to himself, constantly evolving with the times, and taking creative risks while maintaining his authenticity. By doing so, he has been able to build a brand that transcends genres and mediums and remains just as relevant and influential in the music and entertainment industry.

Case Study: J. Cole And The Artist Way

The Artist's Way: A Spiritual Path to Higher Creativity, written by Julia Cameron, is a book that has helped countless artists and creatives to unlock their full potential. The book is a guide for anyone looking to tap into their inner creativity and develop a deeper connection with their artistic process.

Finding a practice that realigns you with the creative spark our ideas feed on, is vital to long term creative careers. Our well of ideas is infinite but our ability to receive them and action them can wane with time. We can look at multiple artist across history that have experience burnout or leave the industry due to no longer feeling the love for it that was present when the newness and excitement was first present.

In an interview in 2014, J. Cole discussed his experience with the book "The Artist's Way," and how it helped him overcome creative blocks and find his voice. J. Cole stated that about a year into making his album, he had all this incredible material flowing out like a floodgate, but it hit a point where it stopped. He was under too much pressure, and the people in the studio were bothering him. He needed to get away, and that's when he discovered "The Artist's Way."

The book is a 12-week program that helps readers to identify and overcome the blocks that are preventing them from reaching their full creative potential. It covers a wide range of topics, including self-discovery, artistic exploration, and spiritual growth. One of the key components of the book is the "morning pages" exercise, which encourages readers to write three pages of stream-of-consciousness writing every morning. This exercise is designed to help readers clear their minds, explore their thoughts and feelings, and tap into their inner creativity.

He read the book, and one highlight the regular practice of writing three pages a day, also known as morning pages. J. Cole started to wake up in the morning and write these pages freehand non-stop. He said that *"you can't stop, and you have to write the first thing that comes to your head"*. This exercise helped him get back into writing, and he started to fill up notebooks with lyrics. J. Cole realized that he enjoyed writing stuff down better than typing it out on his phone. He found it more intimate, and it reminded him of when he was a kid.

The book has been praised for its practical and holistic approach to unlocking creativity, and for its ability to help readers to develop a deeper understanding of themselves and their artistic process. For many people, it has been a powerful tool for self-discovery and spiritual growth, and has helped them to reconnect with their inner creativity and to develop a more meaningful connection with their art.

The Role Of A Record Producer

The role of a record producer is to help artists and bands reach their full potential by overseeing their work in the recording studio. This involves not only supervising the recording process itself, but also working with artists in preparation before the actual recording takes place. The producer's job is to be supportive, inspiring, and demanding, in order to bring out the best in the artist and capture the highest level of performance possible.

Producers may come from a background in musical composition and live performance, or may have arrived via the studio route, having spent time as recording engineers and studying the work of other talented producers. Regardless of their background, all producers must develop a range of skills including musical analysis, song arrangement, technical fluency, familiarity with the latest studio techniques, and the ability to combine these factors in a skilful and creative manner.

There is no single approach to studio techniques and style, as each producer works in their own way. Some producers are very hands-on, involving themselves in every detail of the musical arrangement and becoming an extra member of a band. Others take a more subtle approach, guiding the artist through the many options available when making contemporary records. Some producers move between these roles depending on the needs of the artist and the music being created. Ultimately, the role of the producer is to help artists and bands achieve their full potential, and create great music that resonates with listeners.

Music Production And Technology

Music production and technology refers to the processes and tools that are used to create, record musical works in the UK. Music production and technology involves a wide range of activities, from composing and arranging music, to recording and mixing audio.

In the UK, we have seen many artist go from creating in their bedrooms to becoming chart topping hit makers. Music production and technology plays a vital part, and is essential for the success of indie artists and labels. By using the latest production and technology tools and techniques, artists and labels can create high-quality musical works that resonate with audiences. This can help to drive sales, generate revenue, and build a loyal fan base. Never before has there been more information and technical aides from production, as readily available.

The music market is highly competitive, and music production and technology is a rapidly evolving field. In order to succeed, artists and labels must be knowledgeable and skilled in the use of production and technology tools and techniques. Sites such as Skillshare can be great place to learn the deeper specific skills associated with production and technology, as are YouTube platforms focused on the subjects.

Industry Insight: Sphero

In this industry insight interview with Sphero, known for his unique sound and breakout track Pack and Potions. We cover various aspects of the music production process, including what a producer does, branding and building relationships, finding deeper relationships and placement opportunities, understanding your market and demographic, the future of producers, and connecting with producers as an artist.

What A Producer Does: According to Sphero, beat making is a major requirement for a producer. However, he emphasized that this year, his focus is on elevating production beyond just engineering or composing a track. The overall creation of a track is the job of a producer, with most producer acting almost as A&Rs with the track and session. He went onto say,

"With it becoming so much of a broad term, it's good to understand what type of producer you want to be and which route to take from there".

There are different types of producers, such as bedroom producers, who are different from in-studio or working-with-artist producers.

1. **Bedroom Producers**: They produce music in the comfort of their homes, usually with a computer and a few pieces of equipment.
2. **Beatmakers**: They focus primarily on creating beats and instrumental tracks for artists to use.
3. **In-Studio Producers**: They work in professional recording studios with artists to produce high-quality recordings.
4. **Artist Producers**: They work with an artist to develop their sound and produce their albums.
5. **Mixing and Mastering Engineers**: They specialize in mixing recorded tracks to create a cohesive, polished sound and manage the final mastering stage of the music production process to ensure that the final product is of high quality and ready for distribution.
6. **Film and TV Producers**: They produce music for film and television, often working closely with the director to create a specific sound and mood.
7. **Game Producers**: They produce music for video games, often creating immersive and interactive soundscapes.

Branding And Building Relationships: Sphero stated that branding oneself is about who you are and how you want to be present. If one is not outgoing, they need a team to help push them into rooms they normally wouldn't jump to. This team can be comprised of a manager, agent, or other team members. The key is to figure out what one stands for and who to bounce off of. Building relationships is also important. The producer suggested making one's music undeniable and finding the artists that fit the music.

Understanding Your Market And Demographic: Sphero suggested looking at one's demographic and figuring out what people are here for and what they are expecting. One should connect the world to the imagery of their brand and study the culture around the sound and embed that. Producers are also the inspiration for artists. It can take one instrumental to spark an artist's creative drive. Before music even gets played, one can start the gathering of inspiration. Building from scratch is crucial, and there are two types of building - conceptual and instrumental. Producers give the canvas, the colours, and the brush, and the artist signs their signature at the end.

Finding Deeper Relationships And Placement Opportunities: To find deeper relationships and placement opportunities, Sphero recommended sending an email to grab attention (4 instrumentals in the email) and doing it for a few weeks consistently and staying on top of the follow messages can be crucial to catch the opportunities. Keeping your name relevant in the wider sphere ensures that one's name carries weight during outreach. The producer also advised that one should expect that the majority of emails might not be responded to.

> Hi _____,
> I hope this message finds you well. I came across your music and was really impressed by what I heard. I'm a producer and I think we could create something amazing together. I understand that you might already be working with producers, but if you're ever in need of new beats or sounds, I would love to collaborate. I'm always looking for new artists to work with and create something fresh.
> Let me know if you're interested and we can take it from there. Looking forward to hearing back from you.
> Best,
> [Your Name]

The Future Of Producers: Sphero talked about how producers are becoming more versatile, and the industry is starting to realize that a producer can do more than just make beats. Producers are now getting more involved in the overall creation of a song, including writing lyrics, and even creating references for the artist in some scenarios. Sphero also mentioned that the industry is shifting towards a more DIY approach, with artists and producers taking more control of their careers, rather than relying solely on major labels.

Connecting With Producers As An Artist: Sphero recommended that artists should do their research and figure out who they want to work with. Artists should look for producers who are aligned with their vision and style. It is also important to have a budget and be willing to invest in one's career. He also suggested that artists should not be afraid to reach out to producers directly on social media or through email, but they should make sure that their music is up to par before making contact.

The interview with Sphero provided valuable insights into the production side of the industry. He emphasized the importance of branding and building relationships, finding deeper relationships and placement opportunities, understanding one's market and demographic, and connecting with producers as an artist. Sphero also spoke about the evolving role of producers in the industry, and the need for producers to be versatile and take control of their careers.

Case Study: Steel Banglez

Steel Banglez is a British record producer and musician of Indian Punjabi descent who is known for his work with artists such as Mist, MoStack, J Hus, and Wiley. He achieved his first chart hit as a lead artist with the track "Bad" which reached the top 30 on the UK Singles Chart in February 2018.

Steel Banglez was born in Newham, East London, which was one of the epicentres of grime music in the UK. Banglez was D Double's neighbour, seven years his junior, and produced a track for him while still in his teens, putting the youngster who had grown up on Indian classical music in close proximity with grime's first wave. After a difficult stint in prison in his teens, where he focused on his music, making beats on a keyboard from Argos, Sandhu was able to continue with his passion in his 20s, working with the likes of Wiley and Krept + Konan.

Steel Banglez won Producer of the Year at GRM Daily's Rated Awards in 2017 and Best Non-Traditional Asian Act at Brit Asia TV Music Awards in 2018 and 2019. He produces a YouTube series, The House of Banglez, featuring guest appearances from personalities from the culture. He is climbing the charts with his recent track "Fashion Week" featuring MoStack and AJ Tracey, which topped the official Trending Chart in the UK and entered the main chart at number 7, landing him his first UK Top 10 hit.

Steel Banglez is considered one of the most in-demand producers in the UK, along with the likes of Jae5 and Sevaqk. He is known for being one of the architects of the new and diverse sound of UK rap, which is pick-and-mixed from afrobeats, dancehall, grime and more. He has also struck out as a lead artist with tracks such as "Fashion Week," "Bad" featuring Yungen, MoStack, Mr Eazi and Not3s, and adopted a more pop sound on "Your Lovin'" for MØ and Yxng Bane. Steel Banglez's ascent is particularly pertinent in a time when his home city often feels more fractured and divided than ever.

Steel Banglez's success story serves as a valuable source of inspiration for aspiring producers and musicians alike. With a combination of talent, dedication, hard work, and networking skills, Steel Banglez was able to break through the competitive UK music scene and establish himself as one of the most sought-after producers. His unique approach to music production, which blends various genres and influences, has helped him create a distinctive sound that resonates with audiences across the UK and beyond.

Case Study: Fumez The Audio Engineer

Fumez the Engineer, is a UK-based audio engineer and music producer who has made a significant impact in the music industry with his production skills and signature tags. He rose to fame after working on the Plugged In and Studio with Fumez series and gained wider recognition after engineering the remix of Ed Sheeran's "Bad Habits", featuring Tion Wayne and Central Cee, which remained at number one for eight weeks.

Fumez began his career in a youth club, where he discovered his passion for producing music. He started to learn and experiment with equipment in the underprivileged youth club's recording studio. After two years of volunteering, He was eventually offered a paid job, where he continued to hone his skills and grow his brand. His unique branding strategy, which included tagging his productions with his signature "Fumez the Engineer" tagline, gained traction, and soon he became known as the go-to audio engineer for many artists in the UK music scene.

Fumez's approach to his work is driven by his passion for music and his desire to influence the industry. He is constantly pushing himself to stay relevant, consistent and to knock on doors for new opportunities. Fumez's ability to produce high-quality work has led to collaborations with some of the biggest names in the industry. Despite his successes, he remains humble and continues to look for new ways to grow and improve.

One of his biggest successes was the remix of Ed Sheeran's "Bad Habits." Fumez's contribution to the remix was significant, helping to elevate the song's popularity. The remix not only showcased his production skills but also established him as one of the most sought-after audio engineers in the UK music scene.

Fumez's journey has not been without challenges. He faced setbacks when he went into debt after launching Pressplay Media, which led to him selling his shares in the company. However, Fumez did not let these setbacks define him, and he continued to pursue his passion for producing music. He went on to work for Link Up TV, where he engineered the Mic Check and Behind Barz freestyle series and started the Plugged In series of freestyles on Pressplay, which gained immense popularity, with over 100 million views and streams.

Fumez's experiences have taught him the importance of hard work, perseverance, and a passion for his craft. He remains dedicated to his work and continues to inspire others to pursue their passions. Despite his success, Fumez remains focused on improving and creating new opportunities for himself and others in the industry.

Fumez's story is a testament to the power of hard work and dedication. His journey in the industry, from the youth club to working with some of the biggest names in the industry, shows that anything is possible if you have the drive and passion for it. Fumez's success as an audio engineer and music producer is a testament to his commitment to his craft, and his story is an inspiration to anyone looking to pursue their dreams in music.

Industry Insights: Lotes, Executive Producer And Founder Of BL@CKBOX

In this industry insight interview we sit down Lotes, a seasoned executive producer and founder of BL@CKBOX, During this conversation we covered, importance of maintaining relationships understanding artists as a producer or engineer, executive producing/full AR role, and the shift in UK music.

Importance Of Maintaining Relationships: In the music industry, relationships are vital. As Lotes explains, **"they're friends before they are business for me."** when speaking of the artist he produces and engineers for. It is important to make sure that people are looked after, and to maintain relationships with individuals in the industry. This is why, even after ten years, Lotes still recognizes the same faces. The room hasn't changed. It is crucial to establish and maintain relationships to ensure longevity in the industry.

Understanding Artists As A Producer Or Engineer: The importance of understanding the artist one is working with applies more as an engineer. As a producer, you make your style, and the artist either resonates with it or doesn't. But as an engineer, you have to be able to adapt your style to the artist to get the best out of the work. Lotes resonates with energy and a well-rehearsed artist. It is vital for the producer or engineer to feel the artist to produce the best possible work.

Executive Producing / AR Role: Lotes explains that his role as an executive producer, is to handle the ins and outs of the recording process and curate the sound and feel of the project. To begin with, he will often aim to record 20-30 songs for a 10-15 track project, and he will consistently be listening to the music to pick the track order. Keeping all the songs in a playlist and then start removing songs that don't fit. The listening process highlights any potential issues, that will prompt Lotes to go back over certain mixes, seeing mixing as constantly evoling process. Lotes says was used to a studio from a young age, so he's had a lot of time around music to train his ear.

Visuals: Artists come in with an existing vision. It is a lot of back and forth till everyone's happy. The platform has stayed the same but has evolved over time to match the current era. The label or rapper can lose their identity if they don't stay true to themselves.

UK Music Shift: When ask the question surrounding the direction of UK music, Lotes stated that the UK rap scene is like a relay race with people running with the torch. Whoever is running the race to make the music as commercial as possible opens up the pockets for more subculture to pop in the mainstream.

> **"The scene is so big now that you can have a career without trying to make a hit or a top 10. People who stay true to themselves and build their niche fan bases will succeed."**

YouTube is no longer the best platform for music, and the views don't represent how successful a stream is anymore. Platforms like TikTok, Facebook, and Instagram generate more streams and revenue than YouTube does. Videos play less of a role now, and it's more about your presence across all social media. Videos are now more like your website or advertisement.

Lotes leaves us with powerful words of advice. He encourages artist to never give up and to keep pushing towards our dreams, reminding us that sometimes we have to do things we don't want to do in order to achieve what we truly desire. If music is your passion, he urges them to work hard and invest in yourselves and your craft emphasizing the importance of being willing to put our money where our mouth is and take risks to achieve success.

Music Production Software And Digital Audio Workstations (DAWs)

Music production software refers to the programs and tools that are used to create, record, and manipulate audio in the music production process. Digital audio workstations (DAWs) are a type of music production software that are used to record, edit, mix, and master audio recordings.

Some popular music production software and DAWs include:
- **Pro Tools:** Pro Tools is a professional-grade DAW that is known for its powerful features and professional-grade sound quality. Pro Tools is a versatile program that is well-suited for recording, editing, mixing, and mastering audio, and is used by many professional studios and artists.
- **Ableton Live**: Ableton Live is a popular DAW that is known for its user-friendly interface and real-time performance capabilities. Ableton Live is well-suited for electronic music production, and is used by many electronic music producers and DJs.
- **Logic Pro**: Logic Pro is a professional-grade DAW that is popular among musicians, producers, and audio engineers. Logic Pro is known for its advanced features and flexible workflow, and is used by many professional studios and artists.
- **FL Studio:** FL Studio is a popular DAW that is known for its user-friendly interface and powerful features. FL Studio is well-suited for electronic music production, and is used by many electronic music producers and DJs.
- **Propellerhead Reason:** Propellerhead Reason is a popular DAW that is known for its user-friendly interface and powerful virtual instruments and effects. Reason is well-suited for electronic music production, and is used by many electronic music producers and DJs.
- **Cubase**: Cubase is a professional-grade DAW that is popular among musicians, producers, and audio engineers. Cubase is known for its advanced features and flexible workflow and is used by many professional studios and artists.
- **GarageBand:** GarageBand is a popular DAW that is included with Apple's Mac operating system. GarageBand is known for its user-friendly interface and built-in virtual instruments and is well-suited for beginners and hobbyists.
- **Reaper:** Reaper is a popular DAW that is known for its affordable price and powerful features. Reaper is well-suited for recording, editing, mixing, and mastering audio, and is used by many professional studios and artists.

Music production software and DAWs are essential tools in the field of music production and technology. Using the right software and DAW, artists and labels can create high-quality recordings that connect with audiences and deliver a powerful listening experience.

DAW Pros And Cons

DAW	Pros	Cons
Pro tools	Industry-standard for audio professionals Advanced audio editing and mixing High-quality plugins and virtual instruments Collaboration features Extensive support and resources	High cost Steeper learning curve Hardware compatibility Resource-intensive
Ableton Live	Live performance-focused Unique Session View for improvisation Powerful MIDI capabilities Vast library of third-party plugins Warp feature for flexible audio editing	Costly Less traditional DAW layout Steeper learning curve for some
Fl Studio	User-friendly interface Affordable pricing Lifetime free updates Pattern-based sequencing Extensive virtual plugin collection	Primarily Windows-based Limited audio recording capabilities Less popular for certain professional use cases
Logic pro	Professional-grade features User-friendly interface Powerful virtual instruments Flex Time and Flex Pitch Great MIDI capabilities Large user community Regular updates	Mac-exclusive Learning curve Resource-intensive Cost Limited built-in plugins Notable absence of some third-party plugins
GarageBand	Free for Apple users User-friendly for beginners Basic recording and mixing features Virtual instruments and loops included	Limited advanced features compared to other DAWs Limited compatibility with certain hardware and software
Cubase	Comprehensive MIDI capabilities Advanced audio editing and mixing Virtual instrument library Professional-grade music notation VST Transit for collaboration	Limited compatibility with certain hardware and software Can be complex for beginners
Reaper	Affordable pricing Lightweight and efficient Customizable interface Extensive third-party plugin support Frequent updates and active community	Learning curve for beginners Less extensive virtual instruments Limited built-in effects

Pro Tip: What Makes A Good Engineer

A skilled music engineer is a versatile professional who merges art and musical science to create captivating sonic experiences. They are responsible for manipulating audio files to produce enchanting and transporting soundscapes that resonate with listeners. As audio technicians they must have a strong skill in technical aspects of recording, mixing, and mastering, and can use their knowledge to enhance the sonic qualities of a recording.

Often they are the problem solver who can identify and fix technical issues that could otherwise ruin a recording, they are essential collaborators who works closely with artists and producers to understand their vision and help them achieve their musical goals. In addition, they possess a solid understanding of the physics of sound, which they can use to shape sound waves for specific effects, such as EQ, compression, and reverb. To create a particular mood, emotion or message using sound takes skill and is often brought in during the mix and mastering phase.

Some artists choose to engineer their own recordings, giving them greater control over the creative process and allowing them to experiment with different sounds and techniques. This highlights the importance of a well-rounded skill set in the music industry, where knowledge and expertise in various areas can greatly enhance one's career. It is important for artists and other professionals in the industry to have a basic understanding of the engineering side of music production. This enables them to communicate more effectively with their engineers, ensuring that their creative vision is fully realized. For example, an artist who is able to describe the desired sonic qualities of a recording in technical terms is more likely to get the desired result from their engineer.

Mixing Is A Journey

Mixing music is a profound process that goes beyond simply making the track louder. It involves capturing the essence of a song and bringing it to life, creating a harmonious balance between all the elements, allowing each instrument and vocal to shine in its own space within the mix. The ultimate goal is to enhance the emotion and energy of the performance, immersing the listener in a captivating musical experience.

Visualize mixing as a journey, beginning with the raw tracks and embarking on a voyage of exploration and experimentation with various sounds and textures. Embrace the opportunity to take risks and venture into uncharted territory, for it is in these daring moments that true magic is born. The ultimate reward is crafting a mix that not only sounds pleasing but also complements the emotional intention of the song, leaving a lasting impact on the listener. Remember, the mix is the final representation of the song, the artistic culmination of all the hard work and creativity poured into it. Make it count, for it is the bridge that connects the artist's vision to the audience.

In the world of music mixing, innovation and pushing boundaries are key elements to elevate an artist's work to new heights. We encourage artists to "think outside the box" and explore new mixing techniques. By challenging yourself, you can discover uncharted territory and create soundscapes that set the music apart from the norm.

Collaboration during mixing is equally important. Working with other producers and mixers, bringing fresh perspectives and ideas to the table. Everyone will have their own technique and approach to mixing so such collaboration can lead to exciting opportunities for growth and open doors to new creative possibilities. The manipulation of texture is another area worth exploring. Artists can play with different textures by incorporating unique sounds or experimenting with existing elements in creative ways. This process can add depth and dynamics to the mix, engaging listeners on a deeper level.

Taking risks is crucial in the pursuit of artistic excellence. It's essential for artists to embrace their individuality and be unafraid to incorporate bold, unconventional ideas into their mixes. These courageous choices can lead to ground-breaking sounds and pave the way for ground-breaking music. However, amidst all the innovation and experimentation, never lose sight of the core essence – emotion. Prompt artists to focus on how their mixes can evoke specific responses from their listeners. By infusing elements that tap into moods like suspense, joy, melancholy, or passion, artists can craft a powerful and unforgettable listening experience. Emotion is the fuel that drives the connection between music and its audience, transcending mere auditory sensations to touch the very soul of the listener.

In the dynamic and diverse music business, effective communication is the key to successful collaboration. Professionals in this field often interact with artists and creators from various backgrounds, each with their unique artistic expressions and aspirations. To ensure smooth communication and productive feedback during the recording process, it is essential to be well-versed in the language and techniques commonly used in the industry.

Understanding the intricacies of music production and mixing enables you to offer valuable insights and constructive feedback to fellow colleagues, fostering a collaborative environment where creativity can flourish. Through speaking the same language, professionals can harmonize their efforts, leading to remarkable results that transcend expectations.

The art of music mixing is a transformative journey that demands creativity, innovation, and emotional depth. Artists and industry professionals alike must embrace experimentation, collaboration, and the fearless pursuit of their vision. Through a shared language and a commitment to emotional impact, the music sector can continue to evolve, pushing the boundaries of what is possible and creating unforgettable musical experiences for generations to come.

Industry Insights: Mikey Joe

In this industry insight interview with Mikey Joe is a UK-based music producer who from early developed an unrelenting passion for music, becoming one of the most recognizable figures in UK real rap. In this sit down with Mikey Joe, we gain his perspective on topics such as building a personal brand, working with artist, auxiliary skills, role of an engineer, key trends and business dealings in the industry.

Building A Personal Brand: Mikey stated that his personal brand is built on his outgoing and confident personality, which has helped him build relationships and secure opportunities. He believes that having a logo alone doesn't showcase your whole self, and being seen and putting out levels of content is essential. Your personal brand is how you present yourself to the world, and it's essential to create an image that is consistent with your values, personality, and style. It's not just about having a logo or a tagline; it's about creating a story that people can relate to and connect with.

> *"If I see someone on Instagram, no matter how big or small they are, I'll reach out, won't even ask for anything usually, just lead with a genuine interaction, offering help to artist on their distro, wider relationships. Always been willing to offer help."*

Mikey's approach to keeping himself in the mix and building his credibility is an excellent strategy for new artists. When you're not fully established, it's essential to put yourself out there and showcase your talent in person and through social media platforms.

Working With Artists: When asked about how he works with artist, Mikey notes that prefers to work with artists he has a personal connection with and who share his vision of getting good music out without only focusing on financial gain. He remains an active part in artist careers in all aspects, such as Tal Greazy, to get things aligned for his career, even though he is currently behind bars. Mikey continued on, speaking about his belief that working more in-depth with artists, will get the best out of their music. It's essential to note that branding is not just about the music; it's also about the personality and values that an artist portrays. Mikey's strategy of offering help to talented artists is an excellent way to build relationships and expand your network. It's essential to identify artists with whom you share a connection, and building a strong relationship takes time, effort, and patience. However, once you've established that connection, it can lead to fruitful collaborations and opportunities.

Auxiliary Skills: Mikey recommends that producers learn how to record artists, as it can allow for more moves to be made in different sides of the industry as well as the creative. He followed this up by advising that producers should have other skills that they can fall back on. For instance, he noted another known producer, started doing photography, which gave him access to more clients and ways to provide value to artist in sessions. Mikey suggests branching out beyond beat-making and learning how to record artists can be a great way for producers to start a new skill set. This not only expands your skills but also opens up opportunities on the business side of the industry.

Role Of An Engineer: Mikey highlights two types of producer-engineers:

- Those who record artist in sessions.
- Those who specialize in mixing and mastering.

The specialized engineers in the industry often receive projects and stems to make the sound the most industry-standard it can be. Mikey recommends that producers who are stuck in the beat-making space and want to start recording sessions, should focus on getting clean recordings for artists and making the process smooth, they do not need to be fully trained audio engineers. They can get more placements by hosting recording sessions and showcasing their beats. Mikey emphasizes the importance of networking and putting oneself in the room whenever possible.

Music Business: Mikey Joe understands the music industry as a business, where he recognizes that it is not always stable, and artists' budgets vary as they try to make this work full time. Circumstances and relationships play a crucial role in determining the price artist must work with therefore, he adopts a flexible approach and often negotiates a 50/50 split with the artist when they don't have a set budget. This attitude demonstrates Mikey's willingness to collaborate and support artists who he believes in, even if they may not have the financial means to pay for his services. Mikey stated that major labels have more financial resources and can provide artists with better deals and contracts, while independent artists may have to rely on their network and resources to navigate the industry, so that is often a big factor in pricing different artist.

Key Trends: Mikey Joe emphasized that staying up to date with current trends is critical for success in music. In particular, he discussed the importance of TikTok in the current landscape. TikTok has become a powerful tool for music discovery, where songs can quickly become viral and gain widespread attention. Mikey suggests that artists release short clips and lyric videos on TikTok to interact with a broader audience and generate buzz around their releases. Moreover, the trend of releasing singles instead of full albums has been on the rise, with streaming platforms such as Spotify and Apple Music emphasizing single releases. This change in strategy has allowed artists to maintain a more consistent presence in the industry and avoid the pressure of creating an entire album. Mikey recognizes the importance of this trend and works with artists to produce high-quality singles that can stand on their own and grab the attention of listeners.

Mikey's insights into the music business provide valuable information for producers and artists looking to build their personal brands and make their mark. His emphasis on building personal connections, offering help, and developing relationships can benefit anyone looking to make it in the industry. Mikey's advice on auxiliary skills, working with artists, and the role of an engineer is also valuable to those looking to succeed in the industry.

CHAPTER 3
PUBLISHING, DISTRIBUTION AND LABELS

Introduction To Music Publishing

Music publishing is the business of owning and exploiting musical copyrights, which refer to the exclusive rights granted to the creator of an original composition. These rights include the right to reproduce, distribute, perform, and create derivative works of the song. Every recorded piece of music has two separate copyrights:

- The composition itself, which is owned by the songwriter and/or publisher
- The sound recording, which is owned by the recording artist and/or label

Music publishing involves the monetization of the composition copyright. As a songwriter, music publishing is an important aspect of your career because it allows you to exploit your compositions and earn income from your creativity.

Artists have multiple avenues to generate income through music publishing, including mechanical royalties for song reproduction in physical or digital formats, performance royalties for public performances, synchronization licenses for use in various media, and print rights for sheet music.

Music publishing can also be a powerful tool for growing your career as a songwriter. By working with a publisher, you can gain access to a wider range of opportunities for exploiting your compositions and generating a new source of revenue. A publisher can help you secure sync placements, negotiate licenses, and collect royalties on your behalf, freeing you up to focus on writing and creating new music. Additionally, they can provide valuable resources and expertise in promoting your compositions and building your career as a songwriter.

Music publishing is a vital aspect of the industry, often under utilized by artist and is an important source of income for songwriters. Understanding how to own and exploit your copyrights, and working with a publisher, can maximize your earnings and build a successful career as a songwriter.

Understanding The Different Copyrights Involved In Recorded Music

Every recorded piece of music is subject to two distinct copyrights: the composition and the sound recording. These copyrights are owned separately, with the composition typically belonging to the songwriter and/or publisher, and the sound recording to the recording artist and/or label. This understanding is crucial in the music business, as it entails what can be done with compositions, the different rights and income streams available.

The composition copyright encompasses the song's music and lyrics, granting the songwriter and/or publisher the rights to reproduce, distribute, perform, and create derivative works. Owners of the composition copyright earn mechanical and performance royalties when the song is publicly performed or reproduced. Streaming platforms have become significant sources of mechanical royalties due to the rise of digital music consumption. Performance royalties are another crucial income stream, earned when a song is publicly performed, such as on radio, TV, live shows, or public venues. Performing rights organizations (PROs) play a key role in collecting performance royalties and distributing them to songwriters and publishers based on public performances.

Synchronization licenses offer valuable opportunities for songwriters to earn income through music publishing. These licenses allow songs to be synchronized with visual media like films, TV shows, commercials, or video games. When a song is used in such media, the copyright owner of the composition is entitled to synchronization royalties, which can be significant if featured in popular media.

The sound recording copyright refers to a particular recorded version of a musical composition. It is typically owned by the recording artist and/or label, and it allows the owner to reproduce and distribute the recorded version of the song. The owner of the sound recording copyright is entitled to receive mechanical and performance royalties, as well as other income streams such as streaming royalties and digital download royalties.

In many cases, the same person or entity may own both the composition copyright and the sound recording copyright for a particular song. However, it is also possible for the composition copyright and sound recording copyright to be owned by different individuals or entities. For example, a songwriter may retain ownership of the composition copyright while signing a recording contract with a record label, which then owns the sound recording copyright for the artist's recorded version of the song.

Understanding the distinction between composition and sound recording copyrights is crucial in the music industry to ensure fair compensation for creative contributions. Songwriters rely on composition copyrights to earn income from their works, while recording artists and labels depend on sound recording copyrights to monetize recorded versions of songs.

Music publishing can also open doors to international markets for songwriters. Music publishers have global networks and partnerships that promote and exploit compositions internationally, potentially leading to substantial income from foreign markets.

Collaborating with a music publisher provides songwriters valuable guidance and support in navigating the complex world of copyright and licensing. Publishers are experienced in negotiating licensing deals, ensuring fair compensation, protecting songwriters' interests, and enforcing copyrights against unauthorized use. Partnering with reputable music publishers, can maximize songwriters earnings and focus on creating music that resonates with audiences worldwide.

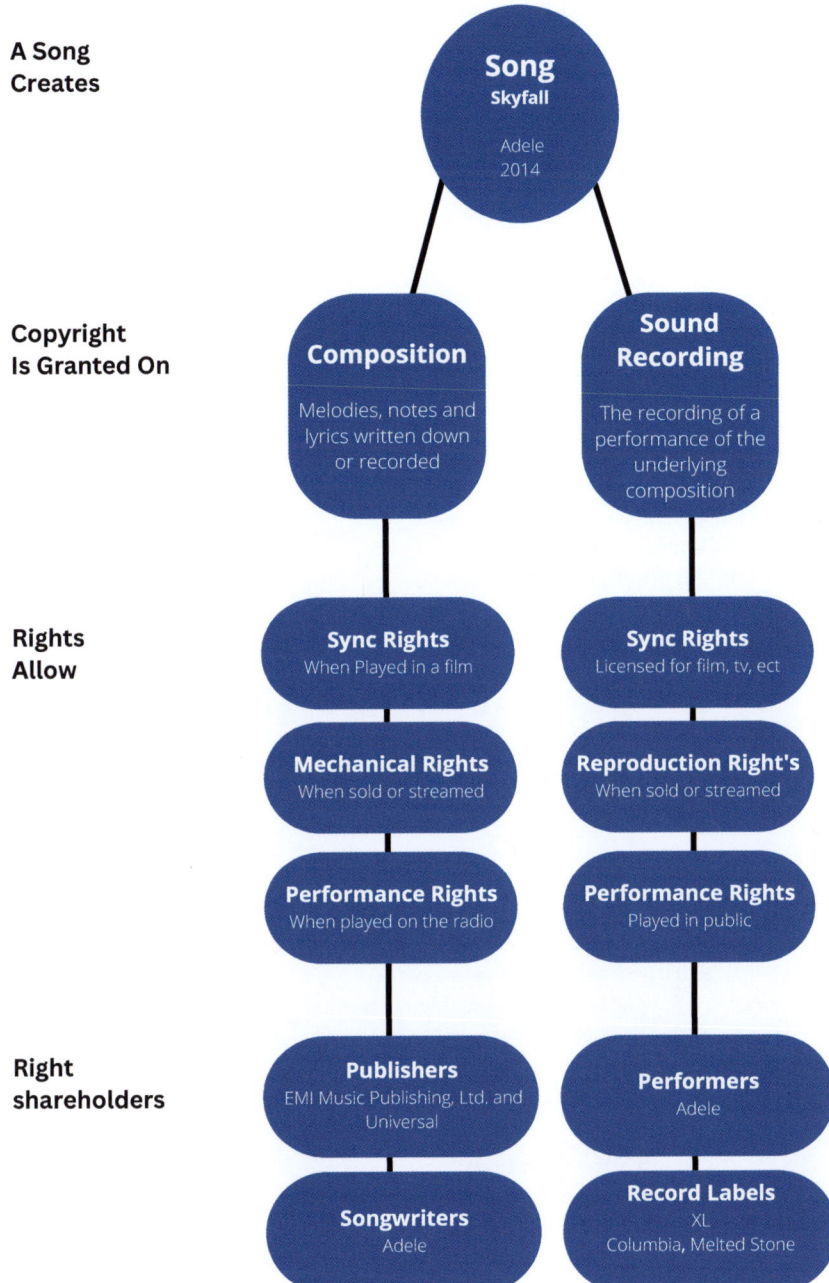

Royalty Management And Distribution In The UK

Royalty management and distribution are integral components of the industry, essential for ensuring that artists and copyright holders receive appropriate compensation for the use of their musical works. In the UK, these processes involve meticulous tracking and accounting for the use of musical compositions and the subsequent distribution of royalties to the rightful parties. Two key aspects that contribute to effective royalty management and distribution are royalty collecting societies and international cooperation.

In the UK, royalty collecting societies play a crucial role, Prominent among them are the Performing Rights Society (PRS) and the Phonographic Performance Limited (PPL). These societies are entrusted with the responsibility of monitoring the use of musical works across various platforms and venues, including broadcasters, live performance venues, and digital music platforms. They collect royalties from these music users and ensure that these earnings are appropriately distributed to artists and copyright holders.

The process of royalty distribution is a crucial step that follows the collection of royalties. Once the societies have amassed the earnings from various sources, they distribute them to the artists and copyright holders entitled to receive them. This distribution can take the form of direct payments to individual artists and copyright holders or disbursing funds to their representatives, such as managers or record labels. By executing a fair and efficient royalty distribution process, the music business strives to ensure that creators receive the monetary compensation they rightfully deserve for the usage of their musical works.

Considering the global nature of the music business, international royalty collection and distribution are equally significant. As musical works gain global recognition and reach audiences worldwide, the need to track and account for international usage arises.

Collaborating with international royalty collecting societies and other organizations becomes necessary to ensure that the use of UK musical works is accurately monitored, and royalties are rightfully paid to the appropriate parties. This aspect of royalty management facilitates equitable compensation for artists and copyright holders on a global scale.

Protecting Your Rights

Protecting the rights of songwriters and creators is of paramount importance in the music industry. To safeguard their interests and ensure fair compensation, songwriters can adopt various proactive strategies:

First and foremost, registering compositions with PROs like PRS for Music, PPL, or the MCPS is a vital step. These organizations diligently collect performance royalties on behalf of songwriters, ensuring they receive rightful payment for the use of their music.

Copyrighting compositions is another crucial measure to establish ownership and protect original works. Copyright protection extends to any original work fixed in a tangible form, such as a recorded or written version of a song. Registering copyrights with the UK Intellectual Property Office provides tangible evidence in case of any disputes.

Careful utilization of contracts and agreements is essential to define the terms of any licensing or publishing arrangements. Prior to signing, it is crucial for songwriters to read and comprehend the contracts fully. Seeking legal advice when required ensures they make informed decisions about their rights and earnings.

Maintaining accurate records of compositions and their usage is essential. By doing so, songwriters can effectively track their earnings and ensure that they receive proper compensation for the use of their music.

Involvement in professional organizations and seeking advice from experienced industry professionals helps songwriters stay informed about their rights and abreast of the latest developments in the music industry.

By diligently following these measures and engaging in robust royalty management and distribution practices, songwriters in the UK can protect their rights, foster a sustainable music industry, and ensure that they receive fair compensation for their creative contributions.

Types Of Income That Can Be Generated Through Music Publishing

As a songwriter or music publisher, understanding the different income streams in music publishing is crucial for maximizing your earnings and effectively managing your music catalogue. These income streams encompass various ways in which you can earn revenue from your compositions and creative works.

Mechanical Royalties: Mechanical royalties constitute one of the primary sources of income in music publishing. These royalties are earned whenever your song is reproduced on a physical or digital format, such as CDs, vinyl records, or digital downloads. With the rise of digital music consumption, streaming platforms like Spotify, Apple Music, and others have become significant contributors to mechanical royalty earnings. The rate at which mechanical royalties are paid per reproduction is determined by factors like the format of reproduction and the geographical territory in which the song is sold.

Performance Royalties: Performance royalties are another essential income stream, are earned whenever your song is publicly performed. This includes live concerts, radio broadcasts, TV appearances, and performances in public venues like bars and restaurants. Performing rights organizations (PROs), such as PRS in the UK and ASCAP, BMI, and SESAC in the US, are the main providers of performance royalties collections, on behalf of songwriters and publishers. These organizations monitor public performances of songs and ensure that the rightful copyright owners receive their royalties based on the frequency of performances.

Synchronization Licenses: Synchronization licenses present yet another avenue for generating income through music publishing. These licenses allow your song to be synchronized with visual media, such as films, TV shows, commercials, or video games. Negotiating sync licenses is an opportunity to generate substantial revenue, especially if your song is featured in high-profile or popular media.

Sheet Music: Print rights for sheet music also offer an income stream for songwriters and publishers. Sheet music refers to printed copies of the music and lyrics of a song, and the owner of the composition copyright receives royalties whenever sheet music is sold. In addition to traditional printed sheet music, digital sheet music platforms have become increasingly popular, opening up new opportunities for earning revenue from sheet music sales.

Beyond these main income streams, there are various other potential sources of revenue in music publishing. Licensing for sampling allows your composition to be used in other artists' works, while print rights for songbooks and other publications can lead to additional income streams.

Understanding and effectively managing these various income streams in music publishing are essential tasks for songwriters and publishers. It involves monitoring and tracking usage of your compositions across different platforms and territories, ensuring accurate royalty collection, and proactively seeking out licensing opportunities.

The Benefits And Challenges Of Self-Publishing

The industry has witnessed a significant shift in recent years, with self-publishing emerging as a viable option for songwriters seeking more control over their creative work. Self-publishing offers a host of benefits that appeal to artists looking to retain autonomy and maximize their earnings. However, it also comes with its fair share of challenges that demand careful consideration and strategic planning.

One of the most compelling advantages of self-publishing is the unprecedented level of creative control it affords songwriters. Unlike traditional publishing deals, where artists may have to compromise on their artistic vision to align with the publisher's commercial interests, self-publishing empowers songwriters to make all the artistic decisions. From choosing the song's arrangement and production style to determining its marketing and promotional strategies, self-published songwriters can fully express their musical identity without interference.

Financial rewards play a crucial role in any artist's career, and self-publishing can potentially lead to greater financial gains. In conventional publishing deals, songwriters typically split their earnings 50/50 with the publisher. In contrast, self-publishers retain full ownership of their compositions, allowing them to keep a more substantial share of the profits generated by their music. Over time, this ownership can translate to higher earnings, especially if the songs gain popularity or are used in lucrative commercial opportunities.

Despite its enticing advantages, self-publishing does come with its set of challenges that aspiring songwriters must be prepared to navigate. One of the primary hurdles is the administrative responsibilities that come with self-publishing. Songwriters take on tasks such as registering their compositions with Performing Rights Organizations (PROs) to collect royalties, negotiating licensing deals, handling copyright issues, and managing financial transactions. For those unfamiliar with the intricacies of the music business, these administrative duties can be overwhelming and time-consuming.

Self-published songwriters might face limitations in resources compared to those signed with established publishing companies. Traditional publishing houses boast dedicated teams that handle marketing, legal support, and industry connections, significantly aiding their songwriters' careers. In contrast, self-publishers often have to wear multiple hats, managing various aspects of their music business independently or seeking external support, which might not be financially feasible for all independent artists.

Another challenge lies in market reach and exposure. Established publishing companies have well-established networks and relationships within the industry, providing their signed songwriters with broader exposure to lucrative opportunities. For self-published songwriters, breaking into these circles might demand extra effort and persistence in building connections and getting their music noticed by industry professionals.

Evaluating personal strengths, resources, and long-term goals is essential in determining if self-publishing aligns with one's artistic vision and career aspirations. Regardless of the chosen path, succeeding demands dedication, talent, adaptability, and a strong entrepreneurial spirit.

Copyright Law And Music Publishing In The UK

Copyright law is a fundamental aspect of music publishing and licensing in the United Kingdom. Governed by the Copyright, Designs and Patents Act of 1988, UK copyright law grants legal protection to original works of authorship, including musical compositions. As per this law, creators of musical works are automatically granted certain exclusive rights, such as the right to reproduce, distribute, and publicly perform their works. These exclusive rights empower the creators to have control over how their works are used and enable them to derive financial returns from their creative endeavours.

In the context of music publishing and licensing, copyright law establishes the legal framework that allows collecting societies like the PRS (Performing Right Society) and MCPS (Mechanical-Copyright Protection Society) to negotiate licensing agreements on behalf of their members, safeguarding the rights and interests of the creators of musical works.

It is essential to recognize that copyright protection for musical works in the UK is not unlimited. In general, copyright protection lasts for the life of the creator plus a certain number of years after their death, commonly referred to as the copyright term. After this period, the musical work enters the public domain, making it accessible to the general public for use without the requirement for licensing. The public domain status allows the work to be freely utilized and even incorporated into new artistic creations.

For creators and copyright holders, maintaining these exclusive rights to their musical works holds immense value. By retaining ownership of their music, they can exercise control over how future artists collaborate with and reinterpret their compositions. This control enables them to ensure continued revenue generation from their works and preserves the cultural relevance and significance of their music over time.

An illustrative example of the significance of copyright in the music business is the emergence of drill artists in the UK and around the world. Drill music, known for its distinctive sound and lyrical content, often samples elements from existing musical works. By maintaining copyright ownership, creators can dictate how artists that sample can interact with and recreate their music, creating a balanced ecosystem that benefits both the originators and the new wave of artists. An excellent illustration of this is Tion Wayne's sampling of La Roux's "In For The Kill," which resulted in a chart-topping hit. The collaboration between Tion Wayne and La Roux not only resonated with the younger audience but also re-engaged La Roux's existing fanbase, adding a fresh and nostalgic dimension to her music.

Copyright law forms the backbone of music publishing and licensing in the UK. Through bestowing exclusive rights upon creators, it allows them to protect their creative works, control their use, and receive fair compensation for their contributions. The continued adherence to copyright law ensures a thriving and dynamic music industry that fosters artistic innovation and financial sustainability for creators and stakeholders alike.

Exploiting Your Own Copyrights

Exploiting your own copyrights as a songwriter offers a powerful avenue to retain control over your musical compositions and maximize your earnings. To effectively own and exploit your publishing rights, it's essential to understand the rights granted to you as the creator of original compositions under copyright law. These exclusive rights encompass the ability to reproduce, distribute, perform, and create derivative works of your songs. By comprehending these rights, you can strategically exploit them to generate income and protect your creative work.

As the owner of your publishing rights, you hold the responsibility of collecting income generated from the exploitation of your compositions. This includes various royalties like mechanical royalties, performance royalties, and licensing fees that you have negotiated. Keeping meticulous records of your income and expenses and managing your finances effectively are crucial to optimizing your earnings as a songwriter. Moreover, it's essential to plan for the long term, as income from your compositions can be passed down to your family for 70 years after the death of the last individual listed as a writer on the record.

Negotiating and issuing licenses for your compositions are essential steps if you desire to license your songs for use in various media, including film, television, commercials, and more. Synchronization licenses enable you to grant permission for the use of your songs in visual media, while mechanical licenses are issued to parties interested in reproducing your compositions on physical or digital formats. Properly negotiating and issuing licenses not only protect your intellectual property but also open up additional revenue streams for you as a songwriter.

Neighbouring rights, often overlooked by songwriters, are equally significant. These rights pertain to performers, producers, and sound recording copyright owners, granting exclusive rights to exploit sound recordings for commercial purposes. Once your tracks have been registered with the PRO, it's vital to report their usage to the society, ensuring accurate payment of royalties to all rights holders. Effectively monitoring and managing the distribution and licensing of your sound recordings ensures they are being used legally and to your financial benefit.

The use of names carries financial implications, particularly concerning taxes. Registered names for songwriters are now required to be human names instead of company names. While the use of pseudonyms is permitted, it's critical to ensure that relevant collecting entities are aware of this arrangement to avoid any complications. For songwriters with common names, like "John Smith," a songwriter identification number is assigned to accurately allocate royalties. If you intend to use multiple names, it's advisable to discuss this matter with a business manager and publisher to ensure proper handling and recognition.

Case Study: Chance The Rapper

Chance The Rapper, born Chancelor Jonathan Bennett, is a multi-Grammy award-winning rapper, singer, songwriter, and philanthropist from Chicago, Illinois. He is one of the most prominent and successful artists in the world of independent music, having gained fame and recognition through his self-publishing endeavours.

Route To Success: Chance The Rapper first gained recognition in 2013 with his self-released mixtape "10 Day." This mixtape helped him build a large local following, and it was followed by two more successful mixtapes, "Acid Rap" in 2013 and "Colouring Book" in 2016. Chance's unique style and innovative approach to music-making earned him critical acclaim, and he soon gained a large and dedicated fanbase. He is best known for his positive, inspiring lyrics and his ability to blend different genres of music in his work.

Chance's approach to community building is deeply intertwined with his independence as an artist. By choosing to remain independent, he has been able to align his music and platform with values that resonate with his fanbase, further strengthening his community ties. His efforts in supporting local initiatives, mental health awareness, and youth empowerment are not only commendable but also reflective of how artists can use their influence to effect positive change within their communities.

His non-profit organization, SocialWorks, has been a key instrument in this effort. Since its inception in 2016, SocialWorks has focused on empowering youth through arts, education, and civic engagement, touching on vital issues like education, mental health, homelessness, and performing and literary arts.

Pros Of Self-Publishing: Chance The Rapper's decision to self-publish his music has allowed him to maintain complete creative control over his work. He has been able to release his music on his own terms, free from the constraints of a traditional label. Additionally, he has been able to build a strong relationship with his fans, and he has used his platform to support various social and political causes.

Cons Of Self-Publishing: While self-publishing has given Chance The Rapper the freedom to create and release his music as he sees fit, it has also meant that he has had to work harder to get his music out to the public. He has had to rely on social media, live shows, and other creative marketing strategies to build his brand and connect with fans. Additionally, without the resources of a major label, he has had to work harder to get his music distributed and sold, which can be challenging for an artist starting out.

Chance The Rapper's success story is a testament to the power of self-publishing. His innovative approach to making and promoting his music has earned him critical acclaim, a dedicated fanbase, and multiple Grammy awards. However, self-publishing is not for everyone, and it requires a lot of hard work, dedication, and creativity to succeed. Nevertheless, for artists who are able to make it work, the rewards can be substantial, both in terms of artistic freedom and financial success.

The Role Of The Publisher In Exploiting And Promoting Your Compositions

If you are a songwriter and/or composer on a record, have the option of owning and exploiting your own publishing rights, or you can work with a music publisher to help expand opportunities to earn money from compositions. In a typical publishing agreement, the songwriter and publisher split the income generated from the exploitation of the copyright, with a typical split of 50/50.

The publisher's role in exploiting and promoting your compositions is to use their expertise and resources to generate income from your copyright. This can include tasks such as registering the compositions with performing rights organizations, negotiating licenses, and collecting royalties. The publisher can also help to promote your compositions by pitching them for sync opportunities in film, television, and advertising, as well as by actively seeking out opportunities for your songs to be covered or performed publicly.

It's important to understand that the publisher is **not responsible for the creative aspects of your compositions**, such as the song writing or production. Their role is to handle the business side of things and to help you maximize the potential income from your copyright. In exchange for their services, the publisher will typically take a percentage of the income generated from your compositions.

It is not mandatory to have a publisher. Both the writer's share and publishing share can be managed by a collection society. However, collection societies do not handle synchronization rights. The role of both collection societies and publishers is to negotiate better royalty rates for the composers. This includes royalty payments for the use of music on various platforms, such as radio stations, streaming services, and even emerging platforms such as TikTok. Additionally, they also ensure that royalties are collected for fan content featuring the composer's music on social media platforms.

The fees charged by collection societies and publishing companies vary based on the type of music involved. The rates for collection societies are listed in the statements they provide. The rate agreed upon by publishing companies is included in the publishing deal that is established between the two parties. The percentage can range from 4% to 30%, but there are no standard rules, as the specifics of the agreement are outlined in the contract between the composer and the publishing company.

Although these entities strive to secure improved rights and compensation for the composers, it remains equally important for the composers to actively engage in the process as well. Although it may seem appealing to grant free access to music on platforms such as Instagram and Tik Tok, it is important to recognize the bigger picture and strive for unity in the industry for the benefit of all parties involved.

The Benefits And Challenges Of Working With A Publisher

Working with a music publisher can offer numerous benefits that can significantly impact a songwriter's career. One of the most appealing advantages of collaborating with a publisher is the expanded reach and increased income potential for your compositions. Publishers possess expertise and resources that allow them to pitch your songs for sync opportunities in various media, such as film, television, and advertising. They can actively seek out opportunities for your compositions to be covered or performed publicly, broadening your audience and increasing your chances of success.

Moreover, a music publisher can effectively handle the administrative tasks related to licensing and monetizing your compositions. This includes registering your compositions with performing rights organizations (PROs), negotiating licenses with various users of your music, and collecting royalties on your behalf. These administrative responsibilities can be time-consuming and complex, but with a publisher's assistance, you can focus more on the creative aspects of your music career, such as writing new songs and honing your craft.

However, while working with a publisher has its advantages, it's crucial to approach any publishing agreement with caution and thorough consideration. Understanding the rights you are assigning to the publisher, the percentage of income they will receive from your compositions, and the duration of the agreement is essential. Be sure to review the terms carefully and seek professional advice, such as consulting with a lawyer or a music business expert, to ensure that the agreement is fair and mutually beneficial.

One potential challenge of working with a publisher is that you may have to relinquish a certain degree of control over the exploitation and promotion of your compositions. It's essential to have confidence in the publisher's expertise and their ability to effectively navigate the music landscape, ultimately generating revenue for your compositions.

Additionally, it's important to recognize that the success of your compositions does not solely rest on the efforts of the publisher. Various factors can influence the income generated from your music, and you must remain proactive in promoting your career and seizing opportunities as they arise. Engaging with your audience, building a strong online presence, and networking within the industry can all contribute to your success as a songwriter.

Balancing the benefits and challenges of working with a publisher can lead to a fruitful and successful collaboration that helps you achieve your aspirations as a songwriter.

Types Of Publishing Agreements

You have four main options when it comes to entering into a publishing agreement. It's important to understand the different types of publishing agreements and how they work in order to make an informed decision about which option is best for you.

Publishing Administration Agreement: A publishing administration agreement is a type of contract in which a songwriter retains ownership of their compositions but hires a third party to handle the administrative tasks related to licensing and monetizing the songs. This can include registering the compositions with performing rights organizations, registering the finished pieces with the copyright office, negotiating licenses, and collecting royalties. The administrator is typically paid a fee or percentage of earnings for their services, and the agreement is usually exclusive to that particular administrator. The main benefit of a publishing administration agreement is that the songwriter retains ownership of their compositions while still receiving assistance with the administrative tasks related to publishing.

Co-Publishing Agreement: A co-publishing agreement involves a collaboration between a songwriter and music publisher, in which the publisher assumes a greater role in the exploitation and promotion of the songwriter's compositions. In this arrangement, the songwriter typically assigns a percentage of their publishing rights to the publisher, who then shares in the income generated from the compositions. Co-publishing agreements can be either exclusive or non-exclusive, and the terms and percentages of ownership can vary depending on the specific agreement. The main benefit of a co-publishing agreement is that the publisher can help to promote and exploit the songwriter's compositions, potentially leading to greater income.

Sub-Publishing Agreement: In a sub-publishing agreement, a publisher licenses the copyrights in a songwriter's compositions to other publishers in different territories. The sub-publisher then assumes the responsibilities of exploiting the compositions and collecting income in those territories. The main benefit of a sub-publishing agreement is that it can expand the reach of the songwriter's compositions and potentially lead to greater income.

Full Publishing Agreement: A full publishing agreement is a contract in which a songwriter assigns all or a portion of their publishing rights to a music publisher. In exchange, the publisher assumes the responsibilities of exploiting the compositions and collecting income on behalf of the songwriter. The terms of a full publishing agreement can vary widely, but typically include an advance payment to the songwriter, a percentage of income collected, and provisions for songwriter royalties and ownership. Full publishing agreements can be either exclusive or non-exclusive, and the percentage of ownership and income being assigned to the publisher can vary. The main benefit of a full publishing agreement is that the publisher can provide resources and expertise to exploit and promote the songwriter's compositions.

With the rise of digital platforms and changing revenue models, it is more important than ever for artists to carefully consider their options. They must weigh the benefits of traditional publishing support against the freedom and potential risks of independent music distribution and self-publishing, keeping in mind that outlier contracts that might offer unique advantages tailored to their specific career path and artistic vision

Pro Tip: Negotiating A Fair Publishing Agreement

Knowing how to negotiating a fair publishing agreement could be make or break in a songwriter's career, as it determines how their creative work will be exploited and how they will be compensated for their compositions. To ensure a successful negotiation, songwriters need to be well-informed, confident in their worth, and clear about their expectations.

Start by educating yourself about the different types of publishing agreements is essential. Familiarize yourself with the intricacies of the deals, the different formats and how they work. Understanding the various terms and clauses will empower you to know what to expect and what to negotiate for, leading to a more favourable outcome.

Seeking legal counsel is highly advisable during the negotiation process. Engaging a lawyer with expertise in music publishing can help you navigate the legal jargon and understand the implications of each clause in the agreement. A lawyer will review the contract, identify any potential pitfalls, and negotiate on your behalf to secure a fair deal.

Knowing your worth as a songwriter is critical when entering into a publishing agreement. Understand the value of your compositions, considering factors such as past successes, commercial potential, and industry demand. Armed with this knowledge, don't hesitate to negotiate for an advance payment, royalty percentages, and ownership rights that align with the value you bring to the table.

Transparency is key during negotiations. Be clear about your expectations and communicate them effectively to the publisher. Discuss crucial aspects of the agreement, including exclusivity, the duration of the contract, and the level of control you will retain over your compositions. This ensures that both parties are on the same page and helps prevent misunderstandings down the line.

Avoid rushing into a publishing agreement without thoroughly reviewing and understanding its terms. Take the time to scrutinize each clause, seeking clarification from the publisher if necessary. Remember, a publishing agreement is a long-term commitment, and you want to ensure that it is a mutually beneficial relationship.

Consider the track record of the publisher. Research their history of working with other songwriters and artists. A reputable publisher with a successful track record of exploiting and promoting compositions can offer valuable support and opportunities for your career growth.
In music publishing, understanding royalty splits and advances is vital for songwriters. Royalty splits refer to how the income from compositions is divided between the songwriter and the publisher. A typical split is 50/50, but this can be negotiated based on the songwriter's leverage, previous successes, and the publisher's commitment to promoting the compositions.

Advances, on the other hand, are upfront payments made to the songwriter by the publisher. These advances are recouped from future royalties earned from the compositions so consider your long term objective before seeking a huge upfront payment. Negotiating the terms of the advance payment is crucial, as it can significantly impact your financial stability as a songwriter.

Case Study: Kamille

Kamille is a UK-based singer, songwriter, and producer who has made a name for herself in the music industry. She has a unique sound that blends elements of pop, R&B, and hip hop, and her music has garnered a large and dedicated following.

Kamille began making music at a young age and started uploading her songs to Soundcloud in her teens. Her music career found major success when she started working as a song writer and went on to have some of the biggest records globally with multiple collaborations with successful artists that have resulted in multiple UK #1 singles and numerous accolades, including Songwriter of the Year at the A&R Awards.

Success in publishing: Kamille began her career as a songwriter in 2013 with the co-write "What About Us" by The Saturdays featuring Sean Paul. This was her first major success and marked the start of her career in music publishing. In the same year, Kamille co-wrote three songs for Little Mix's second album, 'Salute', which began a long-term relationship between the two that has led to worldwide success.

Kamille's most notable work with Little Mix is 'Black Magic', which became her second UK number-one single and gained her her first Brit Award nomination for Best British Single. The track 'Shout Out To My Ex', released in 2016, spent three weeks at #1 in the UK and has since been certified 3x Platinum in the UK. It won Kamille her first Brit Award for Best British Single. Her long-term relationship with Little Mix has resulted in over 30 songs co-written by Kamille, she is considered the group's unofficial 5th member, both publicly by Little Mix themselves and by the national press.

Kamille has collaborated with many other successful artists including Jess Glynne, Clean Bandit, and Mabel. Her 2018 co-write "I'll Be There" for Jess Glynne and "Solo" for Clean Bandit featuring Demi Lovato became UK #1 singles back-to-back. "Solo" was named the 'most-Shazamed' song of 2018. In January 2019, Kamille co-wrote "Don't Call Me Up" for Mabel with Steve Mac. The song became Mabel's most successful to date, peaking at #3 in the UK singles chart, being nominated for a Brit Award for Best British Single, and amassing over 700 million Spotify streams. In November 2019, Kamille launched her own record label and publishing company, Pure Cut, and opened her recording studio, Saint Studios, within London's Metropolis Studios.

In 2020, Kamille was nominated for the Mercury Prize for her work on Dua Lipa's album 'Future Nostalgia' and contributed to five UK Top 10 Singles.

Music publishing is an essential aspect of Kamille's career as a musician. It involves the administration and exploitation of the rights to her original compositions for the artist she writes for. Kamille has a publishing deal with a major music publishing company, which handles all aspects of her publishing rights. This includes securing licenses for the use of her music in various media, such as films, TV shows, commercials, and video games.

Ownership Of Compositions And Masters

Sync licensing involves two key concepts: compositions and masters. Compositions refer to the intellectual property of a song, including the melody, lyrics, and arrangement, while masters refer to the physical recordings of the song. A composition is a piece of intellectual property that exists independently of any specific recording of the song. The copyright holder of a composition is typically the original author or authors, unless there is a written agreement transferring the rights to another person or entity, such as a publishing company.

Masters, on the other hand, refer to the actual, tangible recording of a performance of a composition. If a song is recorded by multiple artists, there will be multiple masters of the same composition. The owner of the master recording is typically the record label or the artist, depending on the terms of the recording contract. The owner of the master recording has the exclusive right to reproduce, distribute, and publicly perform the recording, and to authorize others to do so.

When using a song in sync, it is important to clear the rights to both the composition and the master recording, and negotiate a license with the copyright holders of each. This typically involves contacting the owner of the master or their representative, such as a record label or music licensing agency, and negotiating a license for the use of the song. The terms of the license may include the specific use of the song, the duration of the license, and the territory where the song will be used, as well as the payment of sync fees and royalties. Understanding the key concepts of compositions and masters in sync licensing is crucial for successfully using a song in synchronization with visual media.

How Compositions And Masters Are Used In Sync Licensing

When it comes to sync licensing, both compositions and masters are important to consider. Compositions refer to the intellectual property of a song, such as the melody, lyrics, and arrangement, and the copyright holder has exclusive rights to reproduce, distribute, perform, and authorize others to do the same. To use a composition in sync, you need to obtain permission from the copyright holder and negotiate a license with them or their representative, such as a publishing company or music licensing agency. This license may include the specific use of the song, duration, territory, sync fee, and royalties based on the song's performance.

Masters, on the other hand, refer to the physical recordings of a song, and the owner of the master recording has exclusive rights to reproduce, distribute, perform, and authorize others to do so. In order to use a master in sync, you need to obtain permission from the owner of the master recording, who is typically the record label or the artist, depending on the terms of the recording contract. This involves negotiating a license with the owner or their representative, such as a music licensing agency. The license may include the same terms as a composition license, including specific use, duration, territory, sync fee, and royalties.

Recognizing the significance of both compositions and masters in sync licensing is essential. It ensures acquiring the required rights and fair compensation for all parties involved in the use of their intellectual property and recordings.

Publishing Administration And Covers

Publishing administration involves managing the rights to a composition or a catalogue of compositions. The individual or entity handling the publishing administration is not the owner of the compositions but acts as a representative for the rights holders. Their main objective is to maximize the revenue generated from these compositions. Publishing administrators typically earn a commission from the revenue they help generate for the rights holders.

In the context of sync licensing, publishing administrators play a crucial role in assisting visual media creators. They help identify and clear the rights to suitable compositions for sync projects, ensuring that the appropriate permissions and licenses are obtained for using the music in films, TV shows, advertisements, or other visual media. Negotiating the terms of the license is also a part of their responsibilities, as they work to strike a fair deal for both the rights holders and the visual media creators.

Covers refer to new recordings of existing compositions. Visual media creators may want to use music that sounds similar to a well-known song but find it challenging to obtain the rights to the original composition or recording. In such cases, covers offer a solution. Artists or bands can create their versions of the song, providing a fresh take on the original while making it more accessible for sync licensing purposes.

Using a cover song in sync projects requires clearing the rights to both the composition and the master recording of the cover. This involves negotiating a license for the use of the composition with the copyright holder (or their representative, such as a publishing company or music licensing agency) and a separate license for the use of the recording with the owner of the master recording (or their representative, such as a record label or music licensing agency).

These licenses' terms may encompass various aspects, including the specific use of the song, the duration of the license, the geographic territory where the song will be used, and the payment of sync fees and royalties to the rights holders and master recording owners.

Samples And Clearing Rights

Samples and their use in music, particularly for sync licensing purposes, are subjects that demand careful consideration and adherence to copyright regulations. When incorporating samples into new compositions or recordings, securing the necessary clearance for their use is of utmost importance. To utilize a sample in sync licensing, one must obtain rights for both the composition and the master recording being sampled. This entails negotiating licenses with the copyright holders or their representatives for the composition and contacting the owner of the master recording for permission to use the recording. The license terms will outline the usage of the sample, the duration of the license, the allowed territory of use, and the payment of sync fees and royalties.

The process of clearing rights for samples can be intricate, often involving dealings with multiple parties, including co-authors, producers, and record labels. To navigate this process correctly, it is highly advisable to seek the guidance of a music lawyer or a professional sync licensing agency. Failing to properly clear sample rights can lead to legal consequences for both the creator of the new work and any entity involved in synchronizing the music with visual media.

There are some key considerations that should be kept in mind when using samples in music, particularly for sync licensing. Firstly, copyright law stipulates that using samples necessitates obtaining permission from both the copyright holder of the composition and the owner of the master recording being sampled. This requires acquiring licenses for both the composition and recording and complying with any associated fees or royalties. It is crucial to be thorough and diligent in this process to avoid any copyright infringement issues.

The concept of "fair use" under copyright law may apply to some instances of sample use. However, the fair use doctrine is context-specific and may not be applicable if the use of the sample is not transformative or if it could potentially harm the market for the original work. Therefore, creators should be aware of the limitations of fair use when dealing with samples.

It is essential to budget for sample clearance fees during the music production process. The cost of clearing rights for samples can vary significantly depending on factors such as the popularity and value of the original work and the specific terms of the license. Budgeting for these expenses in advance can prevent unexpected financial setbacks.

The use of samples in music, particularly for sync licensing purposes, requires meticulous attention to copyright regulations and diligent clearance of rights. Make sure to have a thorough understanding of the legal implications and obtain the necessary permissions. Music creators can then ensure that their work complies with copyright laws and that any sync licensing ventures proceed smoothly and successfully.

Releasing A Remix Of A Song In The UK

For music artists and producers, releasing a remix of an existing hit song can be an effective strategy to expand their fan base and establish themselves. However, it is imperative to ensure that the remix is released legally, particularly when incorporating someone else's intellectual property.

In the UK, remixes fall under two types of copyright: the master recording copyright and the song copyright. The master recording copyright pertains to the actual sound recording, while the song copyright covers the composition and its underlying musical and lyrical elements. Both copyrights are crucial in the remix release process, and obtaining permission from the respective copyright holders is mandatory. The fair use policy, although applicable in some situations for certain uses of copyrighted material, may not extend to independent artists seeking to monetize their remixes. Therefore, relying on the fair use doctrine for remix releases is not advisable, and explicit permission from the copyright holders must be obtained.

Obtaining Permission To Remix A Track

Obtaining permission to legally remix a song is a crucial process that requires careful consideration and adherence to copyright laws and the rights of the original artist and copyright holders. To successfully navigate this process, music artists and producers must follow a series of essential steps and consider various factors that could impact the outcome of their request.

The first step in obtaining permission to remix a song is to determine the copyright owner(s) of the original composition. This task can be more complex when dealing with popular songs that involve multiple songwriters or rights holders. Thorough research and investigation are necessary to identify all relevant parties and ensure that permission is sought from each copyright owner. Music artists may utilize various resources, such as online databases, music publishing databases, and official artist websites, to gather information about the copyright ownership of the song.

Once the copyright owner(s) have been identified, the next step is to find the contact details of the artist or the relevant rights holder(s). Direct communication is essential in this process, as it allows for a personalized and professional approach to obtaining permission. Official artist websites, social media profiles, and professional networking platforms may contain contact information for reaching out to the relevant parties. In cases where the artist is signed to a record label, it may be necessary to contact the label or the music publisher to obtain permissions.

When contacting the artist or rights holder(s), it is crucial to present a strong and compelling pitch that clearly outlines the intentions behind the remix. The pitch should highlight the potential benefits of the remix for both the artist and the label, showcasing how the new version of the song can contribute positively to their overall music strategy. Additionally, the music artist should showcase their remixing skills and experience, providing links to their previous remixes or music platforms where their work can be easily accessed and reviewed.

Negotiating the terms of the remix agreement is an essential aspect of the permission process. This involves discussing the scope of the remix, the usage rights, the distribution channels, and any financial arrangements, such as royalty splits or one-time payments. Clarity and transparency in negotiations are crucial to avoid misunderstandings and conflicts later on. Consulting a music lawyer or an experienced industry professional during the negotiation process can provide valuable guidance and ensure that all legal aspects of the agreement are properly addressed.

Regarding the deal, remix licensing in the UK typically involves a 'work-for-hire' based contract. Under this arrangement, the copyright of the remix master, including the original song within it, remains with the original artist or copyright holder. The royalty split for the remix will be distributed among all rights holders, including the artist, music publisher, and the remixer.

Typically, the royalty split for the remix master is evenly divided between the original artist and the remixer, with each receiving 50% of the earnings. However, the royalty split is open to negotiation and will be specified in the licensing arrangement. Clear communication and agreement on the financial aspects are crucial to ensuring a fair and satisfactory collaboration between all parties involved.

To ensure a fair distribution of remuneration, a royalty-sharing agreement is often utilized. However, managing such agreements can pose challenges in terms of accounting and tracking earnings. Therefore, it is crucial for music artists and producers involved in remix releases to register with appropriate performance rights organizations (PROs). By doing so, they can efficiently collect all owed royalties from the remix's performance.

If the artist or rights holder(s) decline the request for permission to release an official remix, it is crucial for the music artist to respect their decision and refrain from using the copyrighted material without authorization. Pursuing the remix without proper permission could lead to legal consequences, including copyright infringement claims and financial penalties. In some cases, the original artist or rights holder(s) may grant permission for a social-only remix. This type of permission allows the remix to be shared on platforms like YouTube and SoundCloud for non-commercial use, providing an opportunity for the music artist to showcase their creativity and remixing skills to a broader audience.

When planning to perform the remix in public, it is essential to clarify the necessary permissions with the venue beforehand. This includes obtaining the appropriate performance licenses and ensuring that all rights holders are properly compensated for the use of their copyrighted material during the live performance.

How To Legally Clear A Sample For A Song Or Beat

In music production, a sample refers to using a portion of a pre-existing song or recording by another artist in a different track. This can include incorporating elements or copying a snippet of another artist's song into the new music. It's important to distinguish between samples and interpolations, where a musician re-records lyrics or music from another artist's song note for note, based on the original composition.

When using a sample, it's necessary to obtain permission for both the master recording and the underlying composition. However, for an interpolation, permission is only required for the underlying composition. Some artists choose to interpolate to reduce the number of permissions needed, saving time and money. It's important to note that licensing for samples/interpolations is different from licensing for cover songs. A mechanical license from the original songwriter and/or publisher is sufficient for a cover version.

Clearing A Sample For A Song

Using music samples without legal permission is against industry law, and rumours about loopholes are false. Obtaining the required licenses is essential to legally use a sample from an existing recording. Clearing a sample requires obtaining two different licenses: a master recording copyright license (typically owned by the artist or label) and an underlying composition copyright license (usually controlled by the songwriter and/or music publisher).

Step 1: Apply For Clearance Well In Advance
Clearing a sample can be a time-consuming process that involves financial negotiations and paperwork. It's crucial to apply for clearance well in advance to avoid delays in releasing the song.

Step 2: Collect Info About The Song You're Sampling
Before contacting the rights holders of a sample, it's essential to gather all the necessary information about the song being sampled. This includes the sample's length, how many times it appears in the song, which part of the original song is being sampled, and the intended use of the new song.

Step 3: Identifying The Master Recording Rightsholder
Identifying the owner of the master recording is a crucial step in the sample clearance process. The owner can be the artist, label, or a third party. Google search can provide the necessary information. Artist and band Wikipedia pages or the linear notes on a song's page on Spotify can also be useful. Once you have found the master recording owner, note down their contact information, including phone number and email address, which is typically listed on their website.

Step 4: Identifying The Publishing Rightsholder

Identifying the publishing rightsholder is another critical step in the sample clearance process. The largest music publishing databases, known as performing rights organizations (PROs), provide a starting point for your search. ASCAP, Harry Fox & BMI in the US, SOCAN in Canada, and PRS in the UK are some of the PROs available.

To access the full information in these databases, you must be a member of the relevant PRO in your area. If you are using a music publishing service like Ditto Music Publishing, they will sign you up on your behalf.

If you are not a PRO member, you can use Google to find the composition owner's name. It may be difficult to locate direct contact information, such as phone numbers or email addresses, but it is worth the effort.

Step 5: Contacting The Rightsholders And Negotiating A Price

Once you have identified the rightsholders, you need to provide them with a copy of your track that features their sample and negotiate the costs. Most publishers will require an upfront advance and a percentage of all revenue generated from the song, based on factors such as how prominently the sample is used, its recognizability, and whether it includes vocals, instrumentation, or both.

Similarly, the label will demand an upfront fee or advance, along with a "rollover" royalty rate calculated based on a sales threshold. If both rightsholders refuse permission, it is best to abandon the project. Releasing a song with uncleared samples may lead to severe legal consequences, such as hefty fines and removal of your music from all streaming platforms.

If you are unable to obtain clearance for the sample, you may want to consider using pre-cleared samples from websites such as Citizen DJ, Tracklib, and DMG Clearances. It is important to remember that obtaining legal clearance for a sample is crucial in avoiding any potential copyright infringement issues. If obtaining clearance is not possible, it is better to create an original element for your music rather than risking your reputation and potential legal troubles by using unapproved samples.

Using samples in music production can be a great way to enhance creativity, but it's crucial to obtain the necessary rights and budget for any associated costs. Following both legal and practical guidelines can help you steer clear of any legal issues and make sure that all parties involved receive fair compensation for their intellectual property and recordings.

Royalties And Sync Fees

In the world of sync licensing, there are two fundamental payment types that play a pivotal role: royalties and sync fees. These payments are crucial as they are made to the respective copyright holders of compositions and owners of master recordings in exchange for using their music in sync with visual media, such as films, TV shows, advertisements, video games, and more.

Payment Types

Royalties: Royalties are payments disbursed to the copyright holders of compositions. These can be songwriters, composers, or the publishing company representing the musical work. When a piece of music is synchronized with visual media, such as a movie scene or a commercial, royalties are typically paid to the copyright holder as compensation for the use of their musical work. The payment amount can vary, and it might be based on a percentage of revenue generated from the music's use or a flat fee, depending on the specific terms negotiated in the sync license agreement.

The frequency of royalty payments can also differ. In some cases, they are paid periodically, such as quarterly or semi-annually, while in other instances, a one-time payment might be agreed upon. These royalties contribute to the financial well-being of the copyright holders and incentivize them to continue creating exceptional musical works for potential sync licensing opportunities.

Sync Fees: Sync fees, are payments made to the owners of master recordings. The master recording refers to the specific recording of a song, which is usually owned by the record label or the artist who produced it. When a sync license is granted for the use of a particular master recording in synchronization with visual media, sync fees are paid to the owner of the master recording or their designated representative, such as the record label or a music licensing agency.

As with royalties, the payment amount for sync fees can also vary and may be based on a percentage of revenue generated from the music's use or a flat fee, depending on the specific terms agreed upon in the sync license agreement. Similar to royalties, sync fees can be paid periodically or as a one-time payment.

These payments ensure that the copyright holders of compositions and the owners of master recordings receive fair compensation for their valuable contributions to the visual media projects. Properly budgeting for these payments during the sync licensing negotiations is essential to ensure a smooth and successful licensing process, benefiting both the copyright holders and the creators of the visual media.

Royalties and sync fees are vital components of the sync licensing landscape. By comprehending these payment concepts and their respective roles, artists, music publishers, and record labels can navigate the sync licensing world effectively and ensure that all parties involved are rightfully compensated for their creative contributions.

Factors That Can Affect The Amount Of Royalties And Sync Fees

Sync licensing allows artists and copyright holders to monetize their compositions by synchronizing them with visual media such as films, television shows, commercials, video games, and online content. The process involves negotiating licenses with the rights holders of the music to use their works in these visual media projects. The amount of royalties and sync fees payable in sync licensing can vary significantly based on some key factors, each of which plays a crucial role in determining the value of the music being licensed.

One of the primary factors that can impact the amount of royalties and sync fees payable is the popularity of the music being licensed. Music that is well-known and widely recognized by the public can command higher fees compared to lesser-known or less popular music. The fame and cultural significance of the music contribute to its value and influence the fees that can be charged for its use in visual media projects.

Project type: The specific type of use of the music also plays a significant role in determining the amount of royalties and sync fees payable. Different types of uses, such as a major motion picture, a TV commercial, a video game, or an online advertisement, can have varying degrees of exposure and reach, which can impact the licensing fees. For instance, licensing music for a major Hollywood film with a wide theatrical release may have higher fees than licensing the same music for a local TV commercial with a limited audience.

Term of the agreement: The duration of the license agreement is another essential factor to consider. Longer term licenses, such as those for feature films or ongoing television series, typically command higher fees than shorter term licenses. The longer the music is used in a visual media project, the more valuable it becomes, warranting higher compensation for the copyright holders.

Territory: Geographic considerations also come into play when determining the amount of royalties and sync fees. The territory of the license refers to the geographic region where the music will be used. Licenses for global or widespread use, such as for international films or advertisements, may command higher fees than licenses for more limited use in specific countries or regions.

Production Budgets: The value of the visual media project in which the music is being used can significantly impact the licensing fees. Projects with higher production budgets, larger audiences, and greater commercial success can justify higher fees due to the increased exposure and potential financial returns for the music copyright holders.

In addition to these factors, the structure of sync licensing agreements can include different royalty and sync fee arrangements that are dependent on a variety of considerations. Some common structures include flat fees, percentage of revenue, tiered structures, and advances.

A flat fee is a fixed amount paid for the use of the music, regardless of the revenue generated. This structure is often used for shorter term licenses or for less popular music. On the other hand, a percentage of revenue structure involves paying a percentage of the revenue generated from the use of the music. This structure may be based on total revenue or specific types of revenue, such as advertising or merchandise sales. Percentage of revenue structures are commonly used for longer term licenses or for more popular music.

Tiered structures involve paying different amounts of royalties or sync fees based on different levels of use or revenue. This arrangement may incentivize greater use of the music or provide rewards for higher levels of success.

When negotiating the terms of a sync license, all these factors and considerations must be taken into account to determine a fair and mutually beneficial arrangement. The popularity of the music, the type of use, the duration of the license, the territory, the value of the visual media, and the chosen fee structure will collectively shape the final licensing agreement. Proper understanding and consideration of these factors are crucial for both artists and copyright holders to receive appropriate compensation for the use of their music in visual media projects. To ensure a successful and fair negotiation process, it is advisable to consult with experienced music lawyers or sync licensing experts who can navigate the complexities of the licensing landscape and maximize the value of the music being licensed.

Music Distribution

Music distribution allows artists and record labels to get their music to listeners all over the world. While the role of distributors has evolved over time, the core purpose has remained the same: to facilitate the distribution of music to consumers.

The History Of Music Distribution

Music distribution has a long history dating back to the early days of the music industry. In the 19th and early 20th centuries, music distribution was largely handled by sheet music publishing companies, which printed and distributed scores to stores and other outlets. As recording technology improved, record labels began to emerge, and the distribution of music shifted from physical scores to recorded music on vinyl records, cassette tapes, and eventually CDs.
During this time, music distribution was primarily handled by record labels, who would manufacture and distribute physical copies of albums to stores and other outlets. Record labels would typically sign distribution deals with distributors, who would handle the physical distribution of the music to stores and other outlets. This model allowed record labels to focus on the creative aspects of music production, while leaving the logistical aspects of distribution to the distributors.

The Rise Of Digital Music Distribution

In the 21st century, the industry has undergone a significant shift towards digital distribution. With the proliferation of the internet and the rise of streaming platforms, more and more music is being consumed digitally rather than as physical copies. This shift has had a major impact on the way music is distributed, as well as on the role of distributors.

In the digital age, music is typically distributed through online platforms such as streaming services, online stores, and social media. These platforms allow artists and labels to make their music available to listeners all over the world, instantly and at little cost. While this has made it easier for artists to reach a global audience, it has also led to a highly competitive and complex music market.

To navigate this market, many artists and labels turn to distributors or aggregators to handle the technical aspects of digital distribution. These distributors act as intermediaries between the artist or label and the various platforms, handling tasks such as uploading and formatting releases, ensuring that the correct metadata is included, and allocating royalties to rights holders.

Types Of Music Distribution Models

There are 4 major types of music distribution models that exist today, each with its own unique characteristics and benefits. Some of the most common distribution models include:

- **Major Label Distribution:** Major record labels typically have their own distribution networks and handle the distribution of their own music. This allows them to maintain control over the distribution process and maximize their profits.
- **Independent Label Distribution:** Independent labels may choose to sign distribution deals with major labels or distributors, or they may handle distribution themselves. Independent labels often rely on distributors to handle the technical aspects of distribution and to provide access to a wider range of platforms.
- **DIY Distribution:** Some artists choose to handle the distribution of their music themselves, using direct artist platforms such as Bandcamp or SoundCloud. This approach allows artists to retain control over the distribution process and keep a larger share of the profits, but it also requires a greater level of technical expertise and may limit the reach of the artist's music.
- **Distributed Label:** A distributed label is a small label that relies on a major label or distributor to handle the distribution of its music. This allows the label to focus on the creative aspects of music production while leaving the logistical aspects of distribution to the distributor.

The Role Of Distributors In Modern Music
In the modern music industry, distributors play a vital role in getting music to listeners all over the world. Some of the key responsibilities of distributors include:

- **Distributing Releases To DSPs:** Distributors are responsible for uploading and formatting releases for different digital service providers (DSPs), such as streaming platforms and online stores. This includes ensuring that the releases meet the technical and formatting requirements of each platform and that the correct metadata is included.
- **Royalties Allocation:** Distributors also handle the allocation of royalties to rights holders. This involves tracking the streams and downloads of each release and calculating the royalties due to each rights holder. Distributors may use proprietary software and algorithms to track and allocate royalties, or they may outsource this task to a third party.
- **Marketing And Promotion:** Many distributors also offer marketing and promotion services to their clients. This may include playlist pitching, social media promotion, and data analysis to help artists and labels understand the performance of their releases.
- **Administrative Services:** In addition to their technical and promotional services, distributors also handle a range of administrative tasks for their clients. This may include invoicing, reporting, and payment processing.

While the specific services offered by distributors may vary, their core goal is always the same: to facilitate the distribution of music to as many people as possible.

While the role of distributors has evolved over time, they continue to play a vital role in getting music to the people who want to hear it. Whether through major label distribution, independent label distribution, DIY distribution, or distributed label distribution, distributors provide the infrastructure and support needed to get music to a global audience.

SoundOn

Launched by TikTok, SoundOn marks a significant foray into the music distribution business. This platform represents a strategic extension of TikTok's influence in the music industry, aligning its prowess as a social media giant with the evolving needs of music distribution. Tracing its roots back to March of 2022, SoundOn was officially introduced, marking TikTok's official entry into music distribution. Its introduction is not just an addition to the array of distribution services but a pivotal moment that reflects the changing dynamics of music consumption and distribution in the digital age.

At its core, the service is more than just a distribution platform; it's a commitment to empowering new and undiscovered artists. This mission is deeply embedded in their ethos, offering a unique blend of distribution services, promotional tools, and direct access to one of the most vibrant music discovery platforms - TikTok.

Integration with a Social Media Powerhouse

SoundOn is ingeniously integrated within TikTok's vast ecosystem. This integration offers artists unparalleled exposure, leveraging TikTok's massive user base for music discovery and promotion. The synergy between SoundOn and TikTok creates a seamless pathway from music creation to global dissemination. The platform boasts some strong features that will be attractive to artist and communities built through their platform. Every aspect of SoundOn, from its user interface to its royalty payouts, is crafted with the artist in mind. The platform is not just a distribution channel but a comprehensive support system, offering;

- Direct Uploads: Artists can directly upload their music to TikTok and Resso, reflecting an ease-of-access that is crucial for emerging artists.
- Royalty Structure: SoundOn stands out with its attractive royalty scheme, offering 100% royalties in the first year and 90% thereafter for catalogues with more than 500 tracks, a testament to its artist-centric approach.
- Global Reach: With its global footprint, SoundOn breaks geographical barriers, allowing artists to reach audiences across continents.
- Promotional Tools: These are tailor-made to enhance an artist's visibility on TikTok and beyond.
- Expert Guidance: SoundOn provides dedicated support, guiding artists through their journey in the music industry.

Understanding the importance of ISRCs and UPCs, SoundOn requires artists to provide original metadata to ensure proper tracking and distribution of their music. SoundOn stands out in the landscape of music distribution platforms. While many distribution platforms offer similar basic services, SoundOn's direct integration with TikTok provides a unique advantage.

SoundOn Compared To Other Music Distribution Platforms

Royalty Structure and Fees
- SoundOn: 100% royalties first year, 90% thereafter.
- Ditto Music: Offers various subscription plans, with artists keeping 100% of royalties.
- SoundCloud: Provides monetization through SoundCloud Premier, with different payout rates based on various factors.

- Audiomack: Free platform offering monetization through its Amplify subscription program.

Platform-Specific Features
- SoundOn: Direct integration with TikTok and Resso.
- Ditto Music: Wide distribution network, pre-release date setup, and chart eligibility.
- SoundCloud: Unique platform combining music distribution with a social media-like environment for music sharing and discovery.
- Audiomack: Focuses on music discovery, allowing artists to upload music for free and reach a community of listeners.

Ease of Use and Artist Support
- SoundOn: User-friendly interface with TikTok-specific promotional tools.
- Ditto Music: Robust support system including label services.
- SoundCloud: Intuitive platform geared towards sharing and community engagement.
- Audiomack: Easy to use, emphasizing accessibility and community.

Global Reach and Market Penetration
- SoundOn: Strong in markets where TikTok is popular, with a focus on social media-driven music discovery.
- Ditto Music: Global distribution, including key markets like the USA, UK, and others.
- SoundCloud: Widespread global reach with a large user base for music sharing and discovery.
- Audiomack: Growing presence, particularly in African markets and among independent artists.

Content Promotion and Marketing Tools
- SoundOn: Integrated promotional tools for TikTok.
- Ditto Music: Marketing services available, including social media promotion.
- SoundCloud: Promotional tools through SoundCloud Premier, including playlist placements.
- Audiomack: Offers promotional opportunities within its community and platform.

Music Rights and Licensing
- SoundOn: Non-exclusive licensing with flexibility for artists.
- Ditto Music: Non-exclusive distribution, allowing artists to retain rights.
- SoundCloud: Rights remain with the artist, with monetization options under SoundCloud Premier.
- Audiomack: Artists retain their rights, with monetization through the Amplify program.

Target Audience and Niche
- SoundOn: Best for artists focusing on leveraging TikTok for growth and visibility.
- Ditto Music: Suitable for independent artists looking for a wide distribution network and additional label services.
- SoundCloud: Ideal for artists emphasizing community engagement and direct fan interaction.
- Audiomack: Great for artists targeting specific markets, especially where the platform has a strong presence, and for those focusing on community-driven discovery.

The choice of a music distribution platform should align with an artist's specific goals, target audience, and desired level of engagement. SoundOn's integration with TikTok makes it highly appealing for artists seeking to tap into the social media platform's user base. In contrast, platforms like Ditto Music, SoundCloud, and Audiomack cater to different aspects of music distribution and artist engagement, each with unique features catering to various artist needs.

Pro Tip: Distribution Strategy

Choosing the right distribution strategy sets the foundation for how your music will reach your audience and how you will generate revenue from your creative work. Before finalizing a distribution strategy, it's essential to align it with your overarching goals as an artist. Are you looking to reach the widest possible audience, maximize your revenue, or build a dedicated fanbase? Each of these goals requires a tailored approach to distribution.

If your aim is to reach the widest possible audience, streaming platforms like Spotify, Apple Music, Amazon Music, and Deezer should be at the forefront of your distribution strategy. These platforms have vast user bases and global reach, making them effective channels for getting your music in front of a diverse audience. Keep in mind that while these platforms offer broad exposure, the revenue per stream may be relatively low, especially for independent artists. However, the potential for discovery and exposure makes them valuable in building brand recognition and attracting new listeners.

If maximizing revenue is a top priority, you may want to consider a mix of distribution channels. While streaming platforms contribute to a significant portion of music consumption today, digital download stores like iTunes and Amazon Music still offer higher royalty rates per download. Additionally, physical distribution through CDs or vinyl records can be a lucrative option, especially if you have a dedicated fanbase that appreciates collectible physical formats.

Building a dedicated fanbase often requires a more personalized and direct approach to distribution. Direct-to-fan platforms like Bandcamp and Patreon enable artists to interact directly with their fans and offer unique experiences and exclusive content. These platforms foster a stronger connection between artists and their supporters, creating a community of loyal fans who are willing to invest in your music and creative endeavours.

As an independent artist, budget considerations are essential when choosing a distribution strategy. Physical distribution can be expensive, involving manufacturing costs, packaging, and shipping. For those on a limited budget, digital distribution services become a more viable option. Platforms like TuneCore, DistroKid, CD Baby, and Amuse offer cost-effective solutions, often charging a flat fee or taking a percentage of the revenue generated from. These services make it accessible for independent artists to distribute their music globally without significant upfront expenses.

Understanding the rights and ownership implications of each distribution channel is vital before making a decision. Some platforms may require you to grant them a percentage of your rights or ownership as part of the distribution deal. This could limit your creative control and financial independence. On the other hand, some platforms enable you to retain complete control over your music and rights, allowing you to make decisions about licensing, sync opportunities, and other potential revenue streams.

Thoroughly examining the terms and conditions of any distribution channel is a must. This includes understanding whether the distribution is exclusive or non-exclusive, what rights you are granting to the platform, and the length of the distribution agreement. Being well-informed about these aspects will ensure that your distribution strategy aligns with your long-term goals and artistic vision. Whether you aim to reach a massive audience, maximize revenue, or cultivate a dedicated fanbase, a well-executed distribution strategy is a crucial element in achieving success.

Distribution Deals

Distribution deals are agreements that exist between record labels, distribution companies, and independent artists. They are popular due to their flexibility, freedom, and ownership. The benefits of signing to a major label have been scrutinized recently as the shift from physical to digital distribution has lowered the cost of producing and distributing music. In the past, a distribution deal was a situation where a distributor paid for the manufacturing costs of an album, including pressing and printing labels, when the upfront costs of making physical copies of music used to be a barrier for independent artists, as well as the difficulty of getting their products to retailers, the digital age provided new solutions and access. Distribution is accessible to anyone who has a little bit of money.

Distribution companies acted as the bridge between record labels and retail outlets, including record stores and big-box retailers such as HMV. Today, a distribution deal may be offered by a true distribution platform such as TuneCore, Create Music Group, Unitedmasters, or a distribution subsidiary of a record label such as The Orchard. These companies may also offer advances, albeit not the same amount as a record label would provide, but still enough to own the masters and at worst, a 50/50 royalty split. Deals also include additional services such as marketing, advertising, soliciting sync licensing opportunities, video monetization, performance rights services, as well as other label services.

The role of music distribution companies has changed as distributors are now operating as mini-record labels without owning masters or collecting excessive royalties. However, the challenges in distributing an artist's music successfully still exist, such as having a release strategy, promoting the product, and ensuring the music is of good quality. In many ways, a distributor is in the best position to acquire new talent as it has access to data and analytics on all platforms, knowing whose music is streaming well in what places at what time.

Example

Streaming Service	Rate per stream	0-1M Streams	Distribution Company's Recoupment
Spotify	£0.004 - £0.048	£4,000 - £4,800	15% - 30%
Apple Music	£0.045 - £0.006	£4,500 - £6,000	15% - 25%
Tidal	£0.010	£10,000	30% - 50%

Case Study: Aj Tracey Utilizing Distribution

AJ Tracey is a successful independent UK grime and rap artist who has gained significant attention over the years for his unique style and approach to music. His success in the music industry is partly attributed to his strategic distribution efforts, which have allowed him to gain widespread exposure and increase his fan base.

The definition of independence is subjective and varies depending on the individual. However, in general, it refers to having creative control, owning one's copyright, and not being affiliated with one of the three major labels, Sony, Universal, or Warner. In the early days of his career, AJ Tracey used a DIY distribution model, handling the distribution of his music himself through direct-to-artist platforms such as Bandcamp and SoundCloud. This approach allowed him to retain control over his music and keep a larger share of the profits, but it also limited the reach of his music.

As AJ Tracey gained more popularity, he realized the importance of widening the distribution of his music to reach a larger audience. In 2018, he signed a distribution deal with Caroline International, a subsidiary of Universal Music Group. The deal provided him with access to a wider range of platforms, including physical distribution to record stores and digital distribution to streaming services such as Spotify and Apple Music. This allowed him to reach a larger audience and gain more exposure, while still maintaining control over his music and keeping a larger share of the profits.

For Tracey, being independent means that he has complete control over his music and can release whatever he wants, whenever he wants but as he is independent he requires nerves of steel and the courage to take the hard route on everything. He has said on various occasion that achieving success as an independent artist is much harder than with the backing of a major label and acknowledges that it's not easy. He foots the bill for everything, with no advance or fallback. He spends a lot of money on music videos, which can cost up to £50,000 each, and if he doesn't recoup the costs, he's out of pocket.

AJ Tracey's experience with distribution deals highlights the importance of choosing the right distribution model for independent artists. While a DIY approach can offer more control, it may also limit the reach of an artist's music. On the other hand, signing a distribution deal with a major label or distributor can provide access to a wider range of platforms and increase exposure, but it may also require the artist to give up some control and a percentage of their profits.

AJ's success in the music industry is a testament to the importance of strategic distribution efforts. By carefully considering his options and choosing the right distribution model for his needs, he was able to gain exposure, reach a larger audience, and achieve success as an independent artist.

UPC Barcodes And ISRC Codes In The Music Industry

A UPC barcode, or Universal Product Code, is a code used to identify and track a music product, such as an album or single, as a physical or digital item. It is used by stores, both physical and digital, to track sales of the product. Each release, such as a single, EP, or album, needs its own separate UPC barcode. In the UK, a different UPC barcode is needed for physical CDs and digital releases.

An ISRC code, or International Standard Recording Code, is a unique identification system for individual sound recordings and music video recordings. It is used by music download and streaming platforms to track sales of specific recordings. An ISRC code follows a standard template and consists of a country code, a registrant code, and a unique identifier. It is typically encoded into a product as a digital fingerprint.

It is important to understand the difference between UPC barcodes and ISRC codes. UPC barcodes are used to identify and track complete products, such as albums or EPs, while ISRC codes are used to identify and track individual recordings. Both UPC barcodes and ISRC codes are important for tracking sales and ensuring proper identification in the music industry.

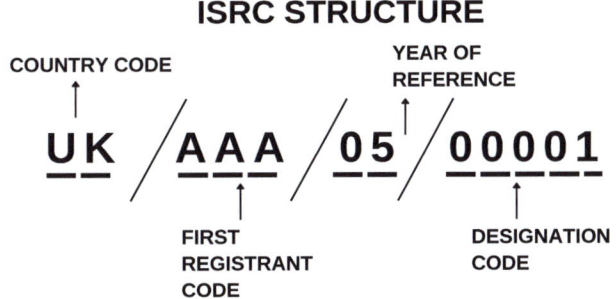

Metadata

Metadata is the essential information that identifies and organizes your music. This data includes vital details like the song title, artist name, album title, and track number. However, metadata goes beyond these basics and can include additional information such as the composer's name, copyright details, and album artwork. Accurate and comprehensive metadata is of utmost importance for effective music distribution, as it ensures that your music is correctly labelled and appropriately categorized across various platforms.

In the digital age, music distribution has evolved significantly, and metadata has become even more critical. Streaming platforms like Spotify, Apple Music, Amazon Music, and others rely on metadata to organize their vast catalogues of songs. They utilize this information to provide seamless user experiences, making it easier for listeners to discover and enjoy music they love. For independent artists, having accurate metadata is a powerful tool that can directly impact their visibility, reach, and revenue potential.

Incorrect or incomplete metadata can lead to significant challenges for artists. When metadata is inaccurate, your music might be mislabelled, making it difficult for listeners to find or identify your work. This can result in missed opportunities for exposure and revenue, as potential fans might be unable to locate your music on their preferred platforms. Additionally, inaccurate metadata might lead to your music being attributed to the wrong artist, affecting your reputation and overall presence in the music community.

Accurate metadata not only ensures proper identification of your music but also influences how it is recommended to listeners. Streaming platforms use metadata to create personalized playlists and recommendations, based on users' listening habits and preferences. By providing detailed and precise metadata, you increase the likelihood of your music being recommended to relevant audiences, helping you grow your fan base.

Key components of metadata that should be included for each song or release are the song title, artist name, album title, track number, composer name, copyright information, and album artwork. These pieces of information collectively create a clear and complete identity for your music, enhancing its discoverability and appeal to potential listeners.

To ensure accurate metadata for your music, it's crucial to pay attention to detail when submitting your work to distribution channels. Working with a reputable distribution company or utilizing a digital distribution platform that allows you to input metadata directly can be beneficial. Regularly reviewing and updating your metadata is also essential, especially when releasing new music or making changes to existing releases.

Metadata is a fundamental aspect of modern music distribution. It empowers artists by providing a well-defined identity for their music, which in turn enhances discoverability and the potential for success.

Industry Insights: A Deep Dive With Craig Evans, Head Of Hip Hop At Believe

In this industry insight we spoke with Craig Evans, a highly experienced industry professional, currently serving as head of hip hop at Believe Digital, based in their London office for the past five years.

With a career spanning multiple notable independent labels and artists, Craig has developed a reputation for working with some of the UK's most successful and ground-breaking names in the music industry. In this Insight we discuss distribution, campaigns, metadata, distribution deals, and mental health.

Distribution: Craig highlighted that before 2013/14, 3rd parties used to create playlists, but after Spotify started creating their own, it became a game-changer. The role a distributor plays often, requires management of existing clients, facilitation of their distribution worldwide and highlighting key tracks and artist to DSP's for potential playlisting, something distributors can never guarantee but with the right efforts and timing, can improve the chances to. From the correct artwork, high quality WAV's, and promo information are the key elements for doing well on DSP's with distributors.

Campaigns: Craig highlighted the importance of going through the label or distributor to communicate with platforms like Spotify and Apple Music. DSPs have stringent requirements, including matching metadata. A good team behind an artist is crucial to engage with DSPs and generate more followers. If artists are not organized, there will be a big line of artists ready to jump in. The interviewee emphasized the importance of digital marketing, including sponsored posts, Google ads, and TikTok. For an album, a 6-month campaign with multiple single releases is the standard time frame.

> *"The right timeline and promo information can increase an artist's chances of success."*

Highlighting releases three weeks before the release date is an effective strategy. For example, Knucks' album had a nearly 12-month campaign, during which communications with DSPs were regular and they would have previews of music before the release.

Metadata: Metadata requirements for artwork include avoiding web links or social media promotion, as the focus should be on the music. Correct product and track details, including the artist's name as the composer, are essential. Metadata is typically completed during the upload process. The interviewee mentioned that UPC gets generated on upload, and ISRC can be obtained without extra cost as part of the terms of the distribution deal.

Distribution Deals: Craig mentioned that established artists often approach them, but the best way to get their attention is to send a direct message with a private listening link and release timeline. When discussing the financials of a deal, the budgets can vary widely depending on the artist and label, so it's important for talent to be realistic about what can be accomplished with the available resources. This approach helps the distributor understand the artist's needs and goals, which enables them to offer better advice and tailor their services accordingly. Believe doesn't prioritize signing artists based solely on TikTok trends or numbers. Instead, they focus on an artist's talent and potential for long-term success. This strategic decision ensures that their roster is made up of artists who are likely to have longevity in the industry, rather than those who might have a brief moment of popularity.

> *"It still is a big numbers game, but people miss the chance to sign artist that could be big in 3-4 years' time. If we like something, let's help it grow."*

The rise of independent artists is a reflection of broader trends in the industry. Many artists are choosing to bypass traditional label systems and find their own paths through independent distribution and marketing channels. This shift has been facilitated by digital platforms and the increased accessibility of tools that enable artists to create and distribute their music independently. From a strategic perspective, this trend underscores the need for labels to adapt and innovate to remain relevant in a changing landscape.

Mental Health: Craig emphasized the need for mental health support, particularly for young artists. Many artists get caught up in the social media side and think they should be further ahead. A good team should highlight everything to artists, and they should focus on their goals instead of comparing themselves to others.

> *"You might see people winning and want to be where they are. Don't worry about the other man, worry about where you're at how you're going to do your thing "*

Craig end the conversation with a reflection on the industry stating that the business is currently saturated, but there is a strong alt hip-hop scene in the UK, which is refreshing for him to see as it gives youth a different side of rap. R&B is also taking a rise again after a knockback with afro and rap, these genres come and go, and the trends move at their own pace. Spotify supports drum and bass, and many other genres are getting more significant support. Craig also mentioned that vinyl is the fasting growing format and encouraged people to buy it. He's unique insights highlights the importance of having a realistic approach when it comes to artists and distribution.

The Major Labels vs Independent Label

When it comes to securing a record finding the right fit and structure with a label is of utmost importance. The decision to sign with a major or independent record company requires a thorough understanding of the differences between the two.

The common perception of a "record label" is that of a major record label, situated in London, Los Angeles or New York, which signs all of the major artists and bands. These major record labels, including Sony, Warner, EMI, Capitol and Universal Records, are major corporations with vast resources to support the projects they choose to invest in. This allows them to fully fund the biggest artists out there. In the eyes of emerging artists, a record deal with a major label was always the big prize to go after.

However, the major labels have been facing significant challenges with the advent of online social networks such as Tik-Tok and digital music retail stores such as Spotify and Amazon. Major releases have been leaked to the internet weeks before their official release date, and this has had a significant impact on music.

Enter the Indie record label. Any music recording label that operates without the funding of the organizations of the major music labels is considered an indie. While major labels are global and operate their own publishing and distribution companies, indie labels work with other smaller companies, either in long-term partnerships or in smaller contractual relationships for their distribution and publishing needs.

Indie labels have created a true niche for themselves in today's music business climate due to the benefits they offer. They generally have the freedom to work with whomever they like and there is no pressure like that found at major labels to sacrifice one's tastes in favour of seeking chart success. When an artist is signed to an indie label, it is almost always because the label is a huge fan of their music. This translates into dedication because they believe in what the artist is doing.

Due to their smaller staffs and tighter rosters, indie labels provide the opportunity for musicians to develop closer relationships with the people working on their record. Although it is not always the case that artists can pick up the phone and get an immediate answer, the odds of closer communication are greater than they are with a major label. Some larger indie labels have relatively complex contracts, but smaller indies often do business on little more than a handshake and a profit split agreement. Indies seldom demand any measure of creative control over their artists, and most don't lock their artists into long-term, multi-album contract deals.

However, indie labels do have their drawbacks. While money is the top reason to sign with a major label, it is also the top negative for indies. It is common to see some indie labels operating stably, but a lot of small operations in the post Covid climate are just trying to stay afloat. They usually don't have the finances to fund an all-out media blitz like the major labels, and they often have to get creative with promotion and PR ideas to stay ahead of the game. Indies also can't afford big advances, fancy packaging, large recording budgets, tour support, and other perks that major labels can offer.

The intimate size of indie labels has its downside in terms of limited purchasing power and fewer strings to pull with the media. The smaller the label, the less influence and power within the music industry and the press.

There are good and bad points to signing with a major or an independent record label, and it is crucial for music professionals in the industry to seek advice from their team of professionals, including music attorneys and accountants, to make informed decisions. Ultimately, finding the right fit and structure with a label is crucial to an artist's success in the industry.

Industry Insights: Despa Robinson, Cultural Icon & BE83 Founder

In this industry insight interview with Despa Robinson, a Birmingham figure head and pioneer in UK culture. After creating Stay Fresh and turning it into a national movement, Despa went on to manage the careers of notable artist Jaykae and build his own label BE83.

During this interview we covered a range of topics from the role of a label today, key factor involved in deals, the common traits in industry professionals, release planning and trends.

Role Of A Label Today: According to Despa Robinson, a label's role today is still centred around artist development, marketing, and financial support. He went to discuss the importance of regular video shoots with different types of artists and keeping them up to date with industry trends. He believes that networking and creative help, especially with the AR side of things, are also essential and with the rise of social media, making it easier for artist to create and distribute their own music, we have seen a significant shift to a more competitive market. As a result, labels need to offer a new array and wider range of services to stand out and add value to their artists' careers.

Key Factors When Offering A Deal: Despa Robinson likes to watch artists for a while before offering them a deal. He believes that the artist must have a clear vision for themselves and demonstrate patience, resilience, and work ethic. While numbers are still important, Despa believes that the artist's mindset and attitude are equally important. This highlights the shift towards a more long-term and sustainable approach to artist development, where labels are investing in artists who have the potential to grow, evolve over time and already have a buzz around them.

Red Thread/Common Trait In Successful People Behind the Scenes: Despa Robinson identifies poise, respect for others, and a good reputation as key traits for people working behind the scenes. He also stresses the power of social media and the importance of finding a balance between letting the work speak for itself and being loud. This shows the importance of building genuine relationships and creating a positive reputation in the industry, as it can lead to long-term success and opportunities. This shows the importance of building genuine relationships and creating a positive reputation in the industry, as it can lead to long-term success and opportunities.

Industry Trends: Despa Robinson highlights the growing trend towards the importance of an artist's personality beyond just their music. He cites KSI as an example of someone whose fans love him for who he is as a person, not just his music. Building a tribe around oneself and being a leader within that tribe is also critical. Despa also predicts that AI will play a more significant role in the industry in the next five years, and artists like Gorillaz, who have always blurred the lines between animated and real-world artists, are great examples we already see in popular culture. This highlights the shift towards building a strong brand identity, where artists are expected to showcase their humanity and values alongside their music and the need for artists and labels to stay up-to-date with the latest technology and tools to remain competitive.

Importance Of Music Videos And Standing Out In A Saturated Market: Despa Robinson acknowledges that music videos are a necessary evil, but the way an artist represents themselves visually is key in today's market. Most people only know about an artist because of their video identity, this is the case for how Despa became aware of the Uk artist Antslive, who recently went viral with a creative visual in the swiss hills. Stardom's advert for a tape is an excellent example of creative thinking outside of the norm. The visual representation of an artist is just as crucial as their music, as it can be the deciding factor for fans to gravitate towards their music. Despa's emphasis on creativity and thinking outside of the norm shows the importance of creating innovative and unique content to capture an audience's attention.

Number Of Tracks An Artist Should Release In A Campaign: Despa Robinson suggests that to stay relevant, an artist should release new content every 60-80 days (6-8 weeks), he noted that it's not just about releasing music, but also being involved in other projects, such as features or collaborations. Drake is a great example of this, as he always has something new in the market, either through singles, features or even content. The key takeaway is that artists must continue to create and put themselves out there to remain relevant. This highlights the importance of diversifying one's portfolio, opportunities to tap in with their audience and building a strong network in the industry.

Despa Robinson's insights provide valuable information for anyone interested in the music industry. He emphasizes the importance of an artist's personality and work ethic, as well as the need for a label's continued support in artist development, marketing, and networking. His analysis of industry trends, the importance of music videos, and the optimal frequency for new releases is also essential information for those aspiring to make a name for themselves in the industry.

Types Of Record Deals

To cater to the distinct needs and aspirations of talented individuals, a range of contract structures has been crafted. These various types of record deals are strategically designed to ensure that artists can navigate their artistic journeys with flexibility and success. Whether you're a budding musician or an established star, understanding these contract options is essential for making informed decisions in your music career.

- **Traditional Record Deal**
- **360 Deal**
- **Distribution Deal**
- **Production Deal**
- **Profit Split Deal**

While there will always be outliers, these are the typical offers you will see. As a reminder, there will never be a one-size-fits-all solution for artists. While sometimes these offers may hinder an artist or limit their creative freedom, a lot of time, they also help to open up doors or increase an artist's platform.

Traditional Record Deal
- Advance: Yes
- Label/Artist Royalty Split: 80/20
- Recoupable Costs: Recording
- Masters Ownership: Label

The classic record deal! And probably the most common among mainstream & major label artists. In this exchange, the record label will grant the artist a hefty advance for their masters' ownership and 80% of their royalties. I have never seen an artist get more than 22% of their royalties, and typically it's much lower than that. Before the artist even sees a dollar of their royalties, they must recoup their advance and recording costs, which rarely ever happens.

While this may seem like a bad deal, sometimes this works out well for the artist. If they can leverage the advance & the marketing support from the label to kick start mainstream success, they have a decent chance of recouping what they owe or receiving better deal offers for their next release.

360 Deal
- Advance: Yes
- Label/Artist Royalty Split: 85/15
- Recoupable Costs: All
- Masters Ownership: Label

360 Deals are a type of partnership between the record label & the artists - where the label operates at a loss for an extended period. There is a massive investment in the artist's development, covering all expenses, including touring, recording, marketing & more. In return, the label then gets to recoup their investment from all forms of revenue that the artist generates, including touring & merchandising. In contrast, traditional record deals recoup based on music sales. A prominent advocate of 360 deals is Lyor Cohen, who has seen great success with 360s at Atlantic & 300 Entertainment. He strongly believes in the label investing in developing a commercially viable artist.

J. Cole is a famous artist who attributes some of his mainstream success today to the 360 deal he signed with Roc Nation back in 2009. On the other hand, independent artist Mac DeMarco has spoken out negatively on 360 deals. He points out that no one should "not sign a 360 deal. I don't care how much money they're offering you, don't [take it]. It's an awful, awful idea... And they own your image." While controversial, sometimes these situations can still be beneficial to an artist. It is up to the artist & their team to ultimately decide their correct route to success.

Production Deal
- Advance: No
- Label/Artist Royalty Split: 50/50
- Recoupable Costs: Recording
- Masters Ownership: Producer

Production deals always fly under the radar but have the potential to be one of the most predatory deals to come across an artist's desk. In a production deal, the artist usually signs a 50/50 deal with a single producer. The producer agrees to produce one or more of an artist's album in entirety but retains 100% ownership of the master recordings. There are multiple producers in the industry that are infamous for trapping up-and-coming artists into these deals. Make sure to ask around & consult friends before arriving at any agreement with these terms.

Distribution Deal
- Advance: Sometimes
- Label/Artist Royalty Split: 75/25
- Recoupable Costs: Recording, Marketing
- Masters Ownership: Artist

Distribution deals are growing in popularity these days & are typically the least predatory offering for independent artists. Simultaneously, they also offer the least amount of resources, so it depends on what type of investment an artist believes they need to do their release justice. Distributors focus on delivering the music to the digital service providers (DSPs) and potentially pressing physical CDs or vinyl, depending on their agreement with the artist.

Distributors typically handle relationships with the representatives at the DSPs to help pitch for playlisting. Meanwhile, the marketing & promotion falls on the artist & their team to complete. If the artist has a strong team & a hungry fan base, partnering with a distributor is an excellent way to increase leverage before seeking a traditional record deal. Some popular distributors include EMPIRE, Sony's The Orchard (& Steak Worldwide!).

Profit Split Deal
- Advance: Yes
- Label/Artist Royalty Split: 50/50
- Recoupable Costs: Recording, Marketing
- Masters Ownership: Label

Profit split deals, highlighted by Russ's 2018 agreement with Columbia, involve a 50/50 royalty division and a substantial advance for the artist. Unlike traditional deals where labels recoup only the advance and recording costs, profit split agreements entail recouping costs for advance, recording, marketing, and more. These deals, offering complete cost recovery for labels and significant benefits for artists, require careful evaluation and legal advice before committing, as the simplicity of their structure can be deceptive.

Key Record Deal Terms

There are specific terms that a common within recording deal terms that we will use throughout our analysis. To make sure that everyone is on the same page, here's a short glossary of the vocabulary you'll need to know:

Advances: Advances are often spoken of in glowing terms, with many artists receiving a significant amount of money upfront. However, it's important to understand that an advance is not actually money, but rather a loan. When a record label or publisher provides an advance, it's essentially an advance on future royalties. If the royalty rate is 20%, for example, the advance is essentially a loan with an 80% interest rate.

In most cases, the record label or publisher will take 80% of the royalties generated during the agreed period of time as repayment for the advance. They argue that this is necessary to cover the significant expenses they incur in promoting and distributing the artist's music, including hiring teams of experts and providing global distribution. They feel that this level of support would not be possible if the artist tried to go it alone, as they could not afford to pay for the same level of expertise and support.

The decision to accept an advance is a personal one, and it's up to the artist to weigh the benefits against the costs. It's also important to keep in mind that recouping an advance can take many years, and is a feat achieved by very few artists. When accepting an advance, it's essential to make it last and use it wisely, as they will expect to see a return on their investment.

Recording Funds: Recording Funds are sometimes referred to as Advances. This can be misleading, as some people assume that the entire amount will be used to fund the recording of the album. This is not always the case, as the artist will still need to live and support themselves during the recording process. An Advance is typically the fee paid to the artist for their time, name, and involvement in the project, while the Recording Fund is the additional amount provided specifically to cover the costs of recording the album. In most cases, both the Advance and the recording fund are fully recoupable, meaning they are loans that must be repaid. The rate of recoupment can vary, but it's usually 100% for both the Advance and the Recording Fund. It's important to understand the terms of the loan, as well as the expected rate of recoupment, before signing any agreements.

The Recouping Process: Recoupable costs is a standard term you'll find most recording contracts, applied to some of the initial investments made by the label. Until the label gets back the recoupable, 100% of the recording royalties will go towards making up for these expenses. In other words, if the label invested £1000 into recording an album and recording costs are recoupable, the artists will start making their share of the revenue only when £1000 worth of recording is sold/streamed.

Depending on the deal type and the contract itself, various costs can be established as either recoupable or non-recoupable. Under a traditional recording deal, only recording costs are recoupable (and even that is not always the case). Under the net profit deal, marketing, promotion, tour support, recording costs, and corporate costs are all recoupable. Sometimes, the label will also include "overhead fees" (calculated as a percentage of the label's gross revenue) as recoupable expenses.

Understanding the recoupable items outlined in your contract with the record label is crucial. These expenses are incurred by the label on your behalf, and they aim to recoup these costs before distributing royalties to you. This practice is prevalent in the industry, though the percentage of recoupable expenses may vary.

To ensure clarity, it's advisable to request a summary page of all recoupable items in your agreement. Be sure to also understand the details of how recouping works, such as whether the costs are deducted from your share of royalties or taken off the top. If the language of the agreement is too complex, don't hesitate to ask the label to explain it in simple terms. Protecting your financial interests is key, and understanding the recouping process is an essential part of that.

Release Commitment: Every agreement should incorporate a clause obligating the label to arrange releases in the UK for recorded tracks, or at the very least, to engage in a contractual arrangement with an established record company that commits to releasing at least one album. it's crucial to include a clause that ensures someone will do so; otherwise, the artist's work might never be made available to the public.

If the record label falls short of accomplishing the above, the artist should secure the right to obtain the unreleased masters. This right would be exercised if an agreement is reached to repay the unrecovered recording costs or provide the production company with an override royalty on these unreleased masters.

The artist should attempt to negotiate to fulfil only one of these conditions, but their success in doing so will ultimately depend on their bargaining leverage. While it's also worthwhile to seek a commitment for releases in major markets such as the USA, France, Germany, and Japan, most production companies are hesitant to commit to this obligation in their contracts, typically opting for a promise to use "reasonable efforts" to secure such releases.

Perpetuity: The term "perpetuity" is often used in the context of music copyright and licensing agreements. A perpetuity clause in a music contract can mean that the rights to a particular piece of music are assigned to the publisher or record label for the duration of the copyright, which can be for the life of the composer plus a certain number of years. This means that the publisher or record label has the right to exploit the music, such as by licensing it for use in films, commercials, or other media, and they can continue to receive revenue from these uses in perpetuity. This can be a disadvantage for the artist, as they may not see any further financial benefit from the use of their work after the initial payment.

> *"In some cases, artists may negotiate more favourable terms in their contracts, such as a shorter term of perpetuity or a higher royalty rate, but this isn't always possible."*

It's important for artists to understand the terms of their contracts and to seek legal advice if necessary. It's also important to be aware of changes in copyright law and the ongoing efforts to reform music industry practices, so that artists can protect their rights and maximize the value of their work.

The Term: The "**Term**" refers to the length of the agreement between the artist and the record label. This term may be specified in years and may also require a minimum commitment for the artist to release a certain number of records during that time. Additionally, the term may also specify a period after the release of the final product, during which the artist cannot release music elsewhere, to allow the record label time to work on promoting the music.

Even after the term has ended, the record label may have a **"Retention Period / Sunset Clause"** during which they have the right to continue collecting royalties from the artist's music. This period is typically around 10 years and is justified by the fact that the label (or management teams) had invested a lot of resources in promoting the artist's music at the start.

A "**Sell Off**" period is an additional 6 months during which the label is allowed to sell off the CDs still in the market. This provision is considered outdated and may no longer be necessary in modern music contracts. It is advised that artists agree on a specific retention period and consider it the end of the agreement.

During the term, it is not possible to release your music for free without the permission of the label and everyone else involved in the project. The same applies to the pricing of your music. Unless there is a specific agreement in the contract that allows you to set the pricing, the label has the final say on the cost of your music. Although they usually aim to be competitive to drive sales, any major changes to pricing, such as lowering the cost on iTunes, will require a corporate decision and may take time to implement.

Options: In the Options section, the label decides the conditions under which they will continue to work with you based on your performance. Note that only the record company has the right to extend or terminate the agreement and you do not have the option to leave. This section covers the following points:

- The time frame within which the label must inform you of their decision to continue working with you. Sometimes, they may request a reminder. It's important to understand the procedure and follow it exactly, including if the notification must be sent as recorded delivery. In that case, keep a copy of the receipt.
- The amount you will be paid for your next commitment and the details of that commitment, which may be based on the performance of your previous work. The record label may agree to pay you a percentage of your previous earnings.
- The targets the record company must reach to secure the option. for example, they may need to sell a certain number of records or receive a certain number of streams or single downloads, which could be counted as one album or one record. Carefully understand this section.

There may be multiple Options. After the first period, the label may choose to continue working with you. Some see options as a motivator for the label to work hard, long-term options can be unhealthy. Ensure that the money offered for new options is not just a percentage of turnover, but also includes a minimum amount or a percentage whichever is greater.

Case Study: The Inspiring Story Of Independent Artist Bugzy Malone

Bugzy Malone is a Manchester-born rapper whose success story is truly inspiring. He has broken barriers and achieved significant success as an independent artist, despite not having the support of a major record label. Malone has been dubbed the "King of the North," and he has come a long way from his humble beginnings on the streets of Manchester.

Malone's childhood was not easy. Growing up, he faced challenges, including poverty, homelessness, and even spending time in prison. However, instead of letting his past define him, Malone used his experiences to fuel his music career. His lyrics are authentic, and he uses them to tell his story and connect with his audience.

Malone's career began in 2010 when he started uploading freestyle videos to YouTube. He quickly gained a following, and his fan base continued to grow with each new release. Malone's hard work paid off when he released his debut EP, "Walk with Me," in 2015. The EP reached the top 10 on the iTunes album chart, and it catapulted Malone into the national spotlight.

Malone's success did not stop there. He continued to release successful projects, and in 2017, he released his album "King of the North." The album debuted at number four on the UK Albums Chart and received critical acclaim. Malone had achieved what many independent artists dream of: mainstream success without the backing of a major record label.

Malone's music has resonated with audiences across the UK, and his live shows are legendary. He has sold out multiple shows at Manchester Arena and performed at festivals across the country. Malone's unique style of music, which blends grime, rap, and hip-hop, has earned him fans from all walks of life.

In addition to his music, Malone has also made his mark in the acting world, with a role in the Guy Ritchie film "The Gentlemen." His acting skills have been praised by critics, and he has expressed an interest in pursuing more acting roles in the future. This is another major move by the artist, as within the movie he was able to sync his own music for specific scene. The relationship with the director has continued, seeing Malone take a centre role in the latest Guy Ritchie film.

Malone's success story serves as an inspiration to independent artists everywhere. His determination and talent have taken him from the streets of Manchester to the top of the UK music industry. Malone's authenticity and passion have connected with fans across the country, proving that success is possible without the backing of a major record label.

In addition to his successful music career, Bugzy Malone has also ventured into the fashion industry, creating his own clothing brand, B Malone. Launched in 2017, B Malone is a streetwear brand that features bold graphics and designs inspired by Bugzy's personal style. The brand has been a huge success, with many of its items selling out quickly after their release.

B Malone's popularity has only continued to grow, with its clothing being worn by many celebrities and influencers. The brand has even collaborated with other well-known brands, such as Footasylum, to create limited edition collections.

Through B Malone, Bugzy has been able to showcase his creativity and passion for fashion. The brand's success is a testament to his talent and ability to connect with his fans not only through music but also through fashion.

Malone's success has also helped to break down barriers in the music business . He has shown that artists can achieve mainstream success without the need for a record label, which has traditionally been seen as the only path to success in the industry. His success has not been without its challenges. He has faced criticism from some in music who have accused him of promoting violence and criminal behaviour in his music. However, Malone has defended his music, saying that it reflects his experiences and is a way for him to express himself.

Bugzy Malone's success story is a testament to the power of hard work, determination, and talent. His journey from the streets of Manchester to the top of the UK music scene is a story of triumph over adversity, and his success has helped to pave the way for independent artists everywhere.

Pro Tip: Deal Or No Deal?

The decision to sign with a record label is a big one for any aspiring artist. While the promise of resources and support may seem enticing, it is important to carefully consider the potential costs involved before signing on the dotted line. As we have discussed, record labels typically offer artists an upfront investment with the expectation of recouping their costs and making a profit. This means that the label will take a significant cut of the artist's earnings, potentially leaving the artist with little creative control or financial ownership.

To truly understand the impact of signing with a label, it is important to dive deeper into the numbers. Let's say a label offers an artist £20,000. Based on industry averages, this likely means that the label sees the potential for at least 3 times that figure in revenue from the artist's music. That £20,000 investment is essentially a loan, with the expectation of a return on that investment. The label will recoup their costs and make a profit before the artist sees any significant earnings.

In contrast, an independent artist who is able to build a dedicated audience can succeed without the help of a label. By securing brand deals and bookings, an artist can fund their career and retain 100% ownership of their music. The key to success is understanding how to monetize their music and audience, which is where labels typically take an 80% cut.

The feasibility of artists building successful careers independently is increasingly evident in the industry. Recent trends show that independent artists comprised a notable 5.5% of total recorded music industry revenue in 2020, with expectations of this share growing to 6.2% by 2022. These figures underscore a significant shift, highlighting that independent artists are not only thriving but also progressively carving out a larger presence in the industry.

One factor that has contributed to the rise of independent artists is the shift in the way music is consumed. Streaming services such as Spotify and Apple Music offer artists the opportunity to earn revenue through streams and downloads, and many artists have been able to build successful careers by leveraging these services and promoting their music through social media and other digital channels.

Beyond streaming, independent artists diversify their income through merchandise sales, brand partnerships, and live performances. In recent years, touring and live shows have become a major revenue source in the industry. They represented a significant majority of the total music sectors revenue, while recorded music contributed a smaller percentage. This trend emphasizes the growing importance of live events and alternative revenue streams for artists in the modern music landscape.

It's essential to understand that when an artist enters into a contract with a record label, they often relinquish a substantial amount of their creative control and music ownership. This can negatively impact the artist's career, limiting their ability to release music on their own terms or make artistic choices aligned with their brand.

The decision to sign with a record label is a complex one that should not be taken lightly. While the promise of resources and support may seem enticing, it is important for artists to consider the potential costs involved and to weigh the benefits against the loss of control and ownership that may come with signing a record deal.

With the rise of independent success stories and the increasing opportunities for artists to monetize their own music, it is becoming more and more feasible for artists to maintain control over their own careers and to build successful, sustainable businesses in music.

As an independent artist, you have the freedom to make creative decisions on your own terms, release music when you feel it's ready, and experiment with different genres and styles without external pressures. Additionally, you retain ownership of your music, allowing you to explore various revenue streams beyond just sales and streams.

The digital age has revolutionized the music business, enabling artists to reach audiences globally without the need for traditional distribution channels. Social media, streaming platforms, and digital marketing tools have become powerful resources for independent artists to connect directly with their fans and grow their fanbase organically.

Building a strong online presence and engaging with your audience through social media platforms can significantly impact your career as an independent artist. Interaction with fans, responding to comments, and sharing behind-the-scenes content can create a deeper connection, fostering a loyal and dedicated fanbase that supports your music and attends your shows.

The rise of crowdfunding platforms like Kickstarter and Patreon provides independent artists with an alternative way to fund their projects and generate revenue. By offering exclusive content, experiences, or merchandise to their supporters, artists can turn their fans into patrons who actively contribute to their creative journey.

As an independent artist, you also have the flexibility to explore various revenue streams. These opportunities can provide additional income and exposure for your music, expanding your reach to new audiences in worlds such as films, TV shows, commercials, or video games.

It is important to acknowledge that being an independent artist also requires significant dedication, hard work, and business acumen. Without the backing of a label, you will be responsible for managing various aspects of your career, including marketing, promotion, booking shows, and handling financial matters. Time management and organizational skills are essential to juggle the creative aspects of your music with the demands of running a business.

Another challenge for independent artists is the sheer volume of competition in the digital space. With a low barrier to entry, many artists are vying for attention on streaming platforms and social media. Standing out in a saturated market requires strategic planning, consistent content creation, and a unique brand identity.

While signing with a record label can offer certain advantages, independent artists have more opportunities than ever before to succeed on their own terms. With the rise of digital platforms, social media, and crowdfunding, independent artists can build successful, sustainable careers without relinquishing creative control or ownership of their music. However, it is crucial for independent artists to approach their careers with a business mindset, leveraging the available tools and resources to maximize their reach and revenue.

*For all your music industry resources and templates, refer to The Music Business Blueprint free resource guide at www.a-krst.com

CHAPTER 4
LEGAL SIDES OF THE INDUSTRY

Lawyers

When executing contractual agreements, it is recommended to seek the assistance of a qualified legal professional. Most contracts require the confirmation that legal advice has been sought, which serves as a protective measure for both parties involved.

There are various ways in which lawyers can charge for their services. Some charge by the hour, while others may request a percentage of the gross revenue generated. In some cases, lawyers may only request a percentage of specific streams of revenue, such as touring. The appropriate method of payment will vary based on the individual needs and circumstances of the client.

Regarding the payment of legal fees, there is no universally accepted solution. Some clients may prefer to cover legal costs from their own income, while others may choose to split the costs with their artist. It is important to have an open and honest conversation with the artist to determine what solution works best for both parties.

You should note that lawyers tend to specialize in the laws and regulations of the country in which they operate. However, many lawyers have a broad understanding of global legal practices and can also call upon local experts as needed. It may be beneficial to utilize the services of a lawyer based in the country where the record deal is based. It is also important to consider if the lawyer requires exclusivity and whether their fees should be factored into the overall costs associated with the contract.

When Legal Representation is Not Required

The negotiation of live performance contracts is typically handled by a talent agent. Basic agreements can be executed without the need for legal counsel, especially as one gains more experience and confidence in these matters. For sample waivers, a template provided by a lawyer or the record label can be utilized and issued after being signed.

Non-Disclosure Agreements (NDAs) can also be created using a template provided by the record label and can be issued by the individual or entity involved. In the event of litigation, a litigation attorney is necessary to represent the individual or entity in court. This type of representation is typically recommended by the primary attorney involved. The issuance of necessary paperwork for each agreement will be discussed at a later time.

Some lawyers may also bring in business opportunities through their connections with brands. It is recommended to inquire about this possibility and communicate your goals regularly with the lawyer to ensure their assistance. Additionally, it is important to be aware that record companies may also provide a budget for legal fees as part of a signing agreement, and it is advisable to look for this and properly invoice the company for these expenses.

Pro Tip: Choosing The Right Lawyer

Selecting the right lawyer for your career is a crucial decision that can significantly impact your success and future opportunities. When evaluating potential lawyers, it is essential to consider various factors to ensure that you choose someone who not only understands your goals but can also navigate the complexities of the music business effectively.

One vital aspect to consider is the lawyer's reputation and track record of securing advantageous deals for their clients. A lawyer with a strong reputation for negotiating favourable contracts can be a valuable asset in maximizing your earnings and protecting your interests. Research their previous work experience and accomplishments to gauge their level of expertise.

Beyond securing favourable deals, it's crucial to assess the lawyer's long-term involvement in your career. Building a successful music career often requires long-term relationships and collaborations. Consider whether the lawyer has a history of maintaining lasting partnerships with their clients, as this can indicate their dedication to fostering sustainable career growth.

Another consideration is the lawyer's relationship with potential labels. Having a lawyer who is respected and trusted by industry professionals can open doors and create opportunities for your music career. A positive relationship with labels can facilitate smoother negotiations and increase the likelihood of landing beneficial deals.

Effective communication is essential in any legal relationship. Evaluate the lawyer's ability to communicate clearly and respectfully. You want a lawyer who can explain complex legal terms in a way that you understand and feel comfortable with. A lawyer who actively listens to your concerns and responds promptly to your inquiries can be a significant asset in building a strong and trusting partnership.

Of course, the affordability of a lawyer's rates is a practical consideration. Legal services can be costly, especially for emerging artists or those with limited financial resources. It is essential to find a lawyer whose rates are reasonable and align with your budget. Balancing cost with quality of service is crucial to ensure you receive the best value for your money.

In the event that you decide to switch lawyers, thoroughly review the termination terms outlined in your agreement with your current lawyer. Some contracts may have specific provisions regarding termination, including notice periods or potential costs associated with ending the relationship. Understanding these terms is essential to make an informed decision and avoid any unexpected consequences.

Before finalizing your decision to switch lawyers, consider seeking assistance from another legal professional to review the agreement with your current lawyer. A second set of eyes can help ensure that the termination process is handled correctly and that you fully understand your rights and obligations.

Conduct thorough research and seek professional advice when necessary to make an informed decision that sets the foundation for a successful and thriving music career. Remember, your lawyer will play a crucial role in protecting your interests and guiding you through the legal complexities of the music industry, so choose wisely.

Contracts In The Music Industry

Contracts are legally binding agreements that outline the terms of a relationship or transaction. They are used to clarify the rights, responsibilities, and expectations of the parties involved and provide a framework for resolving disputes or enforcing obligations. In the music business, contracts are used for a variety of purposes, such as booking shows, recording music, licensing songs, and more. They help to protect the interests of the parties involved and ensure that everyone is clear on their roles and responsibilities.

Contracts are especially important because of the many different parties that may be involved in a project or transaction, such as artists, record labels, managers, venues, promoters, and more. Without contracts, there may be confusion or disputes about who owns what rights, who is responsible for what tasks, and who is entitled to what payment.

Always carefully review and negotiate contracts to ensure that they are fair and in the best interests of all parties involved. It is also important to understand the enforceability of contracts and to be aware of one's rights and obligations under the terms of the contract. Understanding contracts is an important part of business management in music and can help artists and industry professionals to protect their interests and succeed in their careers.

Here is some more information on contracts in the industry:

- **Types Of Contracts:** Contracts can be used for a variety of purposes, such as booking shows, recording music, licensing songs, and more. It's important to understand the different types of contracts you may encounter in your music career and the specific terms and conditions that apply to each one.

- **Key Elements Of A Contract:** A contract should include the terms of the agreement, payment terms, and rights and permissions. For example, a recording contract might specify the length of the contract, the amount of money the artist will receive for their recording, and the rights the label has to distribute and promote the music.

- **Reviewing And Negotiating Contracts**: It's important to carefully review contracts before signing them to ensure that you understand the terms and that they are fair. If you have any questions or concerns, don't be afraid to ask for clarification or seek legal advice. You have the right to negotiate fair terms, and there are resources available to help you with this process, such as templates for contract language and information on how to find a lawyer.

- **Enforceability Of Contracts:** It's important to note that contracts are legally binding agreements, and both parties are expected to fulfil their obligations under the terms of the contract. If one party fails to fulfil their obligations, the other party may have the right to seek legal remedies.

Understanding contracts and the language within them, is a crucial part of business management There will be slight variations of terms and minor details, which can change the entire context and legality of a contract, having a wider understanding will allow you to spot these. Reviewing and negotiating contracts carefully and being aware of your rights and obligations can protect your interests and succeed in your music career.

Pro Tip: Reviewing And Negotiating Contracts

Reviewing and negotiating contracts requires diligence, attention to detail, and a comprehensive understanding of the terms and conditions. Whether you are an artist, manager, producer, or any other music industry professional, it is essential to approach the contract review process with care to safeguard your rights and interests.

The first step in reviewing a contract is to read it thoroughly from start to finish. Pay close attention to every clause, provision, and condition outlined in the agreement. Ensure that you understand the language used and the implications of each term. If any part of the contract is unclear or confusing, don't hesitate to seek clarification from the other party or seek advice from a legal professional familiar with industry contracts. Contracts can be dense and filled with legal jargon, so having someone who can decipher and explain the terms to you can be invaluable.

Seeking advice from a professional is especially crucial when dealing with complex or high-stakes contracts, such as record deals, publishing agreements, or major sponsorship deals. An attorney with expertise in music contracts can help you navigate the intricate language and potential pitfalls of these agreements. They can also ensure that the contract aligns with your goals and protects your rights.

Remember that a contract is not set in stone; it is a mutual agreement between parties, and negotiations are expected. If there are terms in the contract that you are uncomfortable with or that do not align with your interests, be prepared to negotiate. It is essential to be respectful and professional during negotiations while clearly expressing your concerns and priorities. Both parties should be willing to make compromises to reach a mutually beneficial agreement.

Identifying your priorities before entering negotiations can be immensely helpful. Understanding what is most important to you in the contract will allow you to focus on key terms and issues that need attention. This can also prevent you from getting side tracked by minor details and help you negotiate more effectively.

As you negotiate, try to understand the other party's perspective as well. Knowing their needs and motivations can help you find common ground and reach a fair resolution. Asking questions and seeking clarification on certain points can foster open communication and facilitate the negotiation process.

If you encounter complex legal issues or are unsure about certain contract terms, do not hesitate to seek legal advice. An attorney specialized in music industry contracts can provide insights into the legal implications of the agreement and offer guidance on protecting your rights. They can also identify any potential red flags or areas that may require additional negotiation.

Remember that contracts are binding agreements, and signing one without fully understanding its implications can lead to significant challenges and legal disputes down the road. If you have any doubts or concerns about the terms of the contract, take the time to seek advice and gain clarity before making a commitment.

Lastly, be open to compromise during the negotiation process. Both parties should strive to reach an agreement that is fair, equitable, and satisfactory for all involved. It is essential to prioritize the long-term benefits of a balanced and mutually beneficial contract over the rush to finalize an agreement that may not serve your interests in the long run.

Thoroughly understanding the terms and implications of an agreement, seeking professional advice when needed, and engaging in open and respectful negotiations are key to ensuring that contracts are fair, protective, and aligned with your goals.

Understanding Management Contracts

For many artists, working with a manager can be a transformative and essential step towards their career growth and success. A skilled and experienced manager can play a crucial role in handling various business and administrative tasks, securing bookings, opportunities, and navigating the complex landscape. However, before entering into a management contract, it is vital for artists to have a comprehensive understanding of the terms and conditions of the agreement to ensure a fair and mutually beneficial relationship.

A management contract is a legally binding agreement between an artist and their manager. The primary purpose of this contract is to establish clear expectations and responsibilities for both parties involved. It typically covers crucial aspects such as the scope of services the manager will provide, the length of the contract, compensation and payment terms, termination rights and procedures, ownership of intellectual property, and confidentiality and non-disclosure agreements.

The scope of services is a pivotal element in the management contract, as it delineates the specific tasks and responsibilities that the manager will undertake on behalf of the artist. This may encompass a wide range of activities, including booking gigs and performances, negotiating contracts, handling financial matters and budgeting, developing marketing strategies, and assisting with career development and long-term planning.

Compensation and payment terms are another significant aspect of the management contract. It outlines how the manager will be remunerated for their services and the percentage of the artist's earnings that the manager will receive. The standard commission for a manager typically ranges between 15% and 20%. However, this percentage can vary depending on factors such as the manager's experience, the artist's level of success, the specific services provided, and the negotiation skills of both parties.

The ownership of intellectual property is a critical consideration in any management contract. This provision clarifies who holds the rights to the artist's creative work, including songs, compositions, recordings, and other artistic endeavours. Resolving this issue is vital to avoid potential disputes and to ensure that the artist retains appropriate ownership of their intellectual property. In some cases, the manager may have a financial stake in the artist's intellectual property, which should be explicitly addressed in the contract.

Termination rights and procedures are essential provisions in the contract, as they outline the conditions under which either party can terminate the agreement and the steps that must be followed in such situations. Having clear termination clauses in the contract can help protect both the artist and the manager and ensure a smooth process if the need arises. Understanding the terms of termination is crucial as it allows the artist to maintain control over their career trajectory and make informed decisions if the professional relationship is no longer mutually beneficial.

Confidentiality and non-disclosure agreements are significant in maintaining the privacy and protection of sensitive information that may be shared between the artist and the manager during their working relationship. These agreements safeguard confidential data, trade secrets, and other proprietary information to maintain trust and professionalism between the parties. It ensures that both parties can freely share ideas, plans, and strategies without fear of unauthorized disclosure or exploitation.

Having a management contract in place offers numerous benefits for both the artist and the manager. Firstly, it provides clarity by outlining the expectations and responsibilities of each party, minimizing confusion and misunderstandings. This clarity allows both parties to have a shared understanding of their roles and obligations throughout the duration of the contract. Secondly, a management contract offers legal protection for both the artist and the manager in case of a dispute or breach of agreement. It serves as a formal document that can be used to resolve conflicts and protect the interests of both parties.

A management contract adds a level of professionalism to the artist-manager relationship. It demonstrates to industry professionals, potential partners, and stakeholders that the artist is committed to managing their career with the utmost professionalism and strategic planning. The existence of a management contract can enhance the artist's reputation and credibility in the industry.

Understanding the key elements of a management contract is crucial for artists. It empowers them to make informed decisions and ensures that the terms and conditions of the agreement are fair and conducive to their career growth and success. Seeking legal advice, when necessary, can be beneficial in navigating the complexities of the contract and ensuring that the artist's interests are protected. Effective communication, transparency, and trust between the artist and the manager are also vital for building a successful and harmonious professional relationship that contributes to the artist's growth and success in the industry.

Pro's And Cons Of Management Contracts

Management contracts offer numerous advantages and opportunities for artists, but it is equally crucial to be aware of the potential drawbacks and consider both the pros and cons before signing any agreement.

Pros of Management Contracts:
- **Protection:** One of the primary benefits of a management contract is that it provides legal protection for both the artist and the manager. In case of disputes or breaches of the agreement, having a formal contract in place ensures that both parties' rights and interests are safeguarded.
- **Guidance And Support:** A manager can offer valuable guidance and support to the artist throughout their career. They can leverage their industry experience and knowledge to help the artist navigate the complexities of the music business, make informed decisions, and seize opportunities for growth.
- **Business Management:** Entrusting business and administrative tasks to a manager allows the artist to focus on their craft and artistic pursuits. A manager can handle tasks such as booking gigs, negotiating contracts, managing finances, and coordinating marketing efforts, freeing up the artist's time and energy.
- **Networking Opportunities:** A manager often comes with an established network of industry contacts and connections. They can use their network to secure gigs, endorsements, collaborations, and other valuable opportunities that may be challenging for the artist to access independently.

Cons Of Management Contracts:
- **Costs:** Hiring a manager usually involves paying a percentage of the artist's earnings as a commission. While this investment can be beneficial in the long run, it can also be a significant cost for the artist, especially during periods of limited income.

- **Control And Creative Direction:** Some management contracts may grant the manager considerable control over the artist's career decisions and creative direction. This may lead to conflicts if the manager's vision does not align with the artist's artistic aspirations.
- **Compatibility Issues:** Finding the right manager who aligns with the artist's goals, values, and work style can be a challenging process. A lack of compatibility between the artist and manager may result in a breakdown of the professional relationship.
- **Contract Length:** Many management contracts have long-term commitments, which may restrict an artist's flexibility and ability to make changes to their career trajectory. Terminating a contract prematurely may also have legal and financial implications.

Project-To-Project Management Agreements

Project-to-project management agreements offer an alternative approach to artist-manager collaborations. Rather than committing to a long-term partnership, these agreements focus on specific projects or short-term endeavours.

Pros of Project-To-Project Management Agreements:
- **Flexibility:** Project-to-project agreements provide artists and managers with flexibility, allowing them to collaborate on specific projects without entering into a long-term commitment.
- **Cost-Effectiveness:** Artists who do not require full-time management may find project-to-project agreements more cost-effective, as they only pay for the manager's services on a per-project basis.
- **Focus On Specific Goals**: These agreements enable both parties to concentrate on achieving specific goals for a particular project without the distractions of a long-term partnership.

Cons of Project-To-Project Management Agreements:
- **Limited Scope:** Project-to-project agreements may have a more limited scope compared to long-term management contracts. This means that the level of support and guidance provided by the manager may not be as comprehensive.
- **Limited Control:** Managers in project-to-project agreements may have limited control over an artist's overall career, potentially affecting their ability to maximize the artist's long-term potential.
- **Uncertainty**: Artists may experience uncertainty and a lack of stability with project-to-project agreements, as they do not offer the same sense of security as long-term management contracts.

Management contracts, whether long-term or project-to-project, can be advantageous for artists in various ways. However, it is essential for both parties to thoroughly review and comprehend the terms of the agreement before entering into any contractual arrangement. Seeking legal counsel can provide valuable guidance and ensure that the contract is fair, balanced, and protects the interests of both the artist and the manager. Additionally, open communication and mutual understanding are key to establishing a successful and harmonious working relationship between artists and their managers.

Pro Tip: Other Types Of Industry Contracts

Other types of contracts that may be encountered, including booking contracts, recording contracts, licensing contracts, and collaboration contracts. Here is more information on the different types of contracts that may be encountered:

Booking Contracts: A booking contract is an agreement between an artist and a venue or promoter for the artist to perform at a specific event or series of events. The contract will typically outline the terms of the performance, such as the date and time, the fee to be paid to the artist, and any other terms and conditions.

Licensing Contracts: A licensing contract is an agreement between an artist and a third party, such as a film or television production company, to use the artist's music in a specific context. The contract will typically outline the terms of the license, such as the length of time the music can be used, the fee to be paid to the artist, and any other terms and conditions.

Collaboration Contracts: A collaboration contract is an agreement between two or more artists to work together on a specific project, such as a song or album. The contract will typically outline the terms of the collaboration, such as the rights and responsibilities of each artist, the ownership of the resulting work, and any other terms and conditions.

Sync Licensing Agreements: A sync licensing agreement is a contract between an artist or rights holder and a company or individual that outlines the terms under which the artist's music will be used as background music or soundtrack music in films, television shows, commercials, and other media. These contracts typically specify things like the length of the agreement, the rights being granted, and the fees being paid.

Merchandise Agreements: A merchandise agreement is a contract between an artist and a company or individual that outlines the terms under which the artist's merchandise (such as t-shirts, hats, and other items) will be manufactured and sold. These contracts typically specify things like the length of the agreement, the rights being granted, and the revenue sharing arrangements.

Music Production Agreements: A music production agreement is a contract between an artist and a music producer that outlines the terms under which the producer will work with the artist to create music. These contracts typically specify things like the length of the agreement, the rights being granted, and the revenue sharing arrangements.

Co-publishing Agreements: A co-publishing agreement is a contract between a songwriter or composer and a publishing company that outlines the terms under which the publishing company will promote and license the songwriter's or composer's compositions, and the songwriter or composer will retain a percentage of the publishing income. These agreements are often used as an alternative to traditional publishing deals.

Enforceability Of Contracts

Contracts play a fundamental role, governing the relationships between artists, managers, record labels, and other stakeholders. However, even with the best intentions, disputes and breaches of contract can occur. In such cases, understanding the enforceability of contracts and the available legal remedies is crucial to protect the rights and interests of all parties involved.

When one party fails to fulfil their obligations under a contract, the other party may have various legal remedies at their disposal. These remedies are designed to address the harm or losses caused by the breach and ensure fair resolution. Some common legal remedies include specific performance, damages, rescission, and injunctions.

Specific performance is a legal action that compels the party in breach to fulfil their contractual obligations as agreed. It is appropriate when the breach has caused significant harm or when monetary compensation alone cannot adequately remedy the situation. On the other hand, damages come in various types, such as compensatory damages, which aim to cover actual losses, and consequential damages, which address indirect and foreseeable damages at the time of contract formation.

Rescission, another remedy, allows the injured party to cancel the contract and be released from further obligations under its terms. This remedy is typically used when the breach is substantial, and the injured party wishes to discontinue the contractual relationship. Lastly, injunctions are court orders that restrain the party in breach from continuing the actions that violate the contract. This remedy is suitable when immediate action is necessary to prevent irreparable harm to the injured party.

The enforceability of a contract can become a critical issue in various scenarios. Breach of contract is one such situation, wherein one party fails to meet their obligations as stipulated in the contract. The other party then has the right to seek legal remedies to address the breach, which may include specific performance, damages, or rescission.

Payment disputes are not uncommon. In such cases, referring to the contract terms is essential to determine the amount owed and the payment schedule agreed upon by both parties. Similarly, disputes may arise over rights and permissions granted in a contract, making the contract's terms and conditions crucial in clarifying the obligations of each party.

In the event of contract termination, both parties must adhere to the terms specified in the contract. This may include returning any advance payments or addressing the rights to the work produced under the contract. To ensure the enforceability of contracts and to navigate potential disputes effectively, thorough examination of the contract terms is vital. Seeking legal counsel when necessary can provide clarity and insights into the available legal remedies. Moreover, clear and precise contract drafting can help prevent potential disputes and ambiguities in the future.

Case Study: Ivorian Doll

The Ivorian Doll case is a recent example of a music business dispute in which an artist has accused a record label of impeding their career. Ivorian Doll, also known as Vanessa Mahi, is a rising UK rapper who has accused former Radar Radio boss Ollie Ashley and his label Locked In Music of blocking her from signing with other labels and demanding £17,000 in exchange for the rights to her artist names Ivorian Doll and IVD.

The dispute began in 2020 when Ivorian Doll claims that Ashley made false claims of "bullying" against her current manager, which led to a legal row in which Locked In Music attempted to ban her manager from the studio. Ivorian Doll also claims that Ashley tried to force her to sign with a particular label because of his relationship with them and that Ashley's reputation caused other labels to back away from signing her.

Additionally, Ivorian Doll claims that Ashley trademarked the artist names Ivorian Doll and IVD without informing her and is demanding £17,000 in exchange for the rights. Ivorian Doll also claims that she has recorded more than 50 records in 2020, but does not know if they will be released due to the ongoing legal issues.

This case highlights the power imbalance that can exist between artists and record labels. Artists often sign contracts that give record labels significant control over their careers and limit their ability to leave the label or work with other companies. In this case, Ivorian Doll feels that her career is being blocked by Locked In Music and that Ashley is using his power and influence to take advantage of her.

One possible legal remedy for Ivorian Doll would be to seek a release from her contract with Locked In Music. This could involve going to court and arguing that the contract is no longer valid due to the alleged misconduct by Ashley and Locked In Music. Another possible remedy would be to seek damages for any lost income and career opportunities resulting from the actions of Ashley and Locked In Music.

This is a clear reminder of the importance of understanding and protecting one's rights as an artist, and seeking legal advice before signing any agreements or contracts. It also highlights the need for more transparency and fairness in the industry to ensure that artists are able to pursue their careers without undue interference from record labels.

EXAMPLE RECORDING AGREEMENT

Date	Date 20**		
Licensor	NAME OF ARTIST ("Licensor", "you", "your")	Licensee	NAME OF LABEl ("Label", "we", "us", "our", "Company")

Artist	xxxxxxxxxxxxxx
Definitions:	
"Advance"	1. £25,000 in the Initial Period 2. £70,000 in the First Option Period
"Contract Periods"	Two (2), namely: • a "firm" commitment "Initial Period"; and • one (1) optional contract period (each foregoing period a "Contract Period", the option period the "First Option Period"
"Exploitation Period"	The Term plus the later of (i) twenty (20) years thereafter and (ii) recoupment of Licensor's royalty account hereunder continuing in any event thereafter until the Licensor serves three (3) months 'notice of termination thereof.
"Product Commitment"	Shall be the following master recordings (collectively the "Master Recording(s)"): • Initial Period: no less than 8 tracks delivered as minimum 2 tracks per quarter from beginning of the Contract Period in question. • 2nd Period: no less than 8 tracks delivered as minimum 2 tracks per quarter from of the Contract Period in question. Each of the aforementioned tracks and mixtapes shall consist of technically and artistically first class recordings of previously un-released compositions and the Product Commitment of each Period shall be accompanied by a reasonable quantity of bonus mixes.
"Royalty Percentage"	25%
"Term"	A period commencing on the date hereof and expiring six (6) months after the Label's commercial release of the final Master Recording hereunder. During the Term the Artist

	shall not release any master recordings with a third party label and/or "self-release" the same.
Recording Obligation	During each Contract Period the Licensor shall supply the Label with the Product Commitment for the relevant Contract Period at all times treating the production of such Product Commitment as Licensor's first priority over and above other commercial activities.
Rights granted to Label by Licensor	In consideration of the sum of one pound (£1), the receipt and sufficiency of which the Licensor acknowledges and accepts, the Licensor irrevocably grants to Label on a fully sub-licensable basis: a. Exclusive unlimited exploitation rights in the Master Recording(s) during the Exploitation Period in the Territory in any and all formats (now or hereinafter invented including without limitation physical and digital) in whole or in part including without limitation to reproduce, make available, disseminate, commercially release, remix, sync, alter, embellish and to produce audio visual content; b. Rights in the Artist's name, logo, approved likeness and approved biography in connection with the exploitation of the Master Recording(s) and the Label's general publicity for its business; and c. The Licensor hereby irrevocably agrees not to assert any and all moral rights in the Master Recording(s) other than Artist's right to be credited as author of the underlying composition(s) embodied therein to the extent that it is practicable and commercially commonplace to provide such a credit.

EXAMPLE RECORDING
AGREEMENT

Advance	The Label shall pay the Advance to the Licensor: a. In the case of each of the Initial Period and (if Label's option hereunder is exercised) the Option Period: (i) 25% within thirty (30) days of the later of: (i) full execution of this agreement (or in the case of the Option Period, exercise of Option); (ii) the Licensor's complete fully "cleared" delivery of the first single of the Initial Period Product Commitment and the Label's acceptance thereof; and (iii) the Licensor's provision of a valid invoice for the portion of the Advance in question; and (ii) 25% within thirty (30) days of the later of (i) Licensor's complete fully "cleared" delivery of the fourth single of the Initial Period Product Commitment and the Label's acceptance thereof; and (iii) the Licensor's provision of a valid invoice for the portion of Advance in question; (iii) 25% within thirty (30) days of the later of Licensor's complete fully "cleared" delivery of the seventh single of the Initial Period Product Commitment and the Label's acceptance thereof; and (iii) the Licensor's provision of a valid invoice for the portion of the Advance in question (iv) 25% within thirty (30) days of the later of Licensor's complete fully "cleared" delivery of the twelfth single of the Initial Period Product Commitment and the Label's acceptance thereof; and (iii) the Licensor's provision of a valid invoice for the portion of the Advance in question Advances shall be: i. fully recoupable against the Licensor's royalty entitlement hereunder save for mechanical royalties; and ii. fully inclusive of any and all recording costs in connection with the Product Commitment including without limitation costs and fees charged by third parties providing their services (whether artistic or technical) in connection with the Product Commitment.
Territory	The World
Option recordings	All Product Commitment hereunder including without limitation Option recordings shall be artistically and technically commensurate with previous Artist Product Commitment accepted by the Label. The Label shall have a period of six (6) months following the commercial release of the final Master Recording of the previous Contract Period in which to exercise each option hereunder. Notwithstanding the foregoing, in the event that the Label fails to inform the Licensor whether or not it is exercising its option within the aforementioned six (6) month period, the Label's option right under this paragraph shall continue until fifteen (15) working days after the Licensor informs the Label in writing via registered post (with proof of posting) that the Label has failed to exercise its option. If the Label during the aforementioned fifteen (15) working day period exercises its option then the next contract period under this agreement shall be considered to have commenced on the date of such exercise of option.

EXAMPLE RECORDING
AGREEMENT

First and Last Matching Right	Following the First Option Period Licensor hereby grants to Label a first negotiation and last matching right in relation to the Artist's next exclusive recording agreement subject to the following terms:
	Prior to soliciting any offers from any third party in respect of Licensor's subsequent recording agreement first following the Term of this Agreement ("Recording Rights") until nine (9) months from the end of the Term, Licensor shall first notify Label of all the commercial terms which Licensor is seeking in respect of the Recording Rights (the "FN Notification"). Thereafter both parties will negotiate reasonably and in good faith with the intention of granting the Recording Rights to Label on mutually agreeable terms ("First Negotiation Right"). In the event that the First Negotiation Right does not lead to any agreement relating to the Recording Rights within sixty (60) days of Label's receipt of the FN Notification, Licensor may thereafter negotiate with third parties in which event until nine (9) months from the end of the Term the following procedure shall apply:
	a. if Licensor receives any offer from a third party in respect of the Recording Rights, then Licensor shall, within seven (7) days of receipt of such offer or offers, send a copy of such offer or offers ("Offer Notice") to Label.
	b. within fourteen (14) days of receipt of the Offer Notice ("Offer Notice Period"), Label shall be entitled to match the Material Terms of such offer ("Matching Right"), in which event Licensor and Label shall be deemed to have entered into a fully binding agreement upon the Material Terms set out in the Offer Notice, as amended by any other terms and conditions agreed in good faith between Label and Licensor. For the avoidance of doubt, in the event that Label elects to exercise the Matching Right, Label shall not be obliged to agree terms which are not Material Terms.
	c. Label having notified Licensor that it elects to exercise the Matching Right, Licensor shall promptly inform any and all third parties with whom it has been negotiating, and shall desist from any further discussions with any such third parties in respect of the Recording Rights.
	d. if Label does not notify Licensor that it wishes to exercise the Matching Right within the foregoing time period, or notifies Licensor that it does not wish to exercise the Matching Right, then Licensor shall be entitled to enter into an agreement with a third party on Material Terms no less favourable to Licensor than those set out in the Offer Notice.
	e. if, in accordance with the procedure set out above, the Recording Rights are granted to a third party, Licensor shall forthwith upon signature of any agreement, send a fully signed redacted copy of such agreement (such that only the Material Terms may be inspected), to Label.
	f. if Licensor does not conclude an agreement with the third party within a forty five (45) day period upon Material Terms no less favourable to Licensor than those contained in the Offer Notice, until nine (9) months from the end of the Term Licensor shall not be entitled to grant the Recording Rights to any other person unless Licensor again offers to Label a Matching Right as provided for above.
	In this clause "Material Terms" shall mean the advance(s), fees, recording costs and rate(s) of royalty (the deductions, including packaging deductions, made upon which royalties are calculated), the royalty rate base price, the percentage of sales upon which such royalty is payable and any other factors materially affecting the "penny rate" calculation (for example format or territorial reductions) the nature and extent of the rights granted, the geographical territory and exclusivity of the agreement, the term, the product commitment, the nature and extent of any non-recording rights and income entitlement, tour support, controlled composition provisions and shall not, for the avoidance of doubt, contain any terms which it is impossible for Label to match, including by way of example only the provision of a "named" individuals 'services.

EXAMPLE RECORDING AGREEMENT

Release date	Each Master Recording hereunder shall be commercially released in the UK within four (4) months of the later of the complete fully cleared delivery thereof from Licensor and full acceptance thereof by Label provided that Label shall not be obliged to commercially release more than three (3) Master Recordings during any four (4) month period. In the event that the Label fails to fulfil its obligations under the foregoing sentence the Licensor shall serve written notice upon Label via registered post (with proof of posting) instructing Label to commercially release the relevant un-released "Product Commitment" within the next forty five (45) days following the Label's receipt of said notice and if Label fails to so do within this forty five (45) day timeframe the Licensor shall be entitled to terminate the Term, exercisable by Licensor solely within the thirty (30) day period following such failure.
Promotion	The Licensor agrees to provide reasonable assistance in the promotion and marketing of each Master Recording and and shall make themselves available for interviews and promo opportunities (including at Label's request appearance in a video to promote each Master Recording (hereinafter each a "Video")) for no fee, save for reasonable third party expenses to the extent agreed in advance in writing by Label.
Royalties	Label shall account to the Licensor the Royalty Percentage of net income received by Label from all exploitation of the Master Recording(s) in the Territory, calculated as gross income actually received by Label solely and identifiably in connection with the Master Recording(s) (excluding so-called "label's share" of neighbouring rights income, which shall be for Label's sole account) after deduction of, solely, arm's length distributor charges, sales tax and withholding taxes. Notwithstanding the foregoing solely in respect of synchronisation exploitation of the Master Recording(s) Label shall account to Licensor fifty per cent (50%) of Label's actually-received income therefrom after deduction of VAT. The following shall be recoupable against the Artist's Royalties: a) the Advance; b) third party remix costs in connection with any Master Recording; c) third party Video production expenses; d) any recording costs incurred by the Label; and e) One hundred per cent (100%) of the third party marketing campaign costs and expenses for any Master Recording
Composition	The Licensor shall procure the provision to Label and its sub licensees and assigns of the following licences in and to the underlying composition embodied within each of the Master Recording(s): a) first use mechanical licence; b) gratis licence for use in all Videos; c) a mechanical licence in the United States and Canada at 100% of the minimum rate; and d) such commercial sync licences as Label shall request provided on bona fide arm's length commercial terms.

EXAMPLE RECORDING
AGREEMENT

Re-recording	The Licensor and/or Artist shall not (on a case by case basis) re-record the underlying composition embodied within the Master Recording(s) (or parts thereof) or permit re-recording of the same by any third party for a period of five (5) years commencing on the date hereof and expiring five (5) years after Label's UK commercial release of each such Master Recording.
Accounting and auditing	Label shall account royalties hereunder to the Licensor twice per year within 90 days from the end of June and December. Label shall not be obliged to account to the Licensor or provide statements in any bi-annual accounting period when monies owed to the Licensor hereunder are less than one hundred pounds (£1000) and under such circumstances monies owed will be 'rolled over 'to the next accounting period when such threshold has been exceeded. The Licensor shall be entitled to audit Label's books in relation to exploitation of the Master Recording(s) once per year and only once per set of books upon reasonable notice carried out by a suitably qualified chartered accountant with such auditing right limited to two (2) years after the delivery of the accounting statement to be audited.
Reserves	Label shall be entitled to hold back from Licensor accounting 20% of net income calculated in respect of physical formats only which withholding shall be liquidated within the following four (4) accounting periods.
Production Parts	The Licensor shall promptly following the creation thereof deliver to Label in WAV or AIFF format each and every one of the versions, mixes, remixes, edits, production parts and stems controlled by Artist in respect of each Master Recording.
Licensor approvals	The Licensor shall have the right of prior written approval (email and instant messaging being sufficient) not to be unreasonably withheld or delayed in respect of: (a) Synchronisation use of the Master Recording(s); (b) Sample use of the Master Recording(s); (c) The creative content of Videos; (d) The budget of remixes of the Master Recordings; (e) Use of any Master Recording in the endorsement of a third party product or service (f) material changes to any Master Recording save for alterations for the purpose of timing and/or formatting. provided that: (a) Exploitation pursuant to so-called "blanket licences" shall not require Licensor approval; (b) The Licensor's approval shall be deemed granted if the Licensor has failed to respond to a request for approval within three (3) days; and (c) Label's inadvertent failure to seek approval shall not be deemed a breach hereof.

EXAMPLE RECORDING
AGREEMENT

Licensor warranties	The Licensor hereby warrants that: a. Licensor/Artist has the full unencumbered right, power and authority to enter into this agreement and has the exclusive entitlement to fully grant the rights contained in this agreement; b. There are no and will not be any conflicting rights and/or third party claims in respect of the Master Recording(s) and/or the underlying composition embodied therein including without limitation any infringing samples and/or in respect of the Artist's artistic name and branding. c. There are no third party contributors to the Master Recording(s) with un-cleared contributions thereto and to the extent that there are any third party contributors to the Master Recording(s) all remuneration to such contributors will be from Licensor's share of net income hereunder. d. The Label shall be exclusively entitled to the Artist's recording services during the Term. e. The Artist's name and branding does not infringe any third party rights (whether registered or unregistered.
Indemnities	The Licensor/Artist shall indemnify Label and Label's licensees and assigns in respect of any and all third party claims pursuant to the Licensor's breach of any of any of the Licensor's warranties and/or obligations herein provided that such indemnification is pursuant to the judgement of a court of competent jurisdiction or is pursuant to a settlement made with the Licensor's prior consent (not to be unreasonably withheld or delayed).
Agreement	This Agreement shall constitute a binding agreement between the parties.
Ancillary share	Shall be the following (collectively the "Rights Period"): Commencing from the initial period, Label", to source personal appearance bookings, sponsorship and endorsement deals for Artist on a non-exclusive basis (with any such booking or deal always subject to Artist's consent). Where Label", provides this service, Label", shall be entitled to receive a share of income from all such activities and transactions equal to 25% of gross fees. Commencing from the 2nd Period "Label", shall be entitled to receive a share of income arising from all of Artist's other activities in the entertainment industry (*excluding publishing*) equal to 15% of net earnings (calculated on the same basis as and before any deduction of management commission). "Label", entitlement to such share of income shall continue during the Term of the recording agreement and for 24 months thereafter ("Rights Period"). During the Rights Period the Label shall be entitled to 50% of Licensor's Artist merchandise profit (calculated as the gross income received by Artist from Artist merchandise after deduction of, solely, sales tax and the reasonable third party costs actually and verifiably incurred by Licensor solely in connection with such merchandising) (the "Merchandise Right").

EXAMPLE RECORDING
AGREEMENT

Miscellaneous	a. Nothing contained within this agreement shall create a partnership between the parties hereunder nor grant any rights to any third party including without limitation pursuant to the Contracts (Rights of Third Parties) Act 1999. b. This agreement contains the entire agreement between the parties hereto and extinguishes and supersedes all prior discussion (whether written or verbal) regarding the subject matter hereof and neither party has relied on any representation made by the other prior to the signing hereof. c. This agreement may only be amended in writing signed by both parties hereto and no waiver of any right or obligation herein shall be binding unless in signed writing. d. Label may assign and/or licence any and all of its rights under this agreement. The Licensor may only assign this agreement with Label's prior written consent.
Jurisdiction	This agreement shall be subject to the laws of England, whose courts shall have exclusive jurisdiction.

Accepted and agreed as a binding contract

-- --
ARTIST   LABEL

EXAMPLE RECORDING AGREEMENT

Industry Insights: John Sorzano, Sports and Entertainment Lawyer

In this industry insight interview with John Sorzano, a highly accomplished sports, music and entertainment lawyer, we discuss the legal landscape in the entertainment industry, including industry crossover, perpetuity, the use of AI lawyers and tech, and key things to look for in lawyers.

Industry Crossover Between Music, Sports, And Entertainment: John Sorzano explains that the industries operate very similarly with only a few key difference; pointing out that the difference between music, sports and acting is the assignment of rights on the distribution of the property produced. Commissions for agents operate in a very similar way in music and sports, where they were 10%, but have now dropped to around 5% on bigger deals (6/7 figures). If an artist is looking to sign a deal, they should look for deals that exclude or ring-fence previous material, labels can often swoop in, sign talent up and have rights to all of the material that was created before the deal was made. If you're an agent and your talent isn't struggling, we would usually advice to take less payment upfront and look for more points in perpetuity.

> "Take your time, raise the capital, own your production then sell parts of the distribution rights, the proper council will give you that insight."

Key Things People Should Look For In Lawyers: John stressed that it's crucial to look for a lawyer who specializes in the specific industry or field you are working in, as different areas of law have different rules and regulations. For instance, entertainment law is different from corporate law, and a lawyer who specializes in corporate law may not be familiar with the intricacies of the entertainment industry. In addition, he emphasized the importance of having a good rapport with your lawyer, as it helps build trust and makes it easier to communicate effectively. Lawyers should be proactive, responsive, and provide clear explanations of legal concepts to their clients. They should also be able to identify potential issues and provide solutions to mitigate risks.

John stated that people should not be afraid to ask for referrals or do their due diligence when choosing a lawyer. You should look at the lawyer's track record and see if they have experience in handling similar cases or clients. It's essential to choose someone who has your best interests at heart and is committed to helping you achieve their goals.

AI Lawyers And Tech: John Sorzano mentions that AI lawyers and tech are helpful because they provide a base understanding of legal issues. For example, if you don't know much about a topic, they can pop in questions and get a good understanding of it. However, he emphasizes that they cannot litigate or negotiate, and there is a human element that AI will never be able to replace. AI will think black and white, and it may not have the cultural nuances required for outlying individuals. It's also essential to recognize their limitations and not solely rely on them for legal advice.

Perpetuity: John explains that perpetuity can benefit artists by paying them until they die. However, while it can provide a steady stream of income until your death, it also means giving away rights to your work forever. So, it's essential to weigh the long-term benefits against the potential risks and ensure that the terms of the agreement align with your goals and values. John continued to state that ultimately, contracts are all the same, with the person giving the contract trying to lock you in for a good or service that benefits them while limiting their loss or exposure. Talent is also getting into the contract to limit their exposure (financial or legal) and maximize their earnings. The contracts are the middle ground, depending on who is negotiating. It's crucial to understand the implications of signing such a contract.

Taking On Clients: He went on to explained that in football, attitude towards progression and the ability to stand out are critical factors to consider. A good agent can tell when a player has longevity playing and about 4-6 contracts ahead of them. For agents and lawyers in the world of music, actively looking for talent means isolating the genre of music you would like to go for, going to gigs, listening to talent, benchmarking from the top talent selling now, understanding their sound, and then coming down the ladder. They advised that what stands out are the tangibles, such as attitude towards progression.

Aspiring artists and professionals in the entertainment industry should take the time to educate themselves about the legal aspects of the industry and seek out knowledgeable and experienced legal counsel to help protect their interests. With the right guidance and support, they can navigate the legal landscape successfully and achieve their goals in the highly competitive entertainment industry.

Case Study: The Agreement Between Russ Millions And Pressplay Media

Russ Millions is a well-known UK drill rapper who gained prominence in 2018 with his hit single "Gun Lean." However, in an interview with Zeze Millz, he revealed that he signed a 24-album contract with Pressplay Media, a media company specializing in urban music, without fully comprehending the terms of the agreement.

Background: In 2017, Russ Millions collaborated with Loski and Taze to release "Olympic Chinging," which garnered over a million views on the video-sharing platform. This caught the attention of Pressplay Media, who saw his potential and offered him a contract. At the time, Russ Millions was new to the industry and was in a duo, so he believed the contract was for only a few songs. However, he soon discovered that the contract was for 24 albums, which he did not completely understand due to the technical language and fine print.

The Contract: In the agreement, Pressplay Media offered Russ Millions £60,000, which he shared equally with his partner, giving each of them £30,000. It was only after, that Russ Millions discovered the 24-album condition in the agreement.

Outcome: Russ Millions' contract with Pressplay Media was eventually deemed void, but his experience served as a valuable lesson for him and other aspiring musicians. Russ Millions now understands the importance of reading contracts thoroughly and seeking legal advice before entering into any contractual agreement. His story has also become a warning to others who may be tempted to sign contracts without understanding the full terms and conditions.

The experience of Russ Millions is a reminder of the significance of thoroughly reading and comprehending any contractual agreement before signing it. In the music business, where contracts can be complex, seeking professional legal advice before committing to an agreement is critical. It can help artists avoid being bound to unfavourable terms that may restrict their creative freedom or limit their earning potential.

The case emphasizes the importance of understanding contracts before signing them. It highlights the need for clear and concise language in agreements, particularly in music. Furthermore, it demonstrates the importance of seeking legal counsel, especially for inexperienced artists who may not understand the intricacies of the music business.

Pro Tip: Audits

The significance of audits in safeguarding your financial interests cannot be overstated. As an artist, it is imperative to ensure that your contract includes the explicit right to conduct a comprehensive audit every three years. This contractual provision serves as a powerful tool to protect your financial well-being and artistic integrity by verifying the accuracy of the label's financial reporting and ensuring that you are fairly compensated for your creative contributions.

To effectively manage the audit process, it is essential to stay proactive and diligent. Setting a reminder for yourself six months before the audit period begins allows ample time for preparation and notification. In some cases, contractual requirements may necessitate providing written notification to the label, and it is prudent to be cautious and follow their specified communication protocol. If the label requests a paper letter, maintaining a meticulous record, including proof of delivery, becomes paramount in establishing a verifiable audit trail.

Conducting an audit is a proactive measure that empowers you as an artist to gain insight into the financial aspects of your music career. Although audits come with associated costs, artists have the option to consider a more cost-effective "desktop audit," which typically incurs a lower financial burden, around £5,000. For artists with substantial revenue exceeding £100,000, investing in an audit is strongly recommended as it ensures a comprehensive examination of financial records, leading to a deeper understanding of your financial position.

During the audit process, trained professionals will meticulously review the financial records and transactions related to your music career. Any discrepancies found can lead to additional funds being added to your account with the label, ensuring that you receive the appropriate compensation for your artistic efforts. If you find yourself in an unrecouped state, where the revenue from your music has not yet covered the initial investment by the label, the audit can be instrumental in reducing your unrecouped balance and bringing you closer to a recouped status. Conversely, if you have already recouped, the audit may uncover additional revenue that you have not yet received, contributing to your financial well-being.

Beyond financial implications, audits also serve as a mechanism to reinforce trust and transparency between artists and labels. As artists become more proactive in auditing their earnings, labels may be incentivized to maintain accurate and thorough financial records, fostering a more equitable and respectful relationship between both parties.

The right to conduct an audit is a fundamental component of protecting your financial interests. It is a powerful safeguard that ensures you are appropriately compensated for your artistic contributions and enables you to make informed decisions about your music career. By exercising your right to audit, you are taking a proactive stance in securing your financial well-being, asserting your value as an artist, and reinforcing the importance of transparency and fairness in the music industry.

Case Study: Chamillionaire And The Hidden Funds
Introduction

The music industry is a lucrative business that attracts artists from all over the world. Record labels play a crucial role in the success of these artists. However, there have been cases where record labels have taken advantage of artists, leaving them financially crippled or having less than they have rightfully earned.

One such case is that of rapper Chamillionaire, who discovered that his label, Universal Music Group, had been withholding funds from him. Born Hakeem Temidayo Seriki, Chamillionaire is an American rapper who rose to fame with his hit song "Ridin'." Despite his success, Chamillionaire was not satisfied with the way the music business operated. He believed that the industry was designed to scam artists financially. It was only after fellow rapper Nelly introduced him to auditing that Chamillionaire was able to uncover the truth.

Chamillionaire hired Jay-Z's auditor to inspect his accounts. The audit uncovered over £600,000 in hidden funds that Universal Music Group had been withholding from him. This revelation shocked Chamillionaire, who realized that the industry was not as transparent as he thought. He discovered that artists had to pay for their songs to hit number one, and that record labels often took advantage of their artists' lack of financial knowledge.

The audit had a significant impact on his career. He decided to leave Universal Music Group, as he no longer trusted the label's financial dealings. His experience taught him the importance of focusing on equity, rather than just receiving a piece of a show. He also learned that artists needed to have a thorough understanding of record deals, royalties, and contracts before signing anything.

His experience offers multiple learning points for other artists at all levels. First, artists should never sign any contracts without thoroughly understanding the terms and conditions, a full education or expert consultation on specific factors affected by your agreements will only serve to protect you in the long run. Second, artists should consider auditing their accounts to ensure that they are receiving the payment they deserve. Third, artists should focus on equity and take control of their careers to avoid being taken advantage of by record labels.

The case highlights the importance of transparency and accountability in the music industry. It shows that record labels can take advantage of artists financially, and that auditing is a powerful tool for artists to ensure they are receiving the payment they deserve. Chamillionaire's decision to leave Universal Music Group after discovering their financial impropriety shows that artists have power and should not be afraid to assert themselves.

Case Study: Rihanna vs Accountant

When an artist's career takes off, the money often follows. However, success can come with its own set of problems, and financial management can be a challenging aspect for many artists. One artist who learned this lesson the hard way is Rihanna.

Background: In 2007, Rihanna's music career was on the rise, and she had a string of chart-topping hits. However, the Barbadian artist did not limit herself to music alone. She ventured into the world of cosmetics and lingerie with her brands Fenty Beauty and Savage x Fenty. Her business ventures, along with her musical talent, led her to billionaire status in 2021. According to Celebrity Net Worth, Rihanna's net worth is now $1.7 billion. However, Rihanna's success was not always a smooth ride.

The Problem: In 2009, Rihanna's financial situation took a nosedive. According to a lawsuit that was later settled, Rihanna allegedly lost $9 million due to poor financial decisions made by her former accountants at Berdon LLP. Court documents revealed that Rihanna had an estimated $11 million in cash at the beginning of that year, but by the end of the year, she was left with only $2 million. Her former accountants had reportedly recommended that she purchase a new home in Beverly Hills for $7.5 million, despite knowing that she was in financial distress. The purchase left her virtually bankrupt by the end of the year.

The Lawsuit: In 2012, Rihanna filed a lawsuit against her former accountants in Manhattan Federal Court. She accused them of mismanaging her funds, including her 2009 Last Girl on Earth tour, which was reportedly netting losses. The lawsuit also alleged that her former accountants charged excessive commissions and took nearly 23 percent of revenue, while Rihanna only received six percent.

The Outcome: Despite the back and forth and the nasty litigation, Rihanna eventually came out on top. She received a more than $10 million settlement from her former accountants. However, the experience left her with a valuable lesson: the importance of good accountants and accounting practices.

As an artist, it is essential to understand the financial side of the music business and make smart business decisions. This case highlights the importance of having a good accountant to manage one's finances, especially when dealing with large sums of money. Without proper financial management, an artist's success can quickly turn into financial disaster. It is crucial to have a clear understanding of one's financial situation, work with reputable accountants, and maintain proper accounting records to avoid financial mismanagement. Rihanna's experience serves as a cautionary tale for artists and underscores the critical role that good accounting practices play in a successful career.

CHAPTER 5
SYNC AND BRAND PARTNERSHIPS

Sync Licensing

Sync licensing refers to the process of obtaining permission and paying the necessary fees to use a song in synchronization with visual media, such as films, television shows, video games, and advertisements. Sync licensing allows visual media creators to use music to enhance the mood, atmosphere, and overall impact of their work, while also providing revenue for the copyright holders of the music.

As mentioned in our subsection in publishing, the process of sync licensing involves clearing the rights to both the composition (the underlying musical work) and the master recording (the specific recording of the song). The copyright holder of a composition is typically the original author or authors, unless there is a written agreement transferring the rights to another person or entity, such as a publishing company. The owner of the master recording is typically the record label or the artist, depending on the terms of the recording contract. In order to use a song in sync, visual media creators must contact the copyright holders of the composition and the master recording and negotiate a license for the use of the song. The terms of the license may include the specific use of the song (e.g., background music in a television show, theme song in a film), the duration of the license (e.g., one-time use, perpetual use), and the territory where the song will be used (e.g., worldwide, limited to certain countries). The parties may also agree on a sync fee, which is an upfront payment for the use of the song, as well as royalties, which are ongoing payments based on the performance of the song.

Sync licensing can be a complex process, as there are many factors to consider, such as the rights held by different parties, the specific terms of the license, and the availability of the song. It can also be challenging to negotiate fair terms, as the value of a song can vary greatly based on its popularity, the specific use of the song, and the negotiation skills of the parties involved. For these reasons, it is often helpful to seek the advice of a music lawyer or professional sync licensors when working on sync projects.

Why Is Sync Licensing Important For Musicians And Visual Media Creators?

Sync licensing offers an additional revenue stream beyond traditional avenues like album sales and streaming royalties. When a musician's music is used in films, TV shows, commercials, or video games, they earn synchronization fees and royalties, which can significantly contribute to their income. This diversification of revenue sources can help musicians sustain their careers and invest in their artistic endeavours.

Sync licensing presents an opportunity for musicians to gain exposure and expand their fanbase. Having their music featured in popular visual media can introduce their work to audiences that may not have discovered it through traditional means. This exposure can lead to increased recognition, more streaming and sales, and even potential new fans attending their live shows. Additionally, sync licensing can provide a sense of validation for musicians, as it signifies that their music has resonated with creators and aligns with the emotions and themes of various visual projects. This validation can boost their confidence and inspire them to continue producing high-quality music.

For visual media creators, sync licensing is equally valuable. Music plays a pivotal role in setting the mood, tone, and atmosphere of any visual project. Choosing the appropriate music through sync licensing is essential for maintaining artistic integrity and ensuring that the music complements the visuals. It allows creators to evoke specific emotions, build tension, or provide an uplifting background, ultimately enhancing the overall quality of the project.

Sync licensing grants visual media creators access to a vast and diverse catalogue of music from different genres and artists. This breadth of choices enables them to find the perfect fit for their project's specific requirements, style, and target audience. From a financial perspective, sync licensing can be a cost-effective solution for incorporating high-quality music into a project. Instead of commissioning original compositions or hiring composers, licensing existing tracks can fit various budgets and production scales.

In the broader context of the music industry, sync licensing plays a crucial role in supporting artists and sustaining the creation of new music. As the music landscape evolves, sync licensing has become a vital component for artists to remain financially viable and continue producing art that resonates with audiences. For the visual media industry, sync licensing is equally significant as it provides a gateway to a vast pool of talent and musical creativity. It allows creators to use music that aligns with their vision and effectively communicates their message, making their work more captivating and memorable.

Together, sync licensing contributes to the artistic and financial growth of the music and visual media industries, enriching the creative landscape and elevating the overall quality of artistic expression.

Pro Tip: Key Terms And Concepts Related To Sync Licensing

Sync licensing, involves specific terminology and concepts crucial for effectively marrying music with visual media. These terms and ideas underpin the process, safeguarding the rights of artists and creators and ensuring equitable compensation. Let's delve into some pivotal terms in the realm of sync licensing within this context:

Master and Composition: In the context of sync licensing, "composition" refers to the core elements of a song, encompassing its melody, lyrics, and arrangement. Typically, the composition's copyright belongs to its original author(s), unless otherwise transferred through written agreements, often involving publishing companies. On the flip side, "master" pertains to the actual recorded version of a song. In cases where multiple artists record the same song, there can be multiple masters for a single composition. Music labels often own these masters and collect revenue until recouping any advances paid to the artists.

Publishing Administration: Sync licensing involves managing the rights to compositions or catalogs of compositions. Publishing administrators don't own these compositions but rather earn a commission from the revenue generated by them. Their primary objective is optimizing the earnings from the compositions they represent.

Covers and Samples: "Covers" are fresh recordings of existing compositions, and using them in sync requires securing rights to both the composition and the master recording. "Samples" refer to using a portion of an existing sound recording in the creation of a new one. To incorporate a sample into your music for sync use, you must clear the rights to both the composition and the master recording being sampled. Clearing rights involves obtaining permission and paying requisite fees, necessitating negotiations with the copyright holders of both the composition and the master recording.

Sync Fees and Royalties: "Sync fees" constitute upfront payments made for the synchronization rights of a song. These fees fluctuate based on factors such as the specific use of the song, its popularity, and the negotiation process. "Royalties" are payments made to copyright holders for the use of their music in sync. Royalties consider various factors, including the song's duration, media type, and audience reach.

Mechanical Royalties: These royalties pertain to payments made to copyright holders for reproducing their music on physical media, like CDs or vinyl records. Typically, these rates are legally determined and linked to the number of copies produced.

Public Performance Royalties: These royalties compensate copyright holders for the public performance of their music, encompassing instances like radio broadcasts and live venue performances. Such royalties are often collected by performance rights organizations (PROs) such as ASCAP or BMI.

Neighbouring Rights: In select countries, "neighbouring rights" pertain to the entitlements of performers and producers for their music's public performances. These rights exist separately from those of composition copyright holders.

A firm grasp of these key terms and concepts is essential for anyone navigating the intricacies of sync licensing. Effective understanding and application of these principles are fundamental for safeguarding the rights of music creators and ensuring fruitful collaborations between music and visual media.

Case Study: Sync And Vince Staples' Success

Vince Staples is a well-known rapper, singer, and songwriter who has been active since 2011. With standout tracks in popular films such as "Spider-Man: Across The Spider-Verse," "Creed," and "Black Panther," Vince has established himself as a successful artist in the industry.

Vince Staples was initially unaware of the financial potential of sync licensing, which involves the use of music in visual media such as TV, film, advertisements, trailers, or video games. He did not actively pursue sync licensing opportunities, and as a result, he was missing out on a significant revenue stream in the industry. Vince received an offer from the popular "Call of Duty" video game franchise to create music for the platform. Although the track was not used, Vince was still paid a substantial amount, which made him realize the value of sync licensing.

Vince's success in sync licensing is not an isolated case. Many artists have found success in this field, including Pharrell Williams, who has had his music synced in various films and TV shows, including "Despicable Me" and "The Voice." Another example is Mark Ronson, who has had his music synced in numerous films and TV shows, including "Uptown Funk" in "The Lego Movie."

Vince adapted his approach to making music by creating an album with songs that were specifically made to be synced with visual media. He recognized the opportunity to increase his income by creating music that could be used in film, TV, and video games.

Vince's adaptation paid off, as 80% of the songs from his album were synced and placed in popular visual media such as "Baywatch" and "Black Panther." He was able to recoup his album budget and secure heavy-hitting placements that helped him increase his visibility and revenue. Vince's change in approach to making music demonstrates the importance of being adaptable and open-minded in the industry. By recognizing the potential of sync licensing, Vince was able to grow his brand, increase his income, and evolve as an artist.

The success of Vince Staples in sync licensing serves as a reminder of the importance of being aware of different revenue streams in the music business and adapting one's approach accordingly. By continuously educating themselves on industry trends and exploring new opportunities, artists can not only increase their income but also grow and evolve as artists.

Brand Partnerships

Partnerships can take many forms, from record labels partnering with artists, musicians partnering with instrument or equipment manufacturers, music festivals partnering with brands, to artists partnering with brands for commercial campaigns or events. These allow artists and talent to monetize their creations and extend their reach beyond music alone.

There are also new and innovative approaches to partnerships in the music industry, such as virtual events and partnerships with new, emerging sectors. It is important for both artists and brands to be strategic and selective in their partnerships, in order to ensure that they are mutually beneficial and aligned with their respective goals and values. Building long-term relationships and aligning with brands that share a strong personal or creative affinity can create a more consistent stream of revenue and increase an artist or talent's profile in the industry.

Case Study: Central Cee x Trapstar

Central Cee is a British rapper and songwriter known for his unique style and energetic performances. In 2020, he teamed up with Trapstar to release a limited edition line of clothing, featuring Cee's signature logo and artwork inspired by his music. The partnership between Central Cee and Trapstar had a significant impact on the rapper's career, as it helped him reach a wider audience and establish himself as a serious player in the UK music scene. The clothing line, which sold out within hours of its release, generated a significant amount of buzz on social media and helped raise awareness of Cee's music among fans of streetwear and fashion.

The partnership allowed Central Cee to tap into Trapstar's extensive network of fans and followers, many of whom were already familiar with the brand's signature aesthetic and the artists it has collaborated with in the past. This helped Cee connect with new fans and gain exposure in markets outside of his core fanbase. In addition to the immediate impact on his career, the partnership with Trapstar also helped Central Cee establish himself as a serious face in the fashion industry. He has since gone on to collaborate with other brands and designers, using his unique style and image to create clothing and accessories that resonate with his fans and help him stand out from the crowd.

The success of the partnership between Central Cee and Trapstar underscores the importance of collaborations and partnerships for emerging artists looking to establish themselves. Through teaming up with brands and designers that share their vision and aesthetic, artists can expand their reach, connect with new fans, and create new revenue streams that can help sustain their careers over the long term.

Industry Insights: Ephraim Yeboah, Head Of Partnerships At Ground Up Chale

In this industry insight interview with Ephraim Yeboah, we dive into his decade of experience within the industry, where he has worked in numerous creative roles and the world of brand partnerships.

He has worked with international acts and major brands such as Belaire, Bambu, Beats by Dre and the NBA to name a few. During this conversation we covered partnerships, pro bono work, time management, creative directing, and imposter syndrome.

Partnerships: Ephraim emphasizes the importance of partnerships in building a successful career in the music industry. He advises aspiring industry professionals working in this area on behalf of their client, to align them with brands that have synergy with their work, and to show the commonality with the brand. Ephraim points out that companies often have no clear direction of what to do in relations to new information on the ground, and that it is up to the tapped in artist or professional to demonstrate how the partnership can be creative and effective. He continued on to say that brand partnerships are crucial to tapping into new markets and income streams, noting that it can help bring new fan bases to an artist, and validates what an artist is doing.

Pro Bono Work: Ephraim acknowledges that the early stages of building a career may require a lot of free work, but emphasizes the importance of learning during this phase. He advises against forcing sales pitches, and instead, taking a natural approach to networking. Understanding the pain points of the person or company you are reaching out to, and doing research on their work, can help make networking more effective. Ephraim notes that building relationships should not be seen as begging, but rather as an opportunity to tap into new markets and income streams.

Time Management: Ephraim emphasized the importance of work-life balance, even as he continues to hustle daily. Carving out personal time, and decompressing with the help of supportive relationships are a big factor in maintaining a work life balance for Ephraim. He recommended the "***How I Built This***" podcast by Guy Raz as a source of inspiration, and notes that his own routine comes from his background in law and research. Suli Breaks, Ephraim's former client, taught him the importance of constantly doing something, and the value of bad ideas in the creative process. Ephraim believes that one only needs to be right once to succeed. Finding a balance between work and personal time is crucial for staying motivated and avoiding burnout, and by placing yourself around a supportive team, it will give you time and making time for self-improvement can help.

Creative Directing: When discussing creative directing, Ephraim stresses the importance of networking in building a career in creative directing, as he got many of his gigs through his network noting that talent is not the most important factor, and that work ethic takes precedence. We see the mindset instilled by Suli Breaks on staying busy, take it's own form, as Ephraim updates that advice, stating that entrepreneurs and self-starters need to seek out their own opportunities, rather than waiting for someone to give them a job. Research is also key to success in creative directing, as it can help professionals identify new trends and opportunities. Ultimately being proactive and creative in pitching yourself to brands and building your network. Building a portfolio, doing research, and being confident in your ability to learn and grow are crucial.

Imposter Syndrome: When asked about the topic, Ephraim acknowledges the existence of imposter syndrome in the industry, but encourages aspiring professionals to work around it. He advises being confident in one's ability, and recognizing that one already has a lot of information and access. The music business can be intimidating, but Ephraim believes that with hard work, determination, and a willingness to learn, anyone can succeed. Students of the industry should recognise that Imposter syndrome is normal but can be overcome. Acknowledge the feeling but don't let it hold you back from pursuing your goals.

"If you're already a music lover and into business, you will naturally pick up information because it is something that you enjoy and keep abreast of. This in turn means you will probably have more information and access than those people in an office. A fancy office doesn't mean they have more information to give than you"
- Ephrim

Pro Tip: Reach Decision Makers Of Companies On LinkedIn

Forging brand partnerships is a potent strategy for expanding your fan base and presence. Yet, gaining access to decision makers can be challenging, particularly for emerging artists and their teams. Luckily, LinkedIn offers a unique avenue to engage with industry leaders and cultivate enduring brand collaborations. With over 740 million active users and a professional focus, LinkedIn is the ideal platform for connecting with potential collaborators and showcasing your musical prowess.

Optimizing Your LinkedIn Profile

When enhancing your LinkedIn profile, remember the principles of impression management, first impressions count and your profile will do a lot of the speaking for you. Present yourself as a skilled, affable, and trustworthy artist capable of enriching potential collaborations. To achieve this, employ various strategies:
- **Social Proof:** Highlight your industry or musical achievements, featuring testimonials from satisfied fans or collaborators.
- **Authority Indicators**: Embed keywords in your headline and summary, demonstrating your expertise through past experiences, musical education, or certifications.
- **Consistency:** Ensure your profile aligns with your artistic identity and messaging, resonating with your target audience's expectations.

Leveraging LinkedIn's Advanced Search

To harness LinkedIn's advanced search capabilities effectively, grasp the concepts of targeting and segmentation. Narrow your search criteria to locate decision makers compatible with your musical brand. Implement strategies like:
- **Genre-Specific Targeting**: Identify decision makers tied to genres that match your music, tailoring your outreach accordingly.
- **Location Targeting:** Focus your search on decision makers located in regions where your music enjoys a strong presence or where you aim to expand.
- **Label-Specific Targeting**: Locate decision makers affiliated with labels that align with your musical vision, crafting messages that resonate with their musical interests and goals.

Making A Connection

When connecting with decision makers, apply principles of persuasion and influence. Enhance your chances of a positive response by using techniques such as:
- **Social Proof:** Showcase your musical track record, social media following, or other metrics attesting to your musical value and credibility.
- **Reciprocity:** Offer something valuable to the decision maker, such as exclusive musical insights, access to your fanbase, or a sneak peek of your latest tracks.
- **Personal Connection**: Establish rapport by finding common ground with the decision maker, referencing shared musical interests or experiences.

Engaging With Their Content

When engaging with decision makers' musical content, consider principles of social proof and relationship-building. Demonstrate your interest in their musical brand and position yourself as a valuable connection by:

- **Personalizing Responses:** Tailor your comments or shares to the specific musical content, avoiding generic or superficial reactions.
- **Consistency**: Regularly interact with decision makers' musical content, ensuring your engagement aligns with your artistic identity and messaging.
- **Adding Value:** Offer insightful musical perspectives that highlight your expertise and contribute to the musical conversation.

Crafting Compelling Messages for Decision Makers

When composing compelling messages to connect with decision makers, apply communication and persuasion principles. Improve your chances of a response by utilizing techniques like:

- **Personalization:** Address the decision maker by name and reference their musical interests or accomplishments.
- **Clarity:** Keep your message concise and cantered on how your music can provide value, avoiding irrelevant or self-promotional content.
- **Call to Action:** Include a clear, actionable next step, such as a request for a collaboration meeting or a follow-up discussion about music.

Follow-Up

If your initial message receives no response, follow up respectfully without overwhelming them. Effective follow-up tactics include:

- **Polite Persistence:** Send a courteous follow-up after a few days or a week. If still met with silence, consider reaching out through alternative channels, like email or phone.
- **Offer Value:** Provide something valuable in your follow-up, like a relevant music industry article or insights. This demonstrates genuine interest in building a musical relationship.
- **Personalization:** Reference your prior message and the recipient's musical work, illustrating a sincere enthusiasm for their music and rejecting generic outreach.

Building Successful Music Brand Collaborations

Once you've connected with a decision maker and initiated a dialogue, prioritize constructing fruitful music brand partnerships. Follow these tips for nurturing a strong collaboration:

- **Develop a Mutual Agreement:** Ensure that both sides benefit by crafting a mutually beneficial agreement outlining partnership goals and expectations.
- **Set Clear Roles:** Define the responsibilities of each party and establish realistic expectations to prevent misunderstandings.
- **Maintain Open Communication:** Communication is vital; keep your collaborator informed about updates or changes, and address any concerns promptly.

Case Study: AJ Tracey And His Partnership With Tottenham Hotspur

AJ Tracey is a British grime artist known for his unique sound and ability to capture the essence of London in his music. Tracey has released multiple successful tracks, including the hit song "Ladbroke Grove," inspired by his home borough.

AJ Tracey's Background and Connection to Tottenham Hotspur AJ Tracey was born in Brixton, South London, and grew up in Ladbroke Grove, Kensington, West London. His father, who used to live in Broadwater Farm, a housing estate around the corner from White Hart Lane, supported Tottenham Hotspur. Tracey's father put him in a Spurs kit when he was born, and he has been a fan of the club ever since.

AJ Tracey's Involvement in Tottenham Hotspur's Kit Launches AJ Tracey has been involved in the launch of Tottenham Hotspur's new home kit on two occasions. In 2017/18, he was part of the launch event and helped promote the kit on social media. Most recently, he teased the first look of the new kit on his Instagram page, generating a lot of buzz and excitement among his fans and the club's supporters. The partnership between AJ Tracey and Tottenham Hotspur has helped the club gain more exposure to a younger and diverse audience, especially through social media platforms like Instagram.

Tottenham Hotspur has benefited greatly from its partnership with AJ Tracey and has continued all the way to 2023. The club has gained more exposure and increased its fan base, particularly among a younger demographic. AJ Tracey's involvement in the kit launches has helped the club reach a wider audience and generate more interest in its merchandise. The partnership has also helped the club to connect with its fans on a deeper level, as AJ Tracey's music resonates with many of Tottenham Hotspur's supporters.

AJ Tracey's partnership with Tottenham Hotspur is an excellent example of how a football club can work with a celebrity to reach a new audience. By collaborating with a successful grime artist who is also a die-hard fan, Tottenham Hotspur has been able to engage with a younger and more diverse demographic. The partnership benefits both parties by providing a platform to engage with a wider audience and generate more interest in the club's merchandise. Tottenham Hotspur's successful collaboration with AJ Tracey demonstrates the power of celebrity partnerships and the importance of reaching out to new and diverse audiences.

Case Study: Skepta x Havana Club

Skepta, a British-Nigerian grime artist, has made a name for himself in the music industry with his unique sound and style. He is known for his influence on contemporary British popular culture and his role in the grime scene.

Skepta grew up in Tottenham, North London, and has always been passionate about the city's nightlife scene. He has often referenced the city's clubs and bars in his music and has been instrumental in shaping the sound of London's underground music scene. Skepta's partnership with Havana Club was a natural fit, given his background and influence in the city's nightlife culture. In 2019, Skepta visited Cuba and found links between Yoruba culture and Afro-Cuban spirit, such as the importance of bringing people together, joyful energy, and creative essence. Inspired by this, Skepta teamed up with Havana Club, a popular rum brand, to create a bottle design that incorporates their shared values.

The objective of the collaboration was to create a bottle design that represents the values shared by Skepta and Havana Club. The collaboration also aimed to give back to the local community by exclusively dropping the bottles in corner shops, which play an integral role within the locales they serve.

Skepta created a bottle design that features traditional Nigerian symbols, textiles, and drums, inspired by the Cuban concept of ACHÉ, the "creative, universal spirit that binds all of us". The bottle design was a beautiful blue colour and was stunning to look at. To promote the collaboration and the importance of corner shops within local communities, posters and billboards featuring Skepta were put up across London, Manchester, and Birmingham. The posters and billboards showed Skepta outside a corner shop alongside a picture of the bottle.

The collaboration between Skepta and Havana Club was successful in achieving its objectives. The bottle design was well-received and represented the shared values of the two parties. The exclusive drop in corner shops gave back to the local community and highlighted the importance of these shops within the community. The posters and billboards featuring Skepta helped promote the collaboration and the importance of corner shops within local communities.

The collaboration between Skepta and Havana Club was a successful one that highlighted the shared values of the two parties. The bottle design was well-received, and the exclusive drop in corner shops helped give back to the local community. The promotion of the collaboration through posters and billboards helped highlight the importance of corner shops within local communities. Overall, the collaboration was a great success and showed the positive impact that can be achieved through creative collaborations between different parties.

Case Study: Krept & Konan x Puma

In 2015, Krept and Konan were announced as the new ambassadors for Puma's evolution range at Foot Asylum, making them the perfect fit for the PUMA Evolution pack. The collection featured sweat bottoms, hooded tops, sweatshirts, and T-shirts with a camo print throughout. The duo modelled the range in their 'Nigo Duppy' video, showcasing Puma's new 2016 trainer line.

This partnership between Puma and Krept and Konan was successful as it helped to strengthen Puma's position in the UK hip-hop and grime scenes. The collaboration also brought a fresh and edgy perspective to Puma's Evolution pack, which was well-received by fans and helped to boost sales. This partnership demonstrated the impact of partnerships on emerging artists and how brands can leverage these partnerships to expand their market and reach.

For Puma, the partnership with the popular hip-hop duo provided a unique opportunity to tap into the rapidly growing UK grime and hip-hop scene, which was gaining increasing attention and popularity both in the UK and internationally. By aligning itself with one of the most popular acts in the genre, Puma could leverage the group's popularity and influence to reach a wider audience and drive brand awareness. In addition, the partnership helped to position Puma as a brand that was in tune with popular culture and the latest trends in music and fashion, which is essential for any brand looking to remain relevant and appeal to younger audiences.

For Krept and Konan, the partnership with Puma provided a significant boost to their profile and credibility as emerging artists. By being associated with such a well-respected and established brand, they were able to build their reputation and gain exposure to a wider audience. Furthermore, the partnership allowed them to showcase their music and image to Puma's existing customer base, which included a significant number of young people who were already interested in music, fashion, and popular culture. The partnership between Puma and Krept and Konan provided a mutually beneficial opportunity for both parties to increase their brand awareness and exposure, tap into new audiences, and enhance their respective reputations in the music and fashion industries.

Partnerships between brands and artists have the potential to bring mutual benefits. By providing financial support and resources, brands can help artists create high-quality content and expand their reach. In turn, artists can bring a unique and authentic voice to a brand's marketing efforts, connecting with and engaging audiences in a more meaningful way. The campaigns can create buzz and generate media coverage, increasing visibility for both the artist and the brand. Moreover, partnerships can provide exposure for both the artist and the brand, enabling them to tap into each other's audiences and reach new demographics. Artists can also provide valuable feedback and insights to brands, helping them to better understand and connect with their target market. Similarly, brands can provide artists with access to new and diverse audiences, giving them a platform to share their art and connect with new fans.

Pro Tip: Be Brand Ready

Being brand ready is crucial for artists looking to pitch potential brand partnerships or collaborations. It involves ensuring that their image, messaging, and overall brand align with the values and goals of the target brand. To achieve this, artists need to have a well curated, strong online presence and social media following. Additionally, they should be aware of their reputation and take steps to clean up any potentially damaging content that may hinder their chances of securing brand deals.

A significant aspect of being brand ready is having a clear understanding of their brand identity and unique selling points. Artists should be able to effectively communicate these to potential partners, demonstrating how they can add value to the brand and create a mutually beneficial partnership. This includes showcasing a strong portfolio of work that highlights their creativity, skill, and versatility. A compelling portfolio will help capture the attention of potential brand partners and showcase the artist's abilities.

Another critical factor in being brand ready is aligning the artist's personal brand with the values and image of the brand they wish to collaborate with. This alignment ensures a seamless integration of the artist's identity with the brand's messaging and objectives. Furthermore, considering whether the artist's following demographic matches the target audience of the brand is essential for effective marketing and outreach.

The size of the artist's following and their overall reach are significant considerations for potential brand partnerships. Brands are often interested in artists who not only have a substantial social media presence but also wield influence within their industry. Examining the artist's history of previous partnerships and sponsorships can provide valuable insights into their compatibility with brands and their track record of successful collaborations.

Creative collaboration is an aspect that can elevate a brand partnership to new heights. Artists who are open to collaborating creatively with brands can create more authentic and meaningful content that resonates with audiences. This fosters a deeper connection with consumers and reinforces the brand's message in a way that feels genuine and engaging.

In the negotiation process, artists should be willing to agree to reasonable contractual terms, including exclusivity, partnership duration, and compensation. Flexibility and open-mindedness can facilitate a smooth negotiation process and build a positive working relationship between the artist and the brand.

Relevance is key when considering a potential brand partnership. The artist's brand and identity should align with the target audience of the brand, ensuring that the collaboration feels authentic and resonates with consumers. Above all, authenticity is paramount. Artists should genuinely connect with the brand and be able to communicate the brand's message in an authentic way. This ensures that the collaboration feels natural and reflects positively on both the artist and the brand.

Being brand ready is a multifaceted process that requires artists to carefully align their image and messaging with the values and objectives of potential brand partners. A strong online presence, understanding of their brand identity, and a willingness to collaborate creatively are crucial elements of being brand ready.

Navigating Brand Guidelines As An Industry Professional

As an artist or industry professional, navigating legal and brand guidelines is a crucial aspect of your work. Understanding and adhering to these guidelines is essential for various reasons, including protecting yourself from legal issues and ensuring that your work aligns with the client's vision and brand identity.

One of the most critical aspects of navigating legal guidelines is understanding copyright and trademark laws. Copyright laws protect original works of authorship, such as music, lyrics, and artwork, from being reproduced, distributed, or performed without permission. Trademark laws protect brand names, logos, and slogans, preventing others from using similar marks that may cause confusion in the marketplace.

When working with clients or brands, it's essential to ensure that your work does not infringe on any existing copyrights or trademarks. This means avoiding the use of copyrighted material without proper authorization and steering clear of any trademarks that may conflict with the client's brand. Failure to do so can result in legal action and damage your professional reputation.

Many clients and brands have their own specific brand guidelines or style guides that dictate how their brand should be represented visually and verbally. These guidelines often include rules regarding logo usage, colour schemes, typography, and tone of voice. Adhering to these guidelines is crucial to maintain consistency and coherence in the brand's messaging and visual identity. By following the brand guidelines, you demonstrate your professionalism and commitment to delivering work that aligns with the client's brand values and image. This can lead to stronger relationships with clients and potential opportunities for future collaborations.

In some cases, you may be required to sign a non-disclosure agreement (NDA) or other legal document before starting a project. An NDA is a legally binding contract that protects sensitive and confidential information from being shared with unauthorized parties. NDAs are common in the business, especially when collaborating on unreleased music or creative projects that contain proprietary information. When signing an NDA, it is crucial to carefully review and understand its terms. Pay attention to the scope of the confidentiality obligations, the duration of the agreement, and any exclusions to the confidentiality requirements. If you have any concerns or questions about the NDA, seeking legal advice is advisable to ensure that your rights and interests are protected.

Beyond legal considerations, understanding brand guidelines is equally important in creating successful collaborations. By adhering to a brand's visual and verbal identity, you contribute to a cohesive and recognizable brand presence. This consistency helps build brand trust and fosters a positive image in the minds of consumers.

Understanding brand guidelines allows you to tailor your creative work to fit the client's specific brand identity and target audience. By aligning your artistic vision with the brand's values and goals, you can create work that resonates with the brand's customers and enhances its overall brand experience. Navigating legal and brand guidelines is essential for artists and industry professionals to ensure successful collaborations with clients and brands. Understanding copyright and trademark laws, as well as complying with brand guidelines, can protect you from legal issues and enhance your reputation as a professional.

Understanding copyright and trademark laws, as well as complying with brand guidelines, can protect you from legal issues and enhance your reputation as a professional. Additionally, signing NDAs when necessary demonstrates your commitment to confidentiality and can lead to more opportunities in the competitive music industry.

Financial Management

Financial management is fundamental, encompassing the effective handling of financial resources and activities to support the success and sustainability of artists. One crucial element of financial management in the music industry involves understanding and optimizing the various revenue streams.

The industry generates income from various sources, including record sales, merchandise, brand partnerships, streaming platforms, live events, and intellectual property (IP) licensing. Effectively managing these revenue streams involves carefully monitoring their performance, ensuring proper accounting, and exploring opportunities to maximize earnings.

Conversely, financial management also entails controlling and optimizing costs and expenses. The business involves a range of expenses, such as personnel costs, travel expenses, production costs, marketing and promotion expenses, and touring expenses. By diligently managing these costs and expenses, artists can make informed decisions about resource allocation, prevent overspending, and maintain financial stability.

Financial planning and forecasting are also integral to successful financial management in music. Creating budgets and financial plans enables artists and music professionals to set clear financial goals and strategize resource allocation. Forecasting future financial performance allows them to anticipate potential challenges and opportunities, minimizing risk and fostering long-term sustainability. Financial management is essential for working individuals, and artists are no different. For creatives to navigate the complexities of a rapidly evolving landscape, they must have a complete understanding of their revenue streams and outgoings.

The rise of digital platforms and streaming services has transformed the way music is consumed, altering revenue streams and business models. Effective financial management can help music professionals adapt to these changes, identify new revenue opportunities, and remain competitive in the industry. Financial management plays a pivotal role in guiding artists' careers. It empowers them to negotiate favourable contracts, make sound investments in their careers, and plan for the future effectively. Understanding their financial position and performance allows artists to make informed decisions about touring, album production, and promotional activities.

For artist, effective financial management is vital for maintaining financial health and securing investments or loans. Financial institutions and investors often scrutinize the financial performance and projections of music based businesses and artist, before making funding decisions. A solid financial management strategy can instil confidence in potential investors and lenders, increasing the chances of securing financial support.

Adopting sound financial management practices, means that music professionals can navigate the dynamic and competitive music landscape, make informed decisions, and ensure the sustainability of their careers and businesses. Conversely, poor financial management can lead to financial instability, missed opportunities, and potentially hinder the growth and success of music projects and businesses.

Financial Planning For Music Projects

The initial step in financial planning for projects is to identify all costs associated with the music project. This includes recording costs, marketing and promotion expenses, and touring expenditures. Accurately identifying these costs allows for the creation of a comprehensive budget, ensuring that all financial aspects are accounted for. During this phase, it is essential to strike a balance between creativity and practicality, ensuring that the project is both inspiring and feasible within the available resources.

Estimating the revenues generated by the project is equally important. This involves forecasting revenues from various sources, such as record sales, merchandise, streaming, live events, and licensing. Accurate revenue estimation provides insights into the project's potential profitability and enables informed decision-making regarding its financial performance.

Once costs and revenues have been identified and estimated, the next step is to create a budget and financial plan for the music project. Utilizing financial software or other tools, this comprehensive plan outlines the project's financial aspects, offering a clear roadmap for resource allocation and tracking its financial performance. A well-structured financial plan helps avoid overspending and ensures efficient use of available funds.

Financial planning plays a pivotal role in the overall management of music projects, enabling accurate forecasting and resource allocation for successful project completion. By identifying potential financial risks, the project team can implement measures to mitigate them effectively. Regular monitoring and adjustments based on market trends help maintain financial stability and keep the project on track.

Financial planning is a fundamental aspect of managing music projects, ensuring proper resource allocation and financial sustainability. By accurately identifying costs and estimating revenues, a comprehensive budget and financial plan can be created, offering a roadmap for the project's financial success. Careful financial planning allows music projects to navigate challenges effectively and achieve their desired outcomes without compromising on creativity and quality.

Accounting And Record-Keeping

Thorough accounting and precise record-keeping form the cornerstone of a prosperous music career. These practices not only safeguard an artist's financial health but are also instrumental in fostering their long-term viability and success within the industry.

Accounting

Accounting involves the creation and rigorous maintenance of financial records, which, in turn, serve as the backbone for generating essential financial statements. These statements, including income reports, balance sheets, and cash flow summaries, offer invaluable insights into the financial performance of the music business.

One critical area where accounting shines is financial reporting. Precise accounting practices allow artists to establish and maintain accurate financial records. These records, in turn, lay the groundwork for comprehensive financial statements and reports, providing a clear view of the business's financial standing. This empowers stakeholders to make well-informed decisions regarding the financial well-being of the music career.

Tax Compliance

Accounting in the industry extends to tax compliance. Maintaining meticulous financial records ensures adherence to tax laws and regulations. This encompasses precise income reporting, eligible expense deductions, and fulfilling tax obligations. Complying with tax regulations is essential to avoid penalties and legal complications, safeguarding both the artist's reputation and financial stability.

Record-Keeping

Running an efficient music business also hinges on robust record-keeping. This entails systematic and organized management of various records, spanning financial, contractual, and legal documents. Documenting income, expenses, contracts, and other essential information is crucial for accuracy, reliability, and legal compliance in the music career.

A well-maintained record-keeping system simplifies tasks such as tracking revenue streams, monitoring expenses, and managing artist contracts. This, in turn, enhances financial oversight and decision-making within the music business. Meticulous records ensure that critical information is readily accessible, reducing the risk of potential legal disputes.
Streamlined Auditing: Proof of Compliance

Accurate accounting and diligent record-keeping streamline auditing processes. In the event of an audit, having comprehensive financial records readily available expedites the procedure. It also demonstrates the artist's compliance with financial regulations, further bolstering their financial reputation.

Accounting and record-keeping are fundamental pillars of success for music artists. These practices promote financial transparency, ensure compliance with tax regulations, and optimize business management efficiency. By implementing effective accounting and record-keeping strategies, music artists gain invaluable insights into their financial performance, make informed decisions, and establish a strong foundation for long-lasting success in the ever-evolving music industry.

Case Study: J2K - The Entrepreneurial Pioneer In The Music Industry

J2K, whose real name is Jason Black, is a grime artist from East London, Bow E3. He was part of one of the most important collectives in the grime scene, Roll Deep. Despite never fully pursuing a solo career, J2K has made a significant impact in the music industry as an entrepreneur.

Crep Protect: In 2013, J2K co-founded Crep Protect with brothers Nohman, Imran, and Rizwan Ahmed. With his connections in the grime scene, J2K used smart marketing strategies to promote the brand. By having artists pictured with the product and creating viral marketing campaigns, Crep Protect became a household name. Within no time, the product was available in every major shoe retailer in the UK, and the brand became one of the most successful growing brands in the UK. J2K's innovative marketing strategies and product quality saw the brand expand to over 50 countries worldwide.

At Home: After stepping back from the day-to-day running of Crep Protect, Jason founded AtHome, a digital agency, and lifestyle brand. J2K has collaborated with Puma and music collective Vibber to launch a pop-up shop in Box Park Shoreditch for the launch of Puma's Rs-x3 trainers. The company has also put on a drive-in cinema in London during the global pandemic, showing yet again just how innovative J2K is. AtHome has released a string of products, including socks, sliders, a fire hot sauce, and an alcohol dispenser.

Crepes and Cones: In 2018, J2K collaborated with rap duo Krept and Konan to open Crepes and Cones, a dessert shop that has been a success since its launch.

HYPHNT: Jason, has recently launched his own footwear line called HYPHNT. This new line of sneakers is designed to cater to the modern sneaker wearer, from the block to the boardroom. According to Jason Black, creating a brand that tailors to multi-hyphenated individuals in the same way that a sports brand would to athletes has always been a dream of his.

J2K has become a pioneer, trailblazer, and successful entrepreneur in the industry. His innovative marketing strategies and product quality have made him a successful self-made millionaire. He continues to innovate and inspire many, making him an essential figure in the grime scene. Puma continues to work closely with him, and he is about to release his own brand of trainers, fulfilling a lifelong dream. J2K is an inspiration to many, and it's going to be exciting to see what he does in the next ten years.

Case study: Fredo And Kick Game

In 2021, West London's beloved artist, Fredo, made a savvy and forward-thinking business move by entering the thriving sneaker industry through a partnership with Kick Game, a prominent luxury sneaker retailer based in London. This collaboration signifies a potentially lucrative opportunity for both Fredo and Kick Game, as the sneaker industry continues to flourish and evolve.

Fredo's investment in Kick Game is a testament to his sharp business acumen and ability to foresee market trends. As a renowned sneaker enthusiast with a discerning eye for fashion, he recognizes the immense potential embedded within the sneaker industry and capitalizes on it effectively. By doing so, he not only diversifies his investment portfolio but also fortifies his financial future, ensuring long-term stability and prosperity.

Kick Game's remarkable performance during the challenging times of the pandemic underscores the resilience and strength of the company. Despite the economic uncertainties, the retailer achieved a staggering 600% surge in online sales and propelled its revenue from £2 million to an impressive £15 million in just 12 months. This remarkable growth stands as a testament to Kick Game's market positioning and its adeptness at capitalizing on the ever-expanding sneaker industry.

The partnership between Fredo and Kick Game marks a significant milestone for both parties. It underscores the significance of strategic collaborations in driving business success and underscores the power of aligning personal passions with entrepreneurial ventures. This investment is a prime example of a shrewd and calculated business move that not only secures Fredo's financial future but also positions him as a formidable player in the thriving sneaker industry.

Fredo's collaboration with Kick Game also serves as a beacon of inspiration for fellow artists and entrepreneurs. It demonstrates the importance of wisely managing and investing their financial resources. As an artist with a substantial following, Fredo's alliance with a successful sneaker retailer provides an exceptional opportunity to expand his personal brand and resonate with a broader audience. This diversification of revenue streams can pave the way for long-term financial security beyond the scope of his music career.

Given the significant transformations occurring within the music industry, diversifying revenue streams emerges as a prudent and strategic move. By investing in a business venture that aligns with personal passions, artists can leverage their existing fanbase while simultaneously attracting new audiences. This expansion not only broadens their reach but also opens up additional revenue streams. Furthermore, such investments serve as solid foundations for future business endeavours. Building relationships with successful business partners enables artists to tap into their networks, access new opportunities, and amplify their entrepreneurial ventures.

Fredo's investment in Kick Game stands as a compelling case study for business students, budding entrepreneurs, and seasoned investors alike. It underscores the importance of strategic partnerships and showcases the immense potential of niche markets in driving business success. Fredo's venture into the burgeoning sneaker industry exemplifies how smart investments can secure one's financial future while positioning them for long-term prosperity.

Through smart investing in ventures that align with their personal interests and passions, artists can expand their horizons, create new revenue streams, reach new audiences, and establish a robust foundation for enduring success. Fredo's journey into the sneaker industry serves as a testament to the significance of strategic investments and the power of collaboration in navigating the dynamic landscape of business, culture and entertainment.

Case Study: The Entrepreneurial Journey Of Krept
A Musician's Success In Business

Krept is one-half of the renowned rap duo Krept & Konan, and he is not only a successful musician but also a budding entrepreneur. His journey as an entrepreneur is a testament to the idea that success can be achieved in multiple fields with hard work, dedication, and a business mindset.

Krept grew up on council estates in Gipsy Hill and Thornton Heath in south London, where he witnessed the harsh reality of gang violence and its aftermath. This background instilled in him the value of hard work and determination. At the age of 14, he began selling drinks, sweets, and crisps to his schoolmates, which was his first taste of entrepreneurship. He quickly learned the importance of good customer service and providing high-quality products.

Krept's experiences in the industry have been a significant influence on his entrepreneurial journey. As a rapper, he understands the hustle and the importance of building a sustainable future. Many successful hip hop artists like Rihanna, Jay-Z, and Kanye West have set an example for young artists to explore different business ventures. Krept acknowledges that the music business is a hustle, and many industry contracts do not favor artists, leading to many of them becoming entrepreneurs. While music does not guarantee a stable source of income, entrepreneurship offers an opportunity to build a more sustainable future.

Krept's restaurant, Crepes & Cones, opened in 2018 in Croydon, and has since been thriving. Despite his busy schedule as a musician, Krept is passionate about managing his business and ensuring that it provides customers with an excellent dining experience. The restaurant offers a diverse menu, including sweet and savory crepes, ice cream, and milkshakes. The success of Crepes & Cones has served as an inspiration for those who aspire to work hard and achieve their dreams.

Krept's latest business venture is a skincare range for babies named Nala's Baby. Developed with his co-parent and business partner, Sasha Ellese Gilbert, the cream is vegan, animal cruelty-free, and dermatologically approved, making it suitable for babies with eczema issues or sensitive skin. The product is now available in Boots stores across the UK and has been expanding its reach. Krept's daughter, Nala, was the inspiration behind the product, and he wanted to create a high-quality product that would be safe for babies' delicate skin.

Krept believes that the worlds of rap and business are not mutually exclusive. As a father and a rapper, he sees no contradiction between his profession and his business ventures. Krept asserts that music is just entertainment, and the lyrics he writes portray his reality growing up. He hopes to inspire others to work hard and strive for their dreams, irrespective of their upbringing. With his impressive success in both music and business, Krept is a role model for aspiring artists and entrepreneurs alike.

Krept's journey as an entrepreneur is a testament to the idea that one can achieve success in multiple fields with hard work, dedication, and a business mindset. His background, coupled with his experiences in the music industry, has prepared him for the world of entrepreneurship. Krept's success with Crepes & Cones and Nala's Baby serves as an inspiration for those who aspire to work hard and achieve their dreams. Krept hopes to inspire others to pursue their passions and explore different business ventures, regardless of their upbringing or circumstances. His outlook on entrepreneurship reflects a positive attitude towards exploring different fields and using one's skills and experiences to build a successful future. With his impressive success in both music and business, Krept is a role model for aspiring artists and entrepreneurs, showing that there are no limits to what one can achieve with hard work, determination, and a passion for success.

Krept's story also highlights the importance of diversity in entrepreneurship. It's crucial to have individuals from different backgrounds and experiences contributing to the entrepreneurial ecosystem. Krept's unique perspective as a rapper and entrepreneur has enabled him to create businesses that cater to a diverse audience, providing high-quality products and services that meet their needs.

Krept's journey as an entrepreneur is an inspiring story of perseverance, determination, and the ability to thrive in multiple fields. From he's chart topping success   to opening a successful restaurant and creating a skincare range, Krept's entrepreneurial journey is a testament to the power of hard work, dedication, and a business mindset. His success as an artist and entrepreneur serves as an inspiration to aspiring entrepreneurs and creatives, showing that with the right mindset and determination, anything is possible.

Pro Tip: Negotiating And Managing Collaborations

Collaborations in the music world are creative unions that often require intricate negotiations; how well these are managed can define your success. Whether you're an executive with years of experience or an emerging artist, mastering the art of negotiation within the context of collaboration is pivotal. These are the key elements to consider during these negotiations:

Credit: Beyond recognition, credit solidifies your artistic contribution and shapes your industry reputation. Negotiating credit ensures your creative input is rightfully acknowledged. When entering a collaboration, openly discuss the credits you expect based on your role, be it co-writer, performer, or producer. Clarity upfront prevents misunderstandings and preserves professional relationships.

Ownership: Ownership determines who controls the music project and shares in the revenue. Negotiating ownership empowers you in decision-making and income distribution. Collaborating with songwriters or producers? Dive into discussions on both song copyright and recording ownership. Transparent ownership negotiations protect your creative control and financial interests.

Payment: Payment terms should align with your contributions' value. Negotiating payment ensures everyone is fairly compensated. Engage in discussions regarding fees or establish a percentage of project profits. Transparent payment terms prevent disputes and maintain professionalism.

Creative Control: Collaboration often requires creative decisions. Negotiating creative control ensures your artistic vision is honoured. Clearly define the extent of creative control you want to maintain or share, covering aspects like musical direction and production choices. A well-defined agreement protects your artistic integrity.

Future Opportunities: Success may open doors to more collaborations. Negotiating future opportunities can help you capitalize on your expanding network. Consider discussing how future projects will be approached, especially if your current collaboration leads to wider recognition. Being proactive can lead to even more fruitful partnerships.

Termination Clauses: Termination clauses outline conditions for ending the collaboration agreement. Negotiating these ensures you have an exit strategy in case of disputes or unforeseen events. Clearly define when the collaboration can be terminated and establish what happens to ownership, credits, and revenue in such cases. This safeguards all parties involved.

Effective negotiation within collaborations is a skill that can shape your music career. By addressing elements like credit, ownership, payment, creative control, future opportunities, and termination clauses with care and professionalism, you secure favourable terms and foster enduring partnerships.

CHAPTER 6
MARKETING, BRANDING AND PUBLICITY

Introduction To Marketing And Branding

The significance of marketing and branding cannot be overstated, as they play a crucial role in promoting and establishing an artist's career. Marketing is the process of promoting and selling products or services, and in the context of the music industry, it involves the promotion of an artist's music and persona. Branding, on the other hand, is the process of creating and maintaining a distinct image and identity for a product or service, and in the industry, this translates to establishing and maintaining a unique identity and image for an artist.

A strong marketing and branding strategy can facilitate an artist's visibility, attract fans, and build a positive reputation in the music business. This enables them to differentiate themselves from other artists and develop a consistent and compelling image that resonates with their audience. Effective marketing and branding also assist artists in forging connections with their audience and cultivating a loyal fan base.

To effectively promote their music career, artists must possess a comprehensive understanding of their target audience and what sets them apart. In addition, artists must devise a clear marketing and branding strategy that includes social media marketing, website development, and public relations, among other tactics. By implementing a robust marketing and branding strategy, artists can effectively promote their music and establish their presence in the industry.

Developing A Unique Brand Identity

Developing a unique brand identity involves defining what makes an artist unique and creating a cohesive image and message that reflects that identity. This can involve brainstorming ideas for the artist's style, genre, values, and message and creating a "brand statement" that summarizes their brand identity. It's important for artists to be authentic and true to themselves when developing their brand identity, as this can help them create a genuine and meaningful connection with their audience. A unique brand identity is what makes an artist distinct and sets them apart from other artists. Having this is important for artists because it helps them stand out in a crowded and competitive market.

It's the combination of an artist's style, genre, values, and message that defines their brand identity and creates a cohesive image for their career.

For music artists, cultivating a robust and distinctive brand identity holds great significance as it facilitates meaningful connections with their audience and fosters a loyal fan base. A well-defined brand identity enables fans to grasp an artist's essence and anticipate the musical experience they offer. Moreover, a unique brand identity aids artists in establishing their reputation and securing their position in the competitive music sector.

Brand Identity

Branding is often seen as just the logo and colour pallet the artist or brand uses, but it goes a lot deeper. The brand is the spirit of the artist, crafted into a formula and presented in a unique clear language, that is consistent across all their assets and touch points for consumers to engage with. It can inspire others and invoke emotion when done correctly. Famous music producers and creative directors like Rick Rubin, Pharrell, and Virgil Abloh have made significant contributions to the field of branding.

> ***"The thing that makes a good brand is when it's not just a product or a service, but it's an idea."***
> Rick Rubin

> ***"A brand is the set of expectations, memories, stories and relationships that, taken together, account for a consumer's decision to choose one product or service over another."***
> Pharrell

> ***"Branding is not just a logo. It's a feeling, a tone, an attitude, a culture."***
> Virgil Abloh

Some of the key principles used in branding include:
- **Simplicity**: Keep designs simple and straightforward to make them easy to understand and remember.
- **Consistency**: Maintain a consistent look and feel across all marketing materials to build a strong brand identity.
- **Relevance**: Make sure that the brand speaks directly to the target audience and addresses their needs and interests.

To identify your own branding DNA, you need to understand what makes your company unique and what sets it apart from its competitors. You can start by asking yourself the following questions:

- What are your core values and beliefs?
- What are your unique strengths and weaknesses?
- What are the needs and wants of your target audience?
- What are your goals for the future?

By answering these questions, you can start to build a brand that is true to who you are and that resonates with your target audience.

Pro Tip: The Concept Of "Shop Windows"

In the world of marketing and communication, the term "shop windows" refers to the various platforms and channels that an artist or brand uses to communicate their message and showcase their brand image. It is crucial to ensure that each of these platforms is utilized effectively, as each platform can reach different audiences and demographics.

Equitable Treatment of All Platforms It is important to recognize that not all platforms may hold the same level of popularity or relevance to a particular artist or brand, however, it is crucial to treat each platform and its followers with equal respect. This means providing consistent and relevant information, updates, and promotions across all platforms to ensure that no followers are excluded or left feeling unimportant. Examples of Shop Windows would be TikTok, Instagram, WhatsApp, and a brand's website; these are all "shop windows." Facebook holds a significant reach, with ownership over Instagram and WhatsApp, as well as a store and show listing feature. A website, on the other hand, provides the option for followers to sign up for a newsletter, leaving the owner with valuable, direct data to improve their site/business with.

Importance of Consistency To ensure that each platform is utilized effectively and followers are treated equally, it is recommended to set aside a specific time each day to replicate the same updates and posts across all platforms. While there may be exceptions to this, where a specific promotion or update is exclusive to one platform, it is important to ensure that the majority of vital information is shared across all platforms to avoid any feelings of neglect among followers.

The Consumer Journey

Understanding Your Audience In the planning phase of a project, it is crucial to avoid the assumption that fans are familiar with the industry lingo and know what you are referring to. It is not uncommon for fans to be unaware of the latest developments and updates. It is essential to provide clear and straightforward information to your audience. This can be achieved by ensuring that the links and swipe-ups work efficiently, and the website provides clear and accessible information. Do not direct your fans to an unavailable or unorganized page, as this may result in them losing interest and abandoning their journey.

Take into consideration the global reach of your audience, provide time zone and country information, and use subtitles when necessary. The instructions provided should be clear, easy to follow, and limited to two main points, such as posting and hash tagging. The goal is to reward your audience's attention and make it effortless for them to engage with your brand.

Case Study: Virgil Abloh And "Design Language"

Virgil Abloh, "Insert Complicated Title Here" was a seminal event in the design world, showcasing the work and ideas of one of the most influential designers of our time.

Held at a major design school and attended by a diverse group of students, professionals, and industry leaders, Virgil Abloh was the keynote speaker. He delivered a highly anticipated and thought-provoking talk on his approach to design, branding, and creativity. One of the most notable aspects of the lecture was Virgil's unique and boundary-pushing design language. In this context, "design language" refers to the visual vocabulary, style, and unique artistic expression that an artist or designer employs in their work. It's a set of design elements, principles, and aesthetic choices that define their creative identity. He demonstrated how he blends different styles and influences to create designs that are both visually stunning and culturally relevant.

Another highlight of the lecture was Virgil's insights into the world of branding and marketing. He shared his thoughts on the role that brands play in our lives, and the ways in which they can be used to communicate ideas and values. He also discussed the importance of consistency in branding, and how a strong brand identity can help a company differentiate itself from its competitors. The impact of the lecture was significant. The audience was captivated by Virgil's ideas and designs, and many left the event feeling inspired and energized. The lecture also sparked a great deal of discussion and debate among the attendees, and many of Virgil's ideas and insights were widely shared and discussed in the days and weeks following the event.

Based on Virgil's insights and approach, here are six steps that you can follow to create your own design language:

- **Research and Inspiration:** Start by researching different design styles and influences that interest you. This can include fashion, art, architecture, and other creative fields. Look for inspiration in both contemporary and historical sources, and keep a record of the things that catch your eye.
- **Define Your Aesthetic**: Once you have a good understanding of the different styles and influences that interest you, begin to define your own aesthetic. What elements do you like and dislike? What makes a design feel unique to you? What kind of mood or atmosphere do you want to create with your designs?
- **Experiment and iterate:** Once you have a clear understanding of your aesthetic, it's time to start experimenting and iterating. As you experiment and play with different design elements, you will begin to refine and perfect your own design language. Keep a portfolio of your work to see how your style evolves over time.
- **Embrace simplicity:** A strong design language should be simple, clear, and easily recognizable. Focus on creating designs that are visually stunning and impactful, but also easy to understand.
- **Use storytelling**: Storytelling is a powerful tool for engaging your audience and creating a sense of connection. Consider incorporating cryptic messages or references into your designs to add depth and meaning.
- **Stay consistent:** Consistency is key when it comes to branding and design. Ensure that all of your designs adhere to a consistent visual language, and that your brand is represented consistently across all platforms and touchpoints. This includes your website, social media, packaging, and any other areas where your brand is displayed.

Applying Your Design Language To Campaigns: Design language and brand identity are crucial elements in creating effective marketing campaigns that resonate with target audiences. Consider the design language as your basis for creative work in your distinct style, it's the foundation of your continuous development in the industry and how you build your portfolio, style and vision. To incorporate these elements into a campaign, it's important to break down project briefs to their pillars / simplest forms, understand demographics, align design language with trends, and use storytelling. Here are the steps to do so:

Break Down The Project Brief: The first step in applying design language to campaigns is to carefully read and analyze the project brief. Look for key information such as the target audience, the desired outcome, and any specific requirements or constraints. Take note of the project's scope, timeline, and budget.

Understand Demographics And What Will Resonate: Once you have a clear understanding of the project brief, it's time to research and understand the target audience. This involves considering the demographics of the audience, such as age, gender, income, and location, and understanding their needs and desires. Identify what resonates with them, what motivates them, and what type of content they are most likely to engage with.

Align Design Language with Trends, Balancing Personal Taste and Consumer Taste: The next step is to align the design language with current trends, whilst balancing your own personal taste with the consumer's taste. You can achieve this by researching current trends in design, marketing, and pop culture. However, it's important not to lose sight of the brand's identity and message, and to remain true to its values and goals. A design that is trendy but doesn't resonate with the target audience will not be effective. Therefore, it's crucial to balance design trends with the target audience's preferences and needs.

Storytelling and Archetypes: A powerful tool for engaging your audience and creating a sense of connection is storytelling. Consider incorporating cryptic messages or references into your designs to add depth and meaning. Use archetypes to tap into universal human experiences and emotions, such as the hero's journey, the lover, or the rebel. They help designers create a sense of familiarity and consistency in the campaign, making it easier for the target audience to identify with the brand.

Consistency In Design Language And Brand Identity: It's important to ensure consistency in design language and brand identity. All of your designs should adhere to a consistent visual language, with the same fonts, colors, and imagery. Your brand should have a consistent voice and tone, with messaging that is consistent across all channels.

A well-defined design language also allows you to create more efficient workflows and make better design decisions, as you can refer back to your established guidelines for guidance and inspiration. Additionally, a strong design language can help to differentiate your work from that of your competitors, making your brand more memorable and impactful. Ultimately, having a clear and well-executed design language can help to elevate the quality and impact of your work, leading to greater success and recognition in your chosen creative field.

Pro Tip: Critical Thinking

Critical thinking is a paramount skill, whether you're an artist, manager, or industry professional. This skill equips you with the ability to approach projects and challenges with a meticulous and analytical mindset, enhancing your decision-making and problem-solving capabilities.

Critical thinking begins with a deep comprehension of the context. It involves dissecting project briefs to uncover key objectives, target audiences, and desired outcomes. Ambiguities or uncertainties within the brief should be clarified to establish a solid grasp of the problem at hand. This foundational understanding sets the stage for effective critical thinking.

A critical thinker in the music realm leverages data and research. Conducting thorough investigations into target audiences, market trends, and relevant insights is vital. Such information serves as a compass for shaping design choices and crafting strategies that harmonize with project briefs. Critical thinking guides you in using data as a potent tool to inform your decisions.

Critical thinking propels creative ideation. Employing brainstorming techniques and ideation exercises, you can explore a spectrum of potential solutions to challenges. This process encourages you to venture beyond the obvious, nurturing creativity and innovation. Critical thinkers in music continuously push the boundaries of what's achievable.

The critical thinker evaluates generated ideas rigorously. Each idea is scrutinized based on its alignment with project objectives and audience needs. Feasibility, budget, and timelines are weighed for each concept. The cream of the crop, the most promising ideas, is selected for further development. Critical thinking acts as your compass in choosing the path that promises the most significant impact.

After selecting the top ideas, critical thinking guides you through the refinement and iteration process. Feedback from colleagues and clients becomes invaluable in enhancing designs. Continual testing and refinement lead to the creation of a final solution that not only meets project objectives but also resonates deeply with the target audience.

In the music industry, critical thinking is indispensable for success. It empowers individuals to navigate the multifaceted challenges unique to this creative field. Critical thinkers can identify and evaluate diverse options, weighing their merits and drawbacks to make well-informed decisions. This approach encourages thinking beyond conventions and opens doors to fresh, innovative outcomes.

Critical thinking in music acts as a guiding force, enabling adaptability, enhancing learning, and ensuring a competitive advantage. The self awareness it creates, is key to unlocking an artist's highest potential in the ever-changing and diverse music landscape. It enables individuals to recognize their own biases and limitations, propelling them toward personal and professional growth. In an industry where uniqueness and authenticity are prized, critical thinking is the catalyst for continuous improvement.

Industry Insights: Emma Rose, Multi Genre DJ

In this industry insights interview we spoke with Emma Rose, a multi-genre DJ making waves in the music industry based in Manchester. In this sit down with Emma, we cover topics ranging from the change in rave culture, content, experiences In a label environments and regionally.

The Change In Rave Culture: Emma spoke about the impact of the pandemic on the club scene, stating that people are not the same post-COVID and raving has changed. She noted that people in clubs don't receive new music as well as they used to and that the DJ doesn't play as big a role in setting trends due to TikTok. Emma highlighted the importance of how DJs present the music, citing clubs in Paris, as a strong example. There, DJs take on the responsibility of telling the crowd what music is hot and creating an atmosphere that encourages people to dance and have a good time. This reflects a shift away from the traditional role of the DJ as the sole arbiter of taste and towards a more collaborative and interactive approach to music curation. Emma's comments suggest that the DJ's role is evolving in response to changing listener preferences and the impact of technology.

Content: Emma pointed out, finding a balance between the 9-5 and pursuing your passion in music is a challenge. It's important to consider whether traditional radio platforms still hold the same weight they once did in the era of streaming and on-demand content. Emma highlights the cultural significance of music, but acknowledges that big brands no longer hold the same influence as they once did. The UK is in need of platforms that can make it culturally relevant on a global scale. It's crucial for artists to find their market and create content that aligns with their personality. Emma's platform faced some backlash, particularly from men, when it first emerged. This serves as a reminder that the industry still has work to do in terms of gender inclusivity and representation.

"Find your market, make your content fit your personality"

Experiences In A Label Environments: From her experiences working at various labels, Emma had her fair share of AR responsibilities and difficult encounters to gain her position. She was brought into to work as a scout for talent in the Afro, grime and rap genres. Emma recommended finding a job in a label as everyday your learning something, but advises to be cautious and make wise decisions, don't be that desperate or scared to have a normal 9-5 before you find something, recounting an experience of people in positions of power misusing it for personal gain. Emma continued on saying;

"You will find red flag throughout the industry, so don't be afraid to use your voice in those situations."

Emma made the point of the need to promote women within the industry, providing the platform / opportunity and her active role in this; she went onto state that mainly men run the industry, and female artists, especially in rap, are not getting on platforms. They're not getting opportunities to do cultural moments such as a a daily duppy in the same respect as male artist, and maybe they're not welcomed in those environments. She encourages all DJs and platforms to be mindful of this and create more spaces for these artist to show their talents.

Regionally: During the conversation, we touched on DJs working with one another in different cities, to give artist opportunities across the country. Emma emphasized that with TikTok, you can do a lot yourself wherever you are. Some areas aren't big enough to support the complete growth of an artist, and the lack of facilities has a factor, as a content creator Emma highlighted that there are no affordable podcast studios in Manchester. Regions are still going through growing pains as they don't have the infrastructure some cities do, so it's important to find your place within the music industry.

Emma Rose's industry insights provide a unique and valuable perspective on the current state of the music industry. From her experience as a DJ and her work in various aspects of the industry, Emma has identified key trends and challenges facing artists, particularly female artists, in the UK. Her insights offer valuable advice and insights for those looking to succeed in the music industry, and her experience and expertise make her a valuable resource for anyone looking to navigate the complex and ever-changing landscape of the industry

Building A Social Media Presence

Social media platforms, such as TikTok, Instagram, and Twitter, offer powerful tools that enable artists to promote their music, connect with fans, and gain widespread visibility. Through cultivating a robust social media presence, artists can build a loyal fan base, interact with their audience on a more personal level, stay informed about industry trends, and connect with fellow musicians and industry professionals.

To establish and maintain a compelling social media presence, music artists should start by creating and optimizing profiles on different social media platforms. This involves setting up profiles on platforms like TikTok, Instagram, and Twitter, and ensuring that these profiles are complete with relevant information about their music, upcoming shows, and contact details. A well-optimized profile serves as the virtual hub of an artist's online presence, making it easy for fans and industry stakeholders to find and engage with their content.

Consistently posting engaging content is another vital component of a successful social media strategy. Music artists should regularly share a diverse range of content, such as music releases, music videos, behind-the-scenes glimpses, and photos that showcase their journey and experiences. By offering fresh and captivating content, artists can keep their audience interested and invested in their music career.

Interacting with the audience is a fundamental aspect of building a meaningful social media presence. Artists should actively engage with their followers by responding to comments and messages, showing appreciation for their support, and encouraging them to share their thoughts and feedback. This two-way communication fosters a sense of connection and loyalty, creating a dedicated fan base that feels personally invested in the artist's journey.

For artists seeking to amplify their social media presence, utilizing paid promotions can be an effective strategy. Platforms like YouTube and Instagram offer advertising options that enable artists to target specific demographics and reach a larger audience. Paid promotions can boost visibility, attract new fans, and enhance the impact of an artist's social media efforts.

Cultivating a strong social media presence goes beyond mere self-promotion; it's about building a genuine connection with the audience. By sharing authentic stories, emotions, and experiences, artists can create a relatable and personable online persona that resonates with their followers. This genuine approach fosters a strong sense of community and loyalty among fans.

Social media offers artists valuable insights into their audience's preferences and behaviours. Analysing engagement metrics, such as likes, comments, and shares, can provide valuable feedback on the type of content that resonates best with the audience. Armed with this information, artists can refine their social media strategy to deliver content that truly engages and captivates their fans.

Strategically creating and optimizing profiles on various platforms, consistently sharing engaging content, actively engaging with their audience, and utilizing paid promotions, allow artist to leverage the power of social media to promote their music, connect with fans, and propel their careers to new heights. Building a loyal and engaged fan base through social media empowers artists to create a lasting impact on their audience and cultivate a thriving and sustainable music career.

The Dilemma Of "Clout Chasing"

In recent years, the rise of social media and the increasing importance of online presence has changed the way people interact and network in various industries, including the music industry. With the emphasis on growing a large following and gaining recognition, many individuals, particularly musicians and industry professionals, engage in "clout chasing" behaviour. Clout chasing refers to the act of seeking popularity, influence, and recognition often at the expense of authenticity and genuine connections.

Clout chasing has become a prevalent issue, leading to a loss of focus on building genuine connections and networking opportunities. Musicians and industry professionals often engage in this behaviour to gain recognition and improve their chances of success in the competitive industry. However, this approach can have negative consequences, including:

- **Loss Of Authenticity:** Clout chasing often involves curating a particular image or persona online that may not accurately represent the individual. This can lead to a lack of authenticity and genuine connections, as people may not be connecting with the real person behind the persona.
- **Ineffective Networking:** Clout chasing can lead to a lack of genuine relationships and a shallow network. Many individuals engage in this behaviour in pursuit of recognition, but they may not be making meaningful connections with others in the industry that could benefit their careers in the long-term.
- **Decreased Opportunities:** Clout chasing can also lead to a lack of opportunities, as individuals may not be seen as credible or trustworthy in the industry. This can result in missed opportunities for collaborations, gigs, and other important opportunities for growth and success in the music industry.

Popular publicity stunts by artists such as Boonk Gang, Lil Pump, and Mizzy can have a negative impact on the overall movements of new pockets of talent, creating a wider gap between them and the mainstream. These stunts are often centred on "clout chasing", or gaining popularity and recognition through attention-seeking behaviour, rather than showcasing real talent or hard work. This can lead to a perception that all "successful" artists are just involved in superficial stunts, which can make it difficult for genuine artists to network and build meaningful relationships in the industry.

These stunts can create a culture where quick fame and recognition are valued over real talent and hard work, which can be demotivating for artists who are trying to build their careers based on their skills and dedication. This can also lead to a devaluation of the industry as a whole, as people may begin to view it as a place where only superficial and short-lived success is possible.

Ultimately, the popularity of these stunts make it more difficult for artists to network and build meaningful relationships in the industry; clout chasing can have negative effects on the music business, hindering the development of genuine relationships and opportunities for success. It's important for musicians and industry professionals to focus on building authentic connections and networks, rather than seeking recognition and influence through online means. Prioritize genuine relationships and networking opportunities, to increase the chances of success in the competitive and ever-evolving music industry.

Marketing On TikTok

The use of TikTok as a music marketing platform has revolutionized the way in which artists gain exposure and popularity. With over one billion active users, the app provides a unique opportunity for artists to showcase their talent and connect with fans on a global scale. Not only does the platform offer a massive audience, but it also has a highly engaged user base that actively seeks out new and exciting content.

The app's algorithm prioritizes content that resonates with users, which means that even artists who are relatively unknown can potentially go viral and gain significant exposure. As such, TikTok should be considered a vital component of any modern musician's marketing strategy.

TikTok's focus on music content is the main reason why it is an influential platform for upcoming artists. Users create short videos of around 15 seconds in length with a vertical aspect ratio, all backed by an audio snippet, usually music. Authenticity and group participation are more important than getting the perfect shot, and videos can be recorded in parts and edited together in fragments. Popular videos are pushed to a wider audience with TikTok's algorithm, which creates a unique content feed called the "For You Page" (#FYP) for each user. The more users interact with the platform, the more tailored their #FYP content will become.

When a user enjoys a video so much that they want to create their video, there is an easy way on the TikTok app for people to use an audio clip they have heard elsewhere to make a new video of their own. This process of audio copying makes it easy for a song to go viral on TikTok. If a dance challenge or lip-sync inspires one user, there is a good chance that it will inspire others to make their videos. The more times the algorithm sees people using the music, the more it will feed the song to new viewers, which, in turn, inspires more users to create their own content using the track.

To promote your music effectively on TikTok, you should release your music on the platform, focus on TikTok-friendly tracks, use a mix of hashtags, create challenges and contests, follow other musicians, influencers, and followers, and do a duet.

Releasing your music on TikTok is essential because you cannot go viral on the platform without putting your music on it. Your track needs to be TikTok-friendly, which means it needs to be broad, catchy, and relatable enough for users to create their own video content around it. Using hashtags is essential to increase the chances of your video appearing on TikTok's "Discover" and "For You" tabs.

Creating challenges and contests is another way to promote your music on the platform. Challenges tend to be popular when they are fun and can be interpreted in different ways by different people.

Following other musicians and influencers, and following back everyone who follows you is the best way to start building an audience on TikTok. Doing a duet is another easy way to engage with other TikTokers, collaborate with other musicians, reach new listeners, and generate more TikTok content ideas for musicians.

Pro Tip: Growing Your Audience And Getting Your Music Shared

Growing your audience and getting your music shared on TikTok can be a game-changer for music artists. TikTok's "For You Page" (FYP) is a powerful tool that introduces content to users based on their interests and engagement, making it a prime platform for viral content and increased visibility. When a song or video goes viral on TikTok, it can lead to a surge in streams and followers for the artist.

User-generated content plays a significant role in spreading music on TikTok. When users create their videos using an artist's music, it exposes the song to a wider audience and increases the chances of it going viral. To boost the likelihood of your music being used in popular TikTok videos, consider creating catchy and shareable content that aligns with the platform's unique features. Dance challenges, lip-sync videos, funny skits, and how-to videos are some examples of engaging content that can attract attention.

Collaboration with other users is another effective strategy for expanding your reach on TikTok. Partnering with popular creators who share a similar style or message can introduce your music to a new audience and elevate its chances of going viral.

Using hashtags and participating in trending challenges can also enhance the discoverability of your content on TikTok. By aligning your posts with relevant hashtags and popular trends, you can engage users who are interested in specific topics or themes, thereby increasing the visibility of your music.

TikTok provides valuable analytics that allow artists to track their performance on the platform. Monitoring these metrics enables you to assess the success of your content, identify the most popular content formats, and optimize your music promotion efforts accordingly.

To create a compelling presence on TikTok, it is crucial to maintain an up-to-date profile. Ensure that your latest music, shows, and other essential information are readily available. Employ a clear and eye-catching profile picture and include links to your website and other social media profiles to facilitate easy navigation for your audience.

The "duet" feature on TikTok allows users to create videos that appear alongside another user's video. Utilize this feature to collaborate with other users and produce unique content that features your music. Additionally, consider exploring TikTok's "Creator Fund," which provides financial support to popular creators. If eligible, you can use this fund to invest in your music promotion efforts on the platform.

Beyond promoting your music, TikTok can serve as a powerful platform to announce and connect with fans for your live shows. Utilize the platform to share sneak peeks of your performances, interact with your audience, and create exclusive experiences for your fans, such as behind-the-scenes footage.

Authenticity is highly valued on TikTok, so be yourself and engage with your audience in genuine interactions. Respond to comments and messages, and use the platform to showcase your personality and connect with fans on a personal level.

As TikTok is a dynamic platform, don't shy away from experimenting with different types of content. Test out various formats, such as videos, live streams, or polls, to discover what resonates best with your audience. Consistency is key in building a loyal following, so plan your content in advance using a content calendar and maintain a regular posting schedule.

To succeed on TikTok, continuous learning is essential. Stay up-to-date on the latest trends and best practices for music promotion on the platform. Follow other musicians and creators on TikTok and seek out resources and guides that can provide valuable insights to enhance your TikTok strategy.

To get your music on TikTok, you'll need to deliver it to a digital service provider (DSP) that can distribute it to the platform or use their Soundon service. Popular DSPs like Spotify, Apple Music, and Amazon Music offer this service. Once your music is available on TikTok, users can incorporate it into their videos from TikTok's music library. Whenever your music is used in a TikTok video, you'll earn revenue through streaming and licensing fees. Monitoring how your music is being used on TikTok can be accomplished through the analytics provided by your DSP or by utilizing third-party analytics tools.

TikTok presents music artists with an excellent opportunity to grow their audience and get their music shared. By strategizing content creation, engaging with the platform's unique features, and leveraging analytics to fine-tune their approach, artists can make the most of TikTok's vast potential for music promotion and audience expansion. Stay authentic, consistent, and open to experimentation, and keep a keen eye on industry trends to stay at the forefront of TikTok's ever-evolving landscape.

*For a further deep dive on Tik Tok, refer to The Music Business Blueprint free resource guide at www.a-krst.com

Understanding And Utilizing TikTok

Keep it quick and snappy! Attention spans on TikTok are short, and videos that are quick and to the point will be more likely to hold a viewer's attention. Remove any pauses or unnecessary sentences/words to keep the video moving at a fast pace.

Keep it short and sweet: TikTok videos are typically short, around 15 seconds to 1 minute. Keep your videos within this time frame to hold your audience's attention. The goal is to make the viewer want to watch it again, thus boosting the chances of it being shared. Keeping the video under 15 seconds increases the chances of this happening.

Make The Video Loop Seamlessly: Make the end of the video flow seamlessly back into the start to create a continuous loop.

Speed It Up: Speed up clips by 1%-10% to keep the video moving quickly where appropriate

Text & Timing : Most viewers don't have time to read text in a TikTok video, but this can be used to your advantage by including long text that means people need to rewatch to read. Some creators even cut off their sentences when talking, thrusting the viewer unexpectedly back to the start to leave the viewer wanting more or feeling like they've missed something.

Think beyond music! TikTok lets you follow your passions, and find new fans in those communities

TikTok influencer marketing is a powerful tool for music promotion that can help you reach a new audience and drive engagement for your music, which has made it a favourite for label scouts. As a result, success on TikTok can be instrumental in breaking into the music industry in 2023. One of the key factors behind the platforms success is is the ability to shoot video in increments, which allows users to capture a little bit of video, stop, and then pick up the next shot when they are ready.

This makes it easy to change scenes, characters, costumes, etc. in a video. Another feature that is useful for music promotion is the ability to record video to a song. Users can find a song, select the snippet they want, and then shoot the video. If they do cuts, the audio will stop at the appropriate part and then play from where they left off when they hit record again. TikTok also allows users to either produce and post videos within the app or upload videos from other sources. This means that users can create vertical videos using other tools, such as Adobe Premiere Pro, and then upload them to TikTok for promotion.

The TikTok Algorithm

The TikTok algorithm is a recommendation system that determines which videos will appear on your For You page. It decides which videos a user might like based on various factors, including user interactions, the video information, and device and account settings.

User Interactions: which accounts you follow, creators you've hidden, comments you've posted, videos you've liked or shared on the app, videos you've added to your favourites, videos you've marked as "Not Interested", videos you've reported as inappropriate, videos you watch all the way to the end, and videos you re-watch.

Video Information: captions, sounds, hashtags, effects, and trending topics.

Device And Account Settings: language preference, country setting, type of mobile device, and categories of interest you selected as a new user.

Understanding And Utilizing The TikTok Attention Span

What appeals to human attention spans also appeals to TikTok's algorithms, so make sure to keep this in mind when creating your videos.

Use A Catchy Hook: Using a catchy hook in your TikTok videos can help you grab the audience's attention, increase the chances of your video being watched till the end and make it more memorable. Start with a questions or statement, use the story telling narratives of TikTok.

Keep It Quick And Snappy: TikTok videos are typically short, around 15 seconds to 1 minute. Keep your videos within this time frame to hold your audience's attention. The goal is to make the viewer want to watch it again, thus boosting the chances of it being shared. Keeping the video under 15 seconds increases the chances of this happening.

Make The Video Loop Seamlessly: Make the end of the video flow seamlessly back into the start to create a continuous loop.

Speed It Up: Speed up clips by 1%-10% to keep the video moving quickly where appropriate

Text & Timing : Most viewers don't have time to read text in a TikTok video, but this can be used to your advantage by including long text that means people need to rewatch to read. Some creators even cut off their sentences when talking, thrusting the viewer unexpectedly back to the start to leave the viewer wanting more or feeling like they've missed something.

Tik Tok x Spotify integration

TikTok has continued to grow, not only as a platform for entertainment but as a pivotal player in music discovery and artist promotion, with entire specialist companies or label departments being built around the platform. With the launch of its innovative 'Add to Music' feature, TikTok is redefining the relationship between social media and music streaming services, such as Spotify and Amazon Music. The ground-breaking feature seamlessly bridges the gap between discovering a song on a short-form video and adding it to a personal streaming playlist, heralding a new era in how music is consumed and enjoyed.

The 'Add to Music' feature is a testament to TikTok's growing influence in the music industry. It reflects an understanding of how modern audiences discover and interact with music in the digital age. By tapping into TikTok's viral potential, this feature offers an unparalleled opportunity for artists and labels to convert momentary interest into lasting engagement, expanding their reach beyond the confines of the app.

Functionality

The 'Add to Music' feature allows users to save songs they encounter on TikTok directly to their preferred music streaming service. Users can now add songs from TikTok videos directly to their playlists on streaming platforms, thereby reducing the steps required to locate and save the music they love. This integration is designed to enhance the music discovery experience on TikTok and streamline the listener's journey to their chosen streaming platform. The feature appears as a clickable button adjacent to the track name in TikTok videos. This intuitive design makes it easy for users to instantly save the song to their streaming service playlists, enhancing the overall user experience on the app.

Impact on Artists and Labels

For artists and labels, 'Add to Music' serves as a powerful tool to convert TikTok success into measurable streaming numbers. This feature not only aids in increasing song plays on streaming platforms but also enhances the track's overall visibility and accessibility. By facilitating the transition of music from TikTok to streaming services, this feature plays a significant role in revenue generation for artists and labels. It opens up an additional avenue for royalties, particularly benefiting those whose music gains traction on TikTok.

Marketing On Instagram

Instagram is a powerful social media platform that musicians can leverage to promote their music in a variety of ways. One of the most effective ways to do this is through the use of Instagram Reels, a feature that allows users to post short, 15-30 second videos in portrait view, complete with music or audio, editing cuts and stitches, and stickers. By creatively showcasing their music through Reels, musicians can engage their followers visually and effectively promote their music.

Another way to promote music on Instagram is through sponsored posts and ads. These tools can help musicians reach a new audience, with Instagram ads being easy to set up through Facebook Ads Manager. Goals such as Brand Awareness, Engagement, and Video Views can be tracked, allowing musicians to measure the success of their campaigns. By adding tracks to Music in Stories, musicians can further promote their music on Instagram. Platforms like Ditto Music can make a musician's work available in Instagram's "Music in Stories" audio library on upload to their distribution portal..

Going live on Instagram is another excellent way to promote music and connect with fans. Live sessions can include performances of songs, behind-the-scenes content, and Q&A sessions. Furthermore, recruiting Instagram influencers and running giveaways and competitions can incentivize fans to engage more actively with musicians on Instagram.

To achieve the full potential of an Instagram profile, it is essential to optimize it properly. This includes setting up a profile picture that resonates with the brand identity and image, verifying the Instagram account to boost legitimacy and authenticity, and creating a bio that conveys the musician's key information and links to their latest release or upcoming show tickets. Cross-promoting the bio by including links to other social media accounts such as Twitter and TikTok is also an effective way to grow followings elsewhere, so make use of linktree style links to keep your links section clean and multifaceted.

Posting great content is critical to increasing the Instagram following. The content can be backstage photos, live set clips, music promo graphics, funny memes, inspirational posts, or pictures of the musician's heroes. The goal is to create authentic and engaging content that the followers will enjoy, and always having a video teaser of the music within the first six posts.

Investing time in graphic design skills and ensuring all graphics and album art look professional and eye-catching while conveying a consistent brand identity is also essential. Scheduling and planning ahead is another critical aspect of achieving Instagram success, allowing the creation and planning of posts and graphics in advance, and scheduling them to go live at a specific time.

Finally, using hashtags is an effective way to reach new potential fans with Instagram posts. Musicians can use hashtags that align with both their persona and their music, such as #IndieMusic #IndieRock #LiveMusic for an indie band. Hashtagging nearby locations, similar artists, or anything relevant to the musician's music is also recommended.

Optimizing the Instagram profile and following these steps can help musicians promote their music on the platform and increase their following.

For a further deep dive on Instagram, refer to The Music Business Blueprint free resource guide at www.a-krst.com

Understanding YouTube

YouTube is a powerful platform for music marketing, as it allows artists to connect with their audience and increase visibility through various features and tools. The climate of YouTube in relation to music marketing in 2023 is one that is focused on leveraging data to optimize content, utilizing features such as live streaming, YouTube cards, and YouTube Stories to engage viewers, whilst leveraging other social media platforms to reach a larger audience.

Additionally, there will be a focus on creating content that is unique and engaging, and creating content that is optimized for mobile, as mobile devices continue to account for a larger percentage of internet traffic.

Understanding Your Audience

In order to effectively use YouTube for music marketing, it is important to first research and understand your audience. This includes identifying who your audience is, what their interests are, and what type of content they prefer.

The most effective way to research your audience is to use YouTube's analytics tools, which provide information on demographics, location, and viewing habits. Additionally, social media platforms such as Twitter and Instagram can also be used to gain insight into your audience and their preferences.

Creating Channel Content

Creating channel content on YouTube is an effective way for musicians to showcase their talents, reach new audiences, and build a loyal fan base. Here are some tips for creating engaging and effective channel content using business psychology and strategy techniques:

- **Use Your Music Videos As The Centrepiece:** Use your music videos as the centrepiece of your channel content. Make sure they are visually engaging and well-produced, and that they accurately represent your brand and music style. This will help to establish your visual identity and make a strong impression on potential fans.
- **Create Behind-The-Scenes Content:** Create behind-the-scenes content that gives fans a glimpse into your creative process. This can include studio sessions, writing sessions, or even just a day in the life of being a musician. By doing this, you can help to humanize your brand and create a deeper connection with your audience.
- **Collaborate With Other Musicians And Creators:** Collaborating with other musicians and creators can help you expand your reach and give you access to new audiences. This can also help you to establish yourself as a leader in your niche and increase your credibility in the industry.
- **Share Your Live Performances:** Share your live performances on YouTube. This can help build anticipation for your upcoming shows and give fans a sense of what it's like to see you perform live. It can also help you to establish a strong connection with your audience and build a sense of community around your music.
- **Use YouTube's Features To Promote Your Music:** Use YouTube's features such as end screens and annotations to promote your music and merchandise, as well as your social media platforms. This will help you to increase engagement and drive traffic to your other online properties.

- **Leverage SEO Techniques**: Use SEO techniques to make sure your videos are easily discoverable by potential fans. Use relevant keywords in your titles, descriptions, and tags to help your content rank higher in search results.
- **Create Playlists:** Create playlists that group your music by genre, album, or even mood, to make it easy for your audience to find the music they want to listen to. This will help you to increase engagement and keep your audience engaged with your content.
- **Create A Consistent Visual Identity:** Create a consistent visual identity throughout all your videos, artwork, and social media platforms to help people recognize your music and brand. This will help you to establish a strong brand identity and increase your credibility in the industry.
- **Engage With Your Audience:** Engage with your audience by responding to comments, running contests, and hosting live Q&A sessions on your YouTube channel. This will help you to establish a stronger connection with your audience and increase engagement.
- **Stay Up-To-Date:** Finally, stay up-to-date with the latest trends in music marketing and be creative in how you use YouTube to promote your music. This will help you to stay ahead of the competition and maintain a strong presence on the platform.

YouTube Features

Once you've created YouTube content that will appeal to your audience there are various YouTube features you can use to leverage exposure.

This includes live streaming, YouTube cards, and YouTube stories. Live streaming allows artists to interact with their fans in real-time and create a sense of community. YouTube cards and stories provide a way to share additional information and resources related to your music, such as album releases and tour dates.

YouTube Ads: To maximize the effectiveness of YouTube Ads to maximize ROI through audience data, you should do the following:

Utilize Targeting Options: Utilize YouTube's targeting options such as demographic targeting, affinity audiences, custom affinity audiences, and in-market audiences to ensure your ads are reaching the right people.

Set Up Remarketing: Set up remarketing to follow up with people who have already expressed interest in your company. This will help to increase engagement and conversions.

Analyse Results: Analyse the results of your ads to determine what is working and what isn't. This will help you optimize your ads for better results.

Track Conversions: Track conversions to see how many people are clicking on your ads and taking action. This will help you measure the success of your campaigns.

For a further deep dive on Youtube, refer to The Music Business Blueprint free resource guide at www.a-krst.com

Pro Tip: The YouTube Algorithm

Understanding and effectively working with the YouTube algorithm is crucial for increasing visibility and growing your channel. YouTube's algorithm is rooted in user patterns and is designed to recommend videos that users are most likely to watch. This means that connections to other artists can be an important factor in increasing visibility on YouTube. When YouTube recommends your music alongside other artists, fans of those artists may be more likely to discover your music.

Prioritize Audience Satisfaction: To thrive on YouTube, prioritize creating content that delights and satisfies your audience. Focus on building long-term relationships and providing value to your viewers. By understanding their preferences and interests, you can tailor your content to meet their needs and keep them engaged.

Optimize Video Details: Make your videos more discoverable by optimizing video titles, descriptions, and thumbnails. Craft clear, concise, and relevant titles that accurately represent your video's content. Create engaging and informative descriptions that incorporate relevant keywords. Design visually appealing thumbnails that entice viewers to click and watch your videos.

Engage With Your Audience: Foster a sense of community and encourage audience engagement. Respond to comments, ask for feedback, and create opportunities for viewers to interact with your content. By engaging with your audience, you not only build lasting relationships but also signal to the algorithm that your content is valuable and worth recommending.

Create Valuable And Relevant Content: Focus on producing high-quality content that resonates with your audience. Consider their interests and preferences when developing your content strategy. Incorporate captivating elements, think like a viewer, and deliver value in every video. This approach will help you attract and retain viewers, increasing the likelihood of algorithmic recommendations.

Experiment With Different Formats: YouTube encourages creators to experiment with various video formats and languages. Diversify your content to cater to different audience preferences and expand your reach. Be open to trying new ideas, adapting to changes, and staying ahead of the curve. This flexibility will help you align with the evolving algorithm and attract new viewers.

Leverage Available Tools: Take advantage of the tools and features provided by YouTube to optimize your channel. Utilize playlists to organize and highlight your content, and create video transcripts to enhance the viewing experience and improve discoverability. Leverage YouTube management tools like NapoleonCat to streamline comment management and stay on top of audience engagement.

Stay Informed And Evolve: Keep up with the latest trends, algorithm updates, and best practices in YouTube content creation. YouTube's algorithm and platform features continue to evolve, so staying informed is crucial. Engage with the creator community, follow industry resources, and adapt your strategies accordingly. By continually improving and evolving, you can maximize your channel's performance.

Platforms vs Independence

The world of music and entertainment is constantly evolving with technological advancements and changing consumer habits. In this fast-paced world, time convenience has become one of the most important factors in attracting viewers to spend their leisure time watching music videos or other content. With this in mind, it has become increasingly important for artists to take control of their online presence and audience by building their own YouTube channel.

While platforms like GRM, Link Up TV, Mixtape Madness, and Pressplay remain valuable for artist exposure and audience expansion, a delicate equilibrium must be maintained. For every video shared on these curated platforms, strive to present three on your personal YouTube channel. This balance ensures your content reverberates with existing fans and resonates with fresh audiences.

Building up a dedicated YouTube channel allows artists to take full ownership of their brand image and messaging. By curating their own content and engaging directly with their fan base, artists can build a stronger relationship with their audience, leading to increased loyalty and engagement rates. With a dedicated channel, artists can create a consistent look and feel to their content and build a loyal fan base that follows them across various social media platforms.

Having a dedicated YouTube channel provides artists with valuable marketing opportunities, and when they are creating targeted content and leveraging YouTube's algorithm, they increase their exposure and reach a broader audience. After reaching a certain level and passing YouTube's requirements, they can utilize YouTube's monetization features to generate revenue from their content, providing them with a sustainable source of income.

In today's attention focused era, it's essential for artists to recognize that time convenience plays a crucial role in attracting viewers to their content. With the rise of streaming platforms like Netflix and Spotify, consumers are no longer interested in discovering emerging talent the same way as the YouTube market is oversaturated with such content. Instead, viewers prefer to engage with a specific artist or brand they are already familiar with. Artists must provide a more personalized experience for their viewers to increase the likelihood of their content being consumed.

The music industry is highly competitive and cut-throat, and artists must adapt to changing consumer habits and technology to remain relevant and successful. Owning your online presence and audience is your ticket to staying relevant and successful. Strike the right balance between curated platforms and your dedicated YouTube channel to allow you to expand your audience while cultivating a loyal fanbase across various social media platforms.

Music Promotion On Reddit

Reddit is a vast and collaborative social media platform with over 52 million daily users, making it an ideal network for musicians to share their music and engage with passionate and supportive communities.

Market And Promote Your Music

One of the most effective ways to use Reddit as a musician is to self-promote your music to the millions of people who use the platform daily. Like other organic social media marketing, Reddit is free to use and can help increase your popularity and fan base, especially among niche groups within the Reddit community. You can also link your social media profiles and website on Reddit, which can help improve your site's SEO ranking and attract more views.

Networking

Reddit is a collaborative and open forum where musicians can easily find and recruit band members or collaborators. There are various subreddits dedicated to music, including r/musicians, r/bandmembers, and r/WeAreTheMusicMakers, which can help you connect with fellow musicians who are looking to form a band or collaborate with others.

Finding An Artist Manager

Reddit provides a platform to connect with potential managers or other industry professionals. By regularly posting and interacting with other musicians and music enthusiasts, you can build a strong community and come across like-minded individuals who can help you advance your music career. Additionally, the platform allows you to chat with people who attended the same gig, which can help expand your network and exposure to new audiences and musicians.

The Golden Rules For Musicians:

Although self-promotion of your music is welcomed on Reddit, there are some rules and guidelines that you need to follow to maintain a level playing field for all musicians. It is recommended to engage in discussions and support other musicians, rather than solely promoting your work. Additionally, each subreddit has its own guidelines, and you should avoid spamming any channel and adhere to the rules, which are regularly enforced by admins. Subreddits for musicians

Reddit has a vast amount of subreddits that are dedicated to specific topics, making it easier for musicians to connect with the right community. Some useful subreddits for independent musicians include r/IndependentMusic, r/Music, r/WeAreTheMusicMakers, r/NewMusic, and r/PromoteYourMusic. These subreddits provide a space for independent artists to share their music, connect with like-minded individuals, and gain feedback and exposure.

Reddit is a valuable platform for musicians to promote their music, connect with fellow musicians, and expand their network. By following the golden rules and using the appropriate subreddits, you can effectively use Reddit to advance your music career and reach a wider audience.

Discord For Musicians

As a musician in 2023, you are likely already familiar with various social media platforms such as Instagram and TikTok, which have become essential tools for marketing your music. Discord is a conversation based platforms that can create dynamic platforms for community centric conversations.

Discord is a user-friendly social media platform that focuses on live streaming and video content. Originally targeted at video game users, Discord now offers an easy-to-use platform for musicians to present video content, engage with fans through conversation, and connect with other users through voice, video chat and text.

Using Discord To Promote Your Music

Discord provides musicians with an online community of like-minded individuals, where you can join or create a server dedicated to specific topics, including music. You can also start new fanbase conversations through music video releases, track breakdowns, or online Q&A sessions. Utilizing Discord's creator tools and interacting with your audience, you can develop a real online community around your work, basing things around meaningful discussion between fans and creators.

Developing Your Artist Fanbase

Discord's wide array of chat options makes it a great communication tool, combining all the best features of more commonly used programs, such as Skype and Slack, with an easy-to-use social media interface. Many successful electronic musicians, such as Disclosure and Fred Again.., have already established themselves on Discord by personally interacting with their global network through exclusive server conversations, providing advice on production and home studio advice. In addition to building your fanbase and network, Discord provides musicians with a platform to make extra cash by dropping teasers, starting discussion around an upcoming tour, or directing your fans to your site to buy merchandise. Discord's built-in features are geared towards easy linking, so take advantage of that! Discord now also offers creators the option of placing your Discord community behind a paywall, meaning your fans have to pay a subscription to access your content.

How To Grow Your Network On Discord

By participating in Discord server conversations, you can develop new friendships and professional relationships that could help your career. There are countless music servers on Discord that you can discover, such as Music, Music Production, and Music Feedback. These servers offer a home for general music chat, help artists improve their own productions, and provide constructive and in-depth critique of any track you upload, respectively.

Discord is a versatile platform that can help boost your fanbase numbers as well as grow your network of general music lovers. As an emerging artist, you should consider posting video content and starting group conversations on Discord as part of your music marketing strategy. By utilizing Discord's features and connecting with fans on a personal level, you can establish yourself in the music industry and further your career.

Pro Tip: Content Calendar

Artists need a robust strategy to effectively manage and maintain their online presence. One indispensable tool that can make a significant difference in your social media game is the Content Calendar.

Why Use A Content Calendar?

Content calendars are indispensable for music artists seeking to enhance their social media strategy. They provide consistency by allowing you to schedule posts in advance, ensuring reliability in your online presence. Having a tool such as the content calendar enables strategic planning, aligning your content with events, releases, and campaigns to support your goals. Organization is simplified as content ideas and schedules are centralized, reducing stress and last-minute rushes. Efficiency is improved by batch-creating content, freeing time for other career aspects. Consistent posting fosters audience engagement and loyalty, while calendars facilitate collaboration within teams. Finally, they promote diverse content creation and facilitate performance tracking.

How To Use A Content Calendar Effectively

Begin by setting clear social media goals and identifying your target audience's preferences. Plan content weeks or months ahead, deciding on topics, themes, and posting frequency. Utilize tools like spreadsheets or social media management software for organization. Schedule content using platforms like Hootsuite or Buffer to maintain a balanced posting schedule. Regularly review performance, adapt your strategy, and avoid overcommitting to content creation. Balance planning with spontaneity to keep creativity alive.

Potential Challenges And How To Overcome Them

Challenges may arise, but adaptability is key. Combat rigidity by adjusting your calendar for unexpected events. Overcome creative blocks with a reservoir of content ideas and a fresh approach. Avoid content fatigue by prioritizing quality over quantity. Be ready to adjust for external factors like release date shifts. Manage deadline pressure by planning and batching content creation. Set clear audience expectations regarding content frequency and type. By addressing these challenges, content calendars remain invaluable tools for enhancing your online presence and audience engagement.

*For a template content calendar, refer to The Music Business Blueprint free resource guide at www.a-krst.com

How To Create A Wikipedia Page For An Artist

Wikipedia is a widely used platform that is recognized as a reliable source of information across the globe. Therefore, having a Wikipedia page for an artist or band can provide an instant boost to their artistic credibility. However, creating a Wikipedia page is not an easy task, as it requires approval from volunteer editors who carefully evaluate submissions to ensure that they meet the platform's standards.

For independent musicians, having a Wikipedia page can be a game-changer in terms of building their brand reputation and exposure. The platform is known to be a credible source of information about a person, place, brand, or moment in history.

To create a Wikipedia page for an artist, it is essential to prove eligibility and notability. Eligibility refers to the deservingness of a Wikipedia page, while notability is the ability to prove it. Thus, artists who are relatively new to the industry and lack evidence in terms of noteworthy online news stories or PR may consider waiting for some exposure to roll in before creating a page.

To increase the chances of securing a Wikipedia page, artists should follow these five tips:

Be Noteworthy: The page must demonstrate notability or evidence of the artist's claim to fame, such as multiple articles covering their music or tour, albums or singles in the official charts, prominence within a certain genre or subculture, award or competition wins or nominations, music featured in other forms of media, involvement in political activism or controversy, worked with other famous figures, or performed at major festivals or well-known venues.

Keep It Strictly Neutral: The content should be written from a strictly neutral and unbiased point of view. Avoid using promotional language or hyperbole, as Wikipedia accepts and publishes pages on the basis of neutral and unbiased content.

Use Only Verified Sources And References: Provide sources and references that come from trustworthy, verified third parties, such as article reviews in music blogs, online mentions about the brand or music, or press coverage in a well-known magazine or newspaper.

Don't Write It Yourself: To avoid a page sounding overly promotional or biased, it is best to have someone else write the page. By doing so, artists can ensure that the content remains unbiased and neutral.

Be Patient: Creating a Wikipedia page can take time, and it may not be possible to secure one immediately. Therefore, artists should be patient and continue building their reputation until they can provide evidence of their notability.

By following these tips, artists can increase their chances of creating a successful Wikipedia page, enhancing their credibility, and providing a reliable source of information to their fans and followers.

Creating A Professional Landing Page

As you know from our explanation of the shop window concept, your online presence serves as the storefront to your brand. Just as a physical store's façade should captivate and draw in potential customers, your digital landing page or website must exude your brand's essence and guide users on a bespoke journey. Your goal is to not only engage them but to resonate with them in a manner that is meaningful, memorable, and actionable.

With the meteoric rise of social media platforms, the concept of a 'landing page' has been redefined. Platforms like Tumblr and Koji emerged, offering dynamic, immersive experiences distinct from traditional websites. Brands have capitalized on these platforms, providing unique user experiences that are genuine and allow them to embed themselves organically within the broader cultural milieu.

Modern Digital Platforms For Your Brand Presence:
1. **LinkTree**: This is more than just a link hosting site. It seamlessly amalgamates all your online destinations into one consolidated link, making it perfect for a cohesive social media presence.
2. **SquareSpace Or WordPress**: If you're looking for depth coupled with flexibility, these platforms are for you. They offer extensive customization options, allowing brands to craft intricate, layered websites tailored to their identity and vision.
3. **Wix**: Particularly adept for hosting Electronic Press Kits (EPKs) and sleek single-page sites, Wix caters to those wanting a focused, streamlined web presence.

Essential Components:
To resonate with your audience and imprint your brand, ensure your landing page is populated with:
- **Bio**: Who are you? Showcase your story, ethos, and brand journey.
- **Music Portfolio:** If music is your realm, feature tracks from SoundCloud, including your older catalogue, ensuring your musical journey is accessible and celebrated.
- **Downloadable Content**: Offer exclusive downloads, be it tracks, wallpapers, or other brand-relevant content to make your audience feel special.
- **Professional Branding Elements:** High-resolution photos, compelling graphics, and distinctive logos are non-negotiable. They encapsulate your brand's aesthetic and create a memorable visual identity.
- **Embedded Links:** Ensure your audience has immediate access to all facets of your online presence. From social media handles to streaming platforms, present them in an intuitive, user-friendly manner.

As the digital landscape continually evolves, so should your online presence. The key is to be adaptable, authentic, and always centred around offering value to your audience. Remember, your landing page is more than just a digital address; it's a reflection of your brand's true nature, when speaking to a rapidly evolving and growing landscape, in this vast digital cosmos.

Playlist On Spotify

Spotify, the popular music streaming platform, has created a direct route for emerging artists to be featured on its official playlists by opening up playlist submissions to everyone, including artists and labels.

This move has enabled unsigned artists to gain more exposure and recognition. However, it should be noted that submission of a track does not guarantee playlisting, but it is a simple process that is worth doing.

To submit music for consideration, artists and labels need to log in or sign up to Spotify for Artists using a desktop computer. Unreleased music can be found within the 'Music' section of the artist dashboard under 'Upcoming'. The artist can then choose the unreleased track they would like to submit and complete the playlist submission form, providing as much information as possible about the track.

To increase the chances of being considered and featured, some important points should be kept in mind. Firstly, only unreleased tracks can be considered for playlists, and artists must distribute their music and pitch it for playlisting between the time of delivery and the release date. Secondly, only one track can be submitted at a time, and at least seven days before the release date. Moreover, artists should provide detailed information about their music, including genre, mood, and other relevant details, to help Spotify's editorial staff match the music to the right playlists.

It is essential to note that the submission form is not available on mobile, and the process should be done using a desktop computer. If an artist is not able to secure inclusion on an editorial playlist, submitting music through Spotify for Artists at least a week before the release date guarantees the artist's placement on their followers' Release Radar playlists when the music is released.

Spotify for Artists playlist submission requires artists to provide detailed information about the style, genre, mood, and culture of their track. They should also indicate if the music falls into any specific categories, such as covers, remixes, instrumentals, or location-based playlists. A detailed description of the music's production and promotion plans should also be provided to give more context for playlist editors who hear it.

Spotify's decision to open up playlist submissions to everyone is a significant opportunity for emerging artists to gain more exposure and recognition. However, artists should note that there is a lot of competition and may want to consider using a playlisting promotions service to increase their chances of landing a spot on a big playlist, though none can guarantee placement as it is ultimately at the discretion of the curator. Getting playlisted can significantly boost an artist's Spotify pay per stream rate.

*For a guide on Spotify best practices, refer to The Music Business Blueprint free resource guide at www.a-krst.com

The Spotify Popularity Index

The Spotify Popularity Index is a metric that has a significant impact on how and when users discover your music. It is a ranking from 0-100 and a good score increases a track's discoverability across the platform. The higher the score, the better your chances of massive algorithmic exposure. Although it is not shown in many versions of the Spotify app, the index appears to influence almost all aspects of Spotify's discovery, recommendation, and algorithmic playlist generation.

Spotify measures everything a listener does, including how many times they listen to a track, if they listen to completion, if they skip it when it comes up in a playlist, and if they add it to their own personal playlists. The popularity score is a kind of aggregate metric that factors in the age of a track, in addition to the number of streams, saves, listeners, and probably more. It is always changing based on how users interact with your song on Spotify.

The index is especially critical in the first days and weeks after a song's release. If we can affect our song's popularity index shortly after release, we have the ability to gain exposure through two hugely important algorithmic playlists: Release Radar and Discover Weekly.

Release Radar is the first algorithmic playlist that every song gets a shot to be on. When you release a new track, it will appear on most or all of your followers' Release Radar playlist. Not all users listen to their Release Radar, so don't expect a massive bump on that first Friday unless you have a lot of followers already. However, there seems to be a popularity index threshold that will trigger Spotify to put your song on people's Release Radar who are not your followers yet.

Discover Weekly is a personalized, algorithmic playlist that Spotify updates every Monday. Every user gets their own Discover Weekly. Spotify uses this playlist to expose songs to fans who may not have heard them yet, but are likely to enjoy them.

Unfortunately, Spotify does not currently give us enough information to calculate our popularity index. However, the easiest way to find your track's popularity score is a website called Musicstax. If you can reach a popularity score of 25-30 by the first Friday after you release (1 week if you release on a Friday), you have a very good chance of having your song placed on Release Radar for thousands of people who don't even follow you on Spotify. The popularity number for Discover Weekly is definitely higher, but we don't know what it is.

The Spotify Popularity Index is a crucial metric for music professionals to pay attention to. It is important to take action if your popularity score is hovering right below that Release Radar threshold a few days after release. However, remember that you want quality engagement on your tracks, not just a high stream count. By using this knowledge, you can potentially take steps to influence your score and increase your chances of being discovered by new fans.

Pro Tip: Understanding When To Release Music

Finding the best time to release music is crucial for any aspiring artist. From the time of day to the time of year, every aspect counts, and careful consideration is necessary before any release. Rushing to release your music without taking into account the ideal timing can harm your chances of success.

When is the best time to release music? Every month has its benefits and drawbacks, and knowing what's happening in the music scene at specific times is essential to make the best decision possible. You also need to consider what you want to achieve with your release. Let's dive into what's going on in the music industry throughout the year, and when is the best time to release your music.

Why is January and February ideal for your music release? The first two months of the year, from January to March, are often the best for new artists to release music. It's the perfect time to introduce yourself to bloggers, journalists, radio program directors, etc. because the media is looking for what will be popular in the upcoming year. Moreover, your listeners are also looking for fresh sounds and ideas at the beginning of the year.

Valentine's Day is a busy sales period, so think carefully about releasing your music around that time.

If you decide to release your music during this period, upbeat songs that get your body moving and have a positive message tend to do well. Don't forget that many people make "New Year, new me" resolutions, which is why workout songs are very popular at this time of year. However, February is ideal for love or anti-romantic songs, as well as songs about relationships and similar topics.

Outside of a few award shows, March is relatively open month. Use this to release high quality music and captivating visuals. The mood of songs that do well in March is often similar to that of previous months. These are light, feel-good songs with an uplifting message or upbeat, happy, or party-like sounds.

April and May can be great for gaining exposure The touring season has now started, and the summer festival season is just around the corner. Record Store Day is also happening in April, so consider collaborating with your local record shop and doing some related promotion.

Positive and hopeful (the summer banger) songs are suitable for this period. May is an excellent month to release music because the summer festival season is just around the corner. If you want to spread positive summer vibes, now is the time to release energetic music full of summertime celebration.

June, July, and August are festival months June and July are ideal for releasing music because classes are out, and festival season is in full swing. Try to land some festival gigs if possible to promote your music, and consider releasing a summer-themed album or single. Festival-goers are always looking for fresh and exciting music to dance to, so make sure your music fits that bill.

August is also a great month to release music because of the UK's bank holiday weekend. Many people take advantage of the long weekend to attend festivals or go on holiday, making it an ideal time to promote your music and gain more exposure.

After the festival season ends, people tend to go back to their daily routines, making September and October perfect for new music releases. These months are an excellent opportunity to stand out and attract attention, so make sure your music is fresh and original. Remember that people are still in a good mood after the summer, so releasing energetic and upbeat music is a good strategy.

November and December are the worse time to release music as your not competing with every artist and label but every brand and there marketing budget, the wait all year to market around Black Friday, Christmas and new years, The public and the media frequently pay attention to established acts, leaving less room for unsigned or local acts. We recommend holding any major release until the second week in January, unless your are considering releasing a Christmas album or single, or songs that fit with the winter season. However, if you're not releasing holiday-themed music, by all means go ahead.

Carefully consider the timing of your music release. Knowing when to release your music can make a significant impact on your success in music. By following these tips and taking advantage of the specific months throughout the year, you can give yourself a better chance of success.

Crafting A Campaign

There are many different marketing strategies and tactics that can be used to roll out and promote music artists projects. Each one needs to be tailored to the individuals, the audience and the actual music itself. Some common strategies and tactics include:

- **Identifying The Unique Characteristics Of The Project:** This can involve defining the artist's musical style, target audience, and key differentiators. Through clearly defining the artist or project, you can create a consistent and compelling marketing message that resonates with potential fans.
- **Developing A Marketing Plan:** This can include the use of traditional marketing channels, such as print and broadcast advertising, as well as digital marketing tactics, such as social media marketing and email marketing.
- **Building A Strong Online Presence:** This can involve creating a professional website, maintaining an active social media presence, and using digital platforms to distribute and promote the artist's music to reach a wider audience, engage with fans, and generate buzz around the artist or project.
- **Collaborating With Other Artists And Industry Professionals:** Another effective tactic for promoting music artists and projects is to collaborate with other artists and industry professionals.

The essential factors that need to be built into the foundation of a solid campaign, should be based on data and deep understand of the market you're looking to own.

Timing: Timing is crucial when releasing an album, so it's important to plan and schedule the release date carefully. Consider factors such as the time of year, holidays, and other important events that could impact the success of the release. For example, releasing a Christmas album in July may not be the best timing. Understanding the nuances of your audience's lifestyle and preferences can determine the success of a release.

- **Seasonality**: A feel-good summer track might not resonate in the middle of winter. Conversely, a contemplative song might find its best audience during more introspective seasons.
- **Global Events & Festivals:** Avoid clashing with major global events unless your music directly relates to it. Instead, leverage festivals, especially if they cater to your genre.

Amplify Pre-Release Buzz: The phase leading up to your release can be as crucial as the release itself. Encourage fans to pre-save the project on their streaming platforms so that they are notified as soon as it is released. Pre-saving the project on streaming platforms such as Spotify, Apple Music, and Deezer can help to build momentum and generate buzz ahead of the release. Encourage fans to pre-save the album by sharing links on social media and offering incentives, such as early access to exclusive content.

- **Pre-Save Campaigns:** Platforms like Spotify allow supporters to pre-save upcoming tracks. It's akin to bookmarking a song they're excited about.
- **Exclusive Incentives:** Offer behind-the-scenes footage, early access to lyrics, or personal anecdotes about the song-making process to those who commit early.

Offer Artist Packs: Creating special artist packs can be a great way to incentivize supporters to purchase the project. These packs can include exclusive merchandise, such as t-shirts or posters, as well as signed copies of the project.

- **Curate Exclusive Bundles:** Limited edition merchandise, signed vinyl, or even a personal shoutout can make supporters feel special.
- **Record Bundles:** Leverage partnerships with other artists or brands, potentially offering co-branded merchandise or limited-time collaborations.

Make a Splash On Release Day: Plan a big release day event to generate excitement and interest in the project. A big release day event can help to generate excitement and interest in the project. This can include things like album launch parties, live performances, and meet and greets with supporters.

- **Physical Venues**: If feasible, organize launch shows or parties.
- **Digital Domain:** Virtual listening parties, Instagram Lives, or even Reddit AMAs can engage a broader digital audience.
- **Collaborate:** Partner with influencers or other artists for shout outs or appearances.

Empower Your Promoters: Make it easy for supporters and media to promote the project by providing them with promotional materials, such as graphics, or filters for User generated content. Provide them with promotional materials, such as posters, flyers, and social media graphics that they can use to promote the project.

- **Digital Toolkits:** Provide easily shareable social media graphics, snippets, or even GIFs.
- **Physical Promotions:** Stickers, posters, or flyers can still be effective, especially in local communities or niche audiences.

Strategizing Video Releases: The visual representation of your music can sometimes speak louder than the track itself. Decide whether to release a music video for the album now or later, taking into account your budget, schedule, and other factors. Deciding when to release a music video for the album is important so considering factors such as your budget, schedule, and other marketing activities can provide you with more information when deciding whether to release the video now or later.

- **Teasers:** Before the main video, release teaser clips to build anticipation.
- **Engagement Through Visuals**: Host contests or challenges related to the video. It could be a dance challenge or a lyrical interpretation contest.

If you decide to release a music video, create engaging and shareable video assets that fans can share on social media and other platforms.

Maximize Store Presence: Check your album is available in as many stores as possible, both physical and online, to maximize your reach and sales. Making sure that the album is available in as many stores as possible can help to maximize reach and sales. This includes both physical and online stores, such as record shops and online retailers.

- **Physical Stores:** Engage local record shops for exclusive releases or in-store events.
- **Digital Platforms:** Ensure distribution across all major streaming platforms, and check for correct metadata to ensure easy discoverability.

After The Video: Plan additional promotional activities and events after the music video is released, such as pop ups and concerts. Planning additional promotional activities and events after the music video is released can help to sustain momentum and keep supporters engaged. This can include things like album signings, in-store performances, and concerts.

- **Re-engagement Campaigns:** Share trivia, supporters views, or lesser-known facts about the video to re-engage the audience.
- **Tour Or Virtual Concerts:** Organize live shows or virtual concerts to keep the momentum going.

The All-Important One Sheet: Create a one sheet that provides a quick and easy overview of the project and artist, including key information, track list, and quotes from reviewers and supporters. Creating a one sheet can be a useful tool for promoting the album to media and industry contacts. This should include key information about the project and artist, such as the track list, release date, and quotes from reviewers and fans. It should also include contact information for the artist or label.

- **Include Testimonials:** If you've received reviews or shout outs from notable figures, include them.
- **High-Quality Images:** Ensure you have a couple of high-resolution images that media can easily use.

Example Release Strategy: Releasing music in a way that appeals to Spotify and YouTube algorithms, while also taking advantage of your potential fans' attention span, is crucial for a successful music release strategy. One approach is to release a single every 6-8 weeks, and then between singles, keeping consistent but varied promotion.

- Week 1-2: Visual content (Trailers / Photos / Cover arts) for social media promotion
- Week 3-4: Single Release/Music Video
- Week 5-6: BTS of the video shoot, content around the release,
- Week 7-8: Alternate versions/remixes and Lyric Videos cut into shorts for social platforms

Crafting A Journey For Your Audience Keeps Them Hooked: Crafting a journey for your audience in music involves creating a captivating and evolving experience that resonates deeply with them. This concept extends beyond just presenting music; it's about building a narrative that engages listeners consistently. It involves understanding the nuances of audience behavior and preferences, and then tailoring the musical and extra-musical content to match these insights. The goal is to forge a connection that keeps the audience invested in the artist's journey, eagerly anticipating each new chapter and actively participating in the unfolding story.

- **Engagement Peaks:** Understand your audience's habits. If they're most active on weekends, schedule major releases around that time.
- **Varied Content:** While music is the primary focus, interviews, podcasts, or interactive sessions can offer a more holistic view of the artist.
- **Collaborations:** Feature other artists, not just musically, but even in promotions. A cross-pollination of audiences can be beneficial.

This can be repeated but understand audiences are getting fatigued from stagnant content faster and faster these days. Look to plan something eventful every 4 weeks and something smaller at least once a week. Navigating the intricate web of the music industry requires a mix of intuition, understanding of your audience, and strategic planning. Each step, if thoughtfully executed, can ensure that your music finds both ears and hearts.

Case Study: Stormzy's Marketing And Branding Strategies For 'Gang Signs & Prayer'

This case study focuses on the marketing and branding strategies used by Stormzy for his album "Gang Signs & Prayer," which debuted at number one on the UK Albums Chart and received critical acclaim. Stormzy gained recognition in the UK music scene through his mixtapes and freestyle videos posted on YouTube.

Stormzy's label, Merky Records, kickstarted the campaign by partnering with influential radio stations, with BBC Radio 1Xtra being a notable collaborator. Stormzy himself made appearances on the station, including an interview with DJ Semtex. During these conversations, he peeled back the curtain on the album's creation, giving fans a behind-the-scenes look. BBC Radio 1Xtra also played select tracks from the album ahead of its official release. This pre-release airplay not only built anticipation but also widened the audience's curiosity.

Social media platforms, particularly Twitter and Instagram, became Stormzy's playground for promoting "Gang Signs & Prayer." Here, he utilized his existing fan base by dropping intriguing teasers, exclusive behind-the-scenes content, and regular updates about the album's progress. To centralize engagement, Stormzy established a dedicated Instagram account solely for the album. This account served as a hub for exclusive content and direct interactions with his fan community.

He strategically integrated various album tracks into his appearances at prestigious events, including the BRIT Awards and the MOBO Awards. Stormzy went a step further by embarking on a highly sought-after UK tour in support of the album, and tickets sold out in no time. These live appearance served as both a testament to his exceptional talent and a significant catalyst for the album's hype and commercial success.

Stormzy's marketing for "Gang Signs & Prayer" wasn't limited to promotional efforts. He meticulously constructed a distinct visual identity for the album, characterized by captivating billboards interwoven with strong statements from the project. Beyond visuals, the album's title, "Gang Signs & Prayer," artfully encapsulated Stormzy's personal journey, seamlessly bridging street culture and faith. This cohesive branding left an indelible mark, setting the album apart in the competitive UK rap landscape.

Complementing the album was an innovative 15-minute short film directed by Rollo Jackson. Through compelling visuals and Stormzy's emotive voiceover, the film poignantly portrayed the "inner battle" faced by many black youths. This short film not only added depth to the album's storytelling but also significantly amplified its overall marketing impact. The comments reflect the emotional connection forged through his storytelling. Fans praised the brilliance of the video, its powerful messages, and Stormzy's authenticity.

This comprehensive campaign propelled "Gang Signs & Prayer" to the number one spot on the UK Albums Chart. The album's Platinum certification by the British Phonographic Industry and unanimous critical acclaim solidified its monumental success. Stormzy's achievements extended to the awards circuit, where he clinched top honors such as the Best Album at the 2017 MOBO Awards and the British Album of the Year at the 2018 BRIT Awards. By orchestrating this multi-faceted campaign, Stormzy not only cemented his status as a leading artist in the UK music scene but also emerged as a resonant voice for his generation.

Case Study: Central Cee's "Wild West"

Effective marketing and promotion campaigns can make the difference between an artist's success or failure. This case study will examine the marketing and branding strategies used by British rapper and drill artist Central Cee for his debut mixtape, "Wild West," which was released in 2020.

The choice of "Wild West" as the mixtape title was not arbitrary, paying homage to the area of London Cench hails from. Central Cee embarked on a visually striking campaign that began with a horseback ride through deserted streets of West London, perfectly coordinated with a personalized orange Lamborghini and a prominently displayed orange billboard. Shepherd's Bush, his hometown, served as the campaign's epicentre, grounding the mixtape in his roots. This choice wasn't just about aesthetics; it was a reflection of Cee's identity, as he explained, "the tape is bigger than me, it's for my area."

His approach to music energizes this generation and creates what he calls a "pinging" atmosphere. It's a sound that gets people hyped and contributes to his virality on platforms like TikTok and Cench was able to translate this into real life engagement during the campaign. Central Cee's guerrilla marketing tactics were orchestrated to perfection. Old-style 'wanted' posters featuring his image appeared all over London, creating intrigue and curiosity. He then traded the horse for horsepower, parading London with an orange supercar fleet. On March 17, he rewarded his dedicated fans by distributing over 200 meals to those who could locate him quickly. An impromptu outdoor performance followed, left loyal supporters thrilled and police trying to catch up with the swarm of adoring fans that turned. Limited Miniature figurines of himself and life-size 'wanted' posters were sent to his peers in the music and style industries.

Deepening the various culture touch points his brand could have with his fan base, Cee's collaboration with streetwear brands Trapstar and Corteiz gave supporters a piece of his lifestyle through style and fashion sense. The "Wild West" merch collection, including tracksuits and accessories, was an instant hit, with the website crashing due to high demand during the first drop. Central Cee keeps his style relatable and attainable, blending on-the-go, affordable fashion with touches of luxury. His loyalty to Trapstar, a brand rooted in his hometown, was evident, making it a fitting choice for the merch collaboration.

Central Cee's behind-the-scene style net videos served as a captivating window into the intricacies of his "Wild West" campaign. They meticulously documented the entire campaign journey, from the inception of the deal to the prominent billboards and the entire team donning the vibrant merch. The comments on Central Cee's "Fraud" video showcase the immense support and admiration for his work. Fans hail him as one of the biggest independent artists, highlighting his unique approach to both music and business. These videos not only provided a transparent and relatable view of Central Cee's hustle but also engaged his fanbase on a personal level, making them feel like active participants in his success story. Central Cee effectively harnessed the power of storytelling and authenticity to generate excitement and deeper connection with his audience, ultimately contributing to the mixtape's remarkable success.

Central Cee's "Wild West" campaign showcases a masterful blend of authenticity, creativity, and strategic marketing. His success not only as a musician but also as a cultural influencer speaks to his ability to connect with his audience on multiple levels, establishing himself as a prominent figure in music and fashion, and securing his place in the cultural landscape.

Central Cee's success with "Wild West" shows that a cohesive and consistent visual identity can be a powerful tool in creating a memorable brand image for an artist. Additionally, the use of multiple mediums, such as outdoor advertising, music videos, and fashion collaborations, can help to generate interest and buzz around an artist's work. By employing these strategies effectively, artists can establish themselves as rising stars in their respective genres and build a loyal fan base.

Case Study: Adele's Marketing And Branding Strategies For "25" Album

Adele Laurie Blue Adkins, professionally known as Adele, is a British singer-songwriter celebrated for her soulful and emotionally charged vocal prowess. Her third studio album, "25," unveiled in 2015, was hotly anticipated, and its marketing campaign was meticulously designed to heighten that sense of anticipation.

The campaign for "25" harnessed a diverse array of strategies to expand its reach, pique interest, and foster eager anticipation. Integral to this campaign were television advertisements that brilliantly showcased Adele's unique vocal talent and the deeply personal nature of her music. These ads featured emotive and soul-stirring performances, effectively broadcast on prominent television networks such as NBC, ABC, and ITV, all leading up to the album's much-awaited release. This tactic served to engage a broader spectrum of viewers and generate substantial buzz surrounding the album.

Adele's record label, XL Recordings, executed a close collaboration with radio stations, notably BBC Radio 1, as part of their promotional efforts for the album. Adele herself made multiple appearances on the station, including a revealing interview with host Nick Grimshaw, during which she delved into the album's creation process. In addition, BBC Radio 1 played select tracks from the album ahead of its official release, effectively stoking interest and fostering anticipation among its listeners. This strategy facilitated a direct connection with the core audience and contributed significantly to the album's build up.

A pivotal facet of Adele's marketing endeavour for "25" was her live performances. She graced various events, including the BBC Music Awards and The Ellen DeGeneres Show, with heartfelt renditions of tracks from the album. Furthermore, she embarked on a sold-out global tour to champion the album, earning critical acclaim along the way. These live showcases not only spotlighted Adele's exceptional talent but also heightened the excitement surrounding the album. By engaging directly with the audience, this strategy effectively amplified the anticipation for the album's release.

Adele's branding played a pivotal role in the marketing campaign for "25." A distinctive visual identity was crafted for the album, featuring striking artwork that included a captivating black-and-white photograph of Adele, complemented by the album's title in bold white lettering. This branding initiative yielded a cohesive image for the album, setting it apart from the multitude of pop releases. Consequently, this approach helped establish a robust brand identity and enhance the album's allure.

The culmination of Adele's marketing and branding strategies for "25" was nothing short of remarkable. The album made its debut at the zenith of the UK Albums Chart and the US Billboard 200, shattering numerous records in the process. In its initial week of release, the album surged past the 3 million copies sold mark, securing its status as the fastest-selling album in history. Music critics heaped praise on "25," extolling Adele's vocal virtuosity and emotional depth. The album was duly rewarded with numerous accolades, including Album of the Year at the 2017 Grammy Awards. Adele's resounding success with "25" firmly entrenched her as one of the most triumphant and cherished artists in the UK, setting the stage for an array of future accomplishments.

Adele's marketing and branding strategies for "25" embodied a comprehensive range of techniques, meticulously designed to captivate the audience and kindle fervent anticipation for the album's release. Through television advertising, radio promotion, live performances, and the creation of a distinctive brand identity, Adele orchestrated a campaign that achieved staggering success, not only in terms of record-breaking sales but also in the enduring impact it had on her career and status as a beloved artist.

Music Videos

In today's digital age, music videos have become your prime time tv advert for your art that is accessible at any time, due to people consuming most of their content online through social media and other digital platforms. So, it is crucial to put effort into creating a music video that will stand out from the rest.

A great music video can also show that you are a versatile performer who can bring your songs to life visually, potentially leading to live performances and collaborations with other artists. Additionally, creating an outstanding music video can provide you with an opportunity to work with industry professionals such as directors, producers, and editors.

It is important to keep in mind that the primary reason people watch music videos is to enjoy the music. So, when creating a music video, always prioritize the music, and ensure that it complements the visuals both thematically and visually. Although some viewers may appreciate an engaging video, many people watch music videos simply as a means of listening to their favourite tracks. Even if the video is visually impressive, if the music is mediocre, it may not gain significant traction. In contrast, a hit song with a simple video will still be played repeatedly by fans. It is essential to remember that viewers may not watch a video all the way through. With countless videos available on platforms like YouTube, viewers have numerous options to choose from. Therefore, the opening shots of a video are critical to grab the audience's attention and keep them engaged.

Location can significantly enhance the production value of a music video. When choosing a location, consider what would look good around the performer and what mood is to be created. Even with a limited budget, a unique and visually interesting location can make a big difference in the final product. It is also important to keep in mind any necessary permits or permissions required to film in certain locations.

Performance based video: Performance is the most critical aspect of a performance based video. It is vital to prepare and perform the song multiple times, with each take performed with the same energy and enthusiasm as the first. A video's visual appeal may be impressive, but if the performance does not convey the essence of the song, the video will not reach its full potential. A performer's unique style and live performance experience can be utilized to create a compelling video. Whether it is a powerful emotional connection or high-energy rock performance, the performer must bring their best to the video.

Narrative based videos: Story videos require skilful execution, as they aim to tell a story with no dialogue or exposition, relying solely on imagery and music to connect with the audience. While some videos may act out the story in the lyrics, most songs' themes and emotions are conveyed through the video's imagery. It is important to keep the story simple and focus on key moments in the song. Otherwise, the audience may become disinterested and disconnected.

Crafting an exceptional music video holds significant importance for all artists. It can be a powerful tool to introduce yourself to the world, attract attention from industry professionals, build a fan base, and advertise your music. However, it is essential to prioritize the music and ensure that the visuals complement it thematically and visually. Attention-grabbing opening shots, a powerful performance, a simple yet effective story, and a visually interesting location are all essential components of a successful music video. By putting in the necessary time and effort, you can create a music video that will make a lasting and positive impact on your career as an artist.

Pro Tip: Being Resourceful With Music Videos

In the late 90s and early 00s, music videos were an event in themselves, and almost felt like mini-movies with their high production value and engaging visuals. Back then, the only way to view them was on TV channels like MTV and The Box, which made them even more special. Fast forward to today, anyone can stand in front of a camera and record a music video, and upload it to YouTube, making the market even more saturated than before. In such a crowded field, it has become even more critical to have impactful visuals to stand out from the competition.

Creating high-quality music videos can seem like a daunting task, but with a budget of just a couple of hundred pounds and a good network, you can create a visually stunning experience for viewers. With so many venues and brands looking for exposure, most small venues will let you record for free if you ask and offer their brand placement in the video. Similarly, small clothing brands are often willing to send clothing for placements in your videos, providing you with additional resources to enhance your video's visual appeal.

One of the keys to creating compelling music videos is getting creative and making the most of what you have available to you. Building your own props or using smart camera techniques can take your visuals to the next level. For instance, using your smartphone as a camera can work well, especially with the addition of cheap accessories like stabilizers and lens attachments. These tools can help elevate your video production quality without breaking the bank.

In addition to being creative, building a network is also vital to creating impactful music videos. Collaborating with other artists and creators can help you expand your audience and reach new viewers. It is essential to remember that music videos are not just about promoting your music but also about building your brand and image as an artist. By working with other creators, you can tap into their audiences and gain new followers, all while helping to grow your own brand.

While the music video landscape has evolved significantly over the years, with advancements in technology and the proliferation of platforms like YouTube, impactful visuals remain as crucial as ever. By being resourceful, creative, and building a network, you can create visually stunning music videos that stand out from the competition and attract new fans. The key is to stay focused on building your brand and image as an artist and using music videos as a tool to achieve that goal.

Content Outside Of Music Videos

Creating content outside of music videos is an extension of your asset catalogues, artist can lean into to cultivate excitement and anticipation for their music. Artists in todays landscape cannot rely on their music alone to connect with their audience and must use multiple mediums to foster a deeper bond. While music videos are a fantastic medium for artistic expression, diversifying your content strategy allows you to engage your audience in a more personal and relatable way.

The key to successful content creation is to show your authentic self and let your audience into your world. People tend to fall in love with individuals, not just their music. By providing glimpses into your daily life, thoughts, and interests, you give your fans more opportunities to connect with you on a personal level. This connection can be invaluable in building a loyal and dedicated fan base. A shining example of this approach is IShowSpeed, who maintains an ongoing conversation with his audience through live chats and interactions. His ability to engage and magnetize his fans demonstrates the power of creating content beyond music.

History has repeatedly shown that the most humanized individuals receive the highest regard from their supporters. Consider the case of Mike Tyson, whose journey, including both triumphs and struggles, has been openly shared with the public. By participating in podcasts and sharing his personal stories, Tyson allows people to see beyond the flash of his professional career. This transparency and willingness to let people into his life have earned him massive respect and loyalty from fans.

Define Your Target Audience:
- Start by clearly defining your target audience. Who are they? What are their demographics (age, gender, location, etc.)?
- What are their interests, values, and pain points? What motivates them? What do they care about?

Identify Audience Segments:
- Break down your audience into segments based on shared characteristics or interests. For example, you might have different content strategies for hardcore fans and casual listeners.

Research and Understand Your Audience:
- Conduct surveys, interviews, or social media polls to gather insights directly from your audience.
- Analyse data from your website, social media, and email marketing to understand what content is resonating with your audience.

Content Themes and Topics:
- Create a list of content themes and topics that align with your audience's interests and needs. These should be broad categories.

Niche Down Over Time:
- As you gather more data and insights about your audience's preferences, start to niche down your content. Focus on producing content that speaks directly to specific segments of your audience.
- Experiment with different content angles and approaches to see what resonates best.

Stay Agile:
- Be prepared to adjust your content strategy based on changing audience preferences and trends.

Content creation offers artists the opportunity to control their narrative beyond the initial impression created by music videos or billboards. It allows you to connect with your audience on a more profound level, building a lasting and meaningful relationship that extends far beyond your music.

Videographers (In House Media)

Video production, especially in-house media, plays a crucial role in shaping an artist's image and engaging their audience as this is key component of consistency. The content needs of artists vary based on their niche, aesthetic, and scale. This can include tour videos and daily life vlogs, which are typically created by a skilled videographer.

The collaboration with videographers often starts with individuals who resonate with the artist's vision and gradually transitions into a more formalized working relationship. This evolution includes setting day rates for the videographers, which vary depending on their skill level and the intricacies of the project. This professional approach ensures a mutual understanding of expectations and quality of work.

Timeliness in editing and publishing content is crucial for maintaining audience engagement. Videographers must be proficient in creating engaging social media content of varying lengths, suitable for different platforms. Their storytelling ability should align with the artist's brand, effectively conveying the artist's message through visual media.

A professional videographer should balance creativity with practicality, taking calculated risks to capture compelling footage while ensuring safety. Meticulous attention to detail throughout the production process, along with flexibility in scheduling and payment terms, is key to a successful partnership. Discretion is also vital, allowing videographers to integrate seamlessly into the artist's environment when filming fly on the wall style content.

It's essential for videographers to respect the artist's control over content release, aligning with their broader marketing strategy. This includes not publishing any content prior to the artist and sharing links to the artist's posts with management for consistent distribution. In return, artists should credit videographers, recognizing their creative contribution and aiding in their career growth.

The strategic integration of skilled videographers into an artist's team is not just about producing content; it's about crafting a visual identity that resonates with audiences. These professionals are indispensable in translating an artist's musical narrative into compelling visual stories. Through their lenses, videographers not only capture moments but also significantly contribute to the artist's evolving brand, ensuring that each frame aligns with the artist's vision and enhances their connection with their audience.

Industry Insights: J-Mal, Founder Of JFX Visuals

In this industry insights interview we spoke with J-Mal one of the UK leading directors. He provides valuable insight into the music industry, particularly the process of building relationships, finding the right artist/director connection, and personal branding.

He shares his experience of touring in Japan and Korea, finding long-lasting relationships, creating effective treatments, and the importance of personal branding in the industry.

Building Long-Lasting Relationships: J-Mal emphasizes the importance of building relationships based on mutual benefits then continued on highlights that it is easier to find people in the industry that fit into your niche or category with TikTok, but the relationship must be a genuine collaboration. He advises that to build long-lasting relationships, you have to bring value and play on equal fields, stating that you often see new artist looking to work with bigger and more established artist to break out.

> *"Often people take their ideas up the chain, but the ideas aren't enough, you have to build the value to play on equal fields."*

J-Mal expressed that a lot of it comes to numbers these day, which make it more difficult to build certain relationships. You often need to prove your portfolio of has experience and substance before trying to work with those around you. He also stresses that having another skill outside of the music business might be necessary to get things over the line, and the vision used to be enough, but now it's more metric-based.

Finding the Right Artist/Director Connection: J-Mal provided essential tips for finding the right artist/director connection, suggesting that artist should have a realistic budget in mind and directors should be clear with their pricing as well, highlighting cost associated with the shoot considering factors such as parking, or number of revisions.

> *"Don't leave anything up to assumption, communicate everything"*

He emphasized that communication is key to avoid any misunderstanding. An artist should do research and due diligence on the director to make sure the director is capable for matching the vision in their mind as directors may not be able to emulate the styles of examples that artist are looking for. Directors need to be open and honest of their capabilities to bring that shoot to life.

Working In Industry: He shared valuable insights about working in the creative industry. He stressed the importance of having a personal connection with different elements of the creative space, such as models, and having a network of model agencies. J-Mal also pointed out the value of having a source for key production factors such as a car provider and a gaffer (lighting guy), as it can all add move value to you. Having access to a few locations is also essential, as people always want studios, warehouses, and apartments. He continued on to advise that you don't need to have all of these things to start with, as some agencies do all of the production elements.

Corporate Clients: J-Mal stated that at this stage, you will need to be creating treatments based on the song for the artist and pitching it to the commissioners. Networking is key here, and J-Mal made it clear just how important it is, knowing the right people to even be in the running for these jobs. He continued on to recommend using LinkedIn, as it is more professional outreach platform than Instagram, and having a website to show that you're trustworthy. However, J-Mal cautioned that working with corporates can be more time-consuming due to red tape, and directors should be aware that payments may take longer due to complicated invoice systems. While the pay may be higher, it's important to keep in mind that payment may not be immediate and can take up to 90 days. For these types of videos, J-Mal recommended having a good producer to take care of the behind-the-scenes work, and working with a DP if the budget allows,

> *"when you're doing a shoot for 10K, you're not going to be wanting to focus on the minor details during the shoot days, this is where the production companies come into play."*

Having your own network makes the process simpler, as on these jobs J-Mal stressed that there is no room for mistakes.

Backoffice: J-Mal made it clear that back office management is an important aspect of running a successful business. Initially, he was a sole trader which meant freelancers on his team were paid directly by the artist. However, as he transitioned to a limited company (LTD), freelancers now send invoices before they get paid. J-Mal emphasizes the importance of keeping track of these invoices to avoid losing track. He recommends using QuickBooks, which makes it easy to connect invoices with bank transfer payments. J-Mal stated the importance of getting an accountant who can advise on the best way to pay yourself, as this changes every year. He also highlights the benefits of being an LTD from a legal perspective, as it provides greater protection to the individual in the event of debt, incidents or insurance issues. The company can be liquidated and debts absorbed by that, rather than the individual being held liable.

Treatments: In the creative industry, treatments are an essential tool for pitching your creative vision to potential clients. J-Mal emphasizes the importance of having a treatment, but notes that not all directors are willing to create one if there isn't a budget.

> *"You can ask directors, do you provide treatments with your service."*

In this case, he suggests that artists with a lower budget should take the initiative and provide a treatment themselves. He advises that this should be a collaborative process between the artist and director, as the treatment should accurately represent the artist's vision while also incorporating the director's creative input.

Personal Branding: J-Mal stresses that having a website adds an extra layer of professionalism, which can be a deciding factor in whether or not a potential client decides to work with you, but in the modern day using social media platforms such as Instagram and TikTok to build your personal brand can be enough. Many directors use these platforms to showcase their work and attract potential clients. By utilizing these digital platforms, artists can increase their visibility and reach a wider audience. Ultimately, personal branding is essential in establishing oneself as a unique and valuable asset in the industry.

Tour In Japan: J-Mal shares his experience of touring in Japan, which happened organically when he saw cheap flights to Tokyo. He discovered the grime scene in Japan through a music documentary and followed up on the artist via social media. One of the artists shared a video from one of his artist connection in the local London scene, that had uploaded to SBTV. This organic networking opened up the door for a remix, on a track that was doing well. It also provided a new opportunity for a whole new network of connecting Japanese and Korean artists on new remixes that wanted to gain exposure on SBTV. He connected with producers and artists on the ground, and started getting events booked in with the artists he had networked with. J-Mal stated **"Don't get lost in indecision paralysis. Don't do nothing; that's the worst thing you can do,"** provides an important insight into his work ethic and how we can apply these principals to ourselves.

In this conversation, we gained valuable insights into the industry, including the importance of building a network, having access to locations and equipment, building relationships, finding the right artist/director connection, personal branding and understanding the red tape around corporate clients. Jamaal's personal experience and knowledge provide a unique perspective into the industry and its challenges. By following his insights, individuals can establish long-lasting relationships, find the right artist/director connection, create effective treatments, and build a personal brand to advance their careers in the music industry.

> *"Don't overthink and hesitate, make the move your scared to make. Whether you're right or wrong doesn't matter all that matters is you take action"*
>
> J-Mal

Treatments

Making treatments for music videos is a valuable exercise for artists because it helps them to communicate their creative vision to the directors and other members of the video production team. A treatment is essentially a written document that outlines the concept, themes, and visuals that will be used in the video. It can also include a proposed storyboard or shot list, as well as any other important details that will be helpful in bringing the artist's vision to life.

Example Treatment

The process of creating a treatment forces the artist to think critically about what they want to achieve with the video and how they want to tell their story through visual means. By putting their ideas down on paper, they can clarify their vision and communicate it more effectively to the director and other members of the production team. This helps to ensure that everyone is on the same page and working towards a common goal.

Creating a treatment can also help to save time and money during the production process. By having a clear vision of what they want to achieve, the artist can work with the director to develop a realistic plan for bringing the video to life within the constraints of the budget and timeframe. This can help to prevent costly mistakes or delays, and ensure that the final product is on brand and of the highest quality possible.

For example, let's say that an artist is creating a music video for a new single. They have a rough idea of what they want the video to look like, but they are not sure how to communicate this to the director. By creating a treatment, the artist can outline their ideas for the video, including the themes, visual style, and story line. They can also include references to other videos or films that have inspired them.

Once the treatment is complete, the artist can share it with the director and other members of the production team. This will help to ensure that everyone is on the same page and working towards a common goal. It will also give the director a better understanding of the artist's creative vision, which will make it easier for them to bring this vision to life.

EPKS

An EPK is a digital portfolio that includes information and materials about you and your music, such as your biography, fact sheet, official links, promotional photos, album streaming and download links, tour dates, lyrics, press quotes and reviews, and is an essential tool for an upcoming artist to introduce themselves and their music to the industry.

Having an EPK is important for various reasons:

- **Exposure:** An EPK helps you gain exposure by introducing you to journalists, industry professionals, and potential fans. It can be shared with these individuals to showcase your talent and help them learn more about you and your music.
- **Professionalism:** An EPK demonstrates your professionalism and dedication to your career as an artist. It shows that you are organized and prepared, and that you have put in the effort to create a comprehensive portfolio of your work.
- **Opportunities:** An EPK can open up new opportunities for you as an artist. It can help you book gigs, get signed to a record label, or make new connections in the industry.
- **Convenience:** An EPK is a one-stop-shop for journalists and industry professionals to find all the information they need about you and your music. It saves them time and effort by having everything in one place, rather than having to search for information on various websites and social media profiles.

An EPK serves as a vital instrument for artist to gain exposure, demonstrate professionalism, open up new opportunities, and make it convenient for industry professionals to learn about you and your music. Your EPK can help you stand out, be discovered, and book gigs or make new connections.

Example EPKs

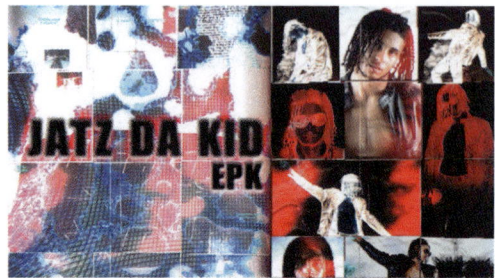
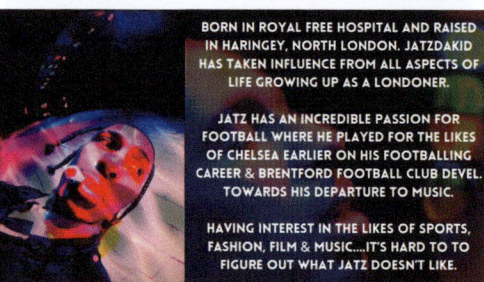

EPK's should reflect the artist style and aesthetic, whilst highlighting key attributes in their careers.

Here are some tips for creating an EPK as an upcoming UK artist:

- **Biography:** This is a great opportunity to share your story and tell the world who you are as an artist. Be sure to include details about your background, musical influences, and the themes and motivations behind your music. You can also mention any previous musical projects or collaborations.
- **Fact Sheet:** This should include your location, artist name, genre, key points of interest, influences, performance style, and any notable facts or achievements. Make sure to include your contact information, such as your website and social media profiles.
- **Official Links**: Include a list of your online presence, including your website, social media profiles, and any other media where your music can be found.
- **Promotional Photos**: High-quality, professional photos that capture your personality and style are essential for your EPK. Include at least two looks and different formats (e.g. vertical, horizontal, square).
- **Project Streaming And Download Links:** Make it easy for journalists and industry professionals to listen to your music by including a streaming link or download link in your EPK. You can use platforms like Soundcloud or Bandcamp to host your music.
- **Press Quotes And Reviews:** If you have received any press coverage or reviews, include a selection of quotes in your EPK. This can help demonstrate the interest and excitement surrounding your music.

Pro Tip: Be Ready - One Sheets & Assets

In the realm of artist management and marketing, being thoroughly prepared with one sheets and assets holds paramount importance. Consistently updating the one sheet on a monthly basis is highly recommended, as it serves as a valuable repository of crucial information, including key statistics, notable achievements, audience size and statistics, and examples of brand collaborations. The availability of a readily updated One Sheet enables artists to seize unexpected opportunities with agility and professionalism.

The significance of having readily available assets cannot be overstated, as they constitute the backbone of an effective marketing plan. However, a comprehensive marketing plan without corresponding material to communicate it is rendered ineffective. Collaborating with a skilled graphic designer to curate a comprehensive list of art requirements is a prudent step. Adhering to deadlines and aligning asset creation with the marketing calendar is essential for seamless campaign execution. Thoughtful naming conventions for the assets foster better organization and facilitate efficient sharing among relevant parties.

Adopting a consumer-centric approach is crucial in managing assets and content. Keeping information up to date is paramount, as outdated content can have adverse effects on an artist's brand image. Ensuring timely updates to the artist's website, and other online platforms, is fundamental in presenting the most current and relevant information to the audience.
In the quest for additional engaging content, it is highly recommended to draw from the artist's own perspectives and experiences. Gathering personal insights from the artist creates an authentic connection with the audience and enhances the artist's online presence. These candid insights can be leveraged across social media platforms, YouTube, and TikTok, forging deeper connections with fans and followers.

When capturing Behind the Scenes (BTS) footage, strategic positioning plays a pivotal role in yielding valuable content. Filming from the side of the set is advised, as it provides unique perspectives and captures genuine moments that resonate with the audience. Such BTS content offers fans a glimpse into the artist's world, fostering a sense of intimacy and exclusivity.

Organizing and saving video clips separately, with clear and descriptive names, serves as a prudent practice for managing assets. A well-organized collection of valuable assets ensures easy retrieval and repurposing for future use. This approach proves invaluable in delivering consistent and engaging content across various platforms and campaigns.

Thorough preparation and effective management of one sheets and assets significantly contribute to an artist's marketing success. Timely updates to the one sheet and the availability of comprehensive assets enable artists to seize opportunities and showcase their achievements and collaborations with finesse. Remaining consumer-centric by maintaining current information on online platforms enhances an artist's brand reputation. Leveraging personal insights and BTS content further strengthens the bond with the audience. Strategic organization and naming of assets optimize efficiency in content creation and ensure a rich and adaptable resource for future campaigns. By adhering to these best practices, artists and their teams can elevate their marketing efforts and leave a lasting impact on their audience.

Decks: Elevating the Artist's Business Arsenal

Within the dynamic music industry, artists constantly explore various tools and methods to engage with their audience. Among these, the "deck" has become a key promotional tool, similar in impact to the "epk" (electronic press kit). Decks, or "pitch decks/presentation decks," serve as vibrant visual stories crafted to captivate, inform, and influence. They are designed to effectively communicate an artist's vision and goals, making them an essential component in modern music promotion.

1. Funding: Decks are potent instruments for securing funding, whether through grants, sponsorships, or investors. They elucidate an artist's vision, showcasing their potential for return on investment, and eloquently persuading financiers.

2. Creating Partnerships: Building meaningful collaborations is at the heart of any artist's journey. Decks provide a compelling platform for proposing partnerships with fellow musicians, brands, and industry influencers.

3. Idea Presentation: Artists often have innovative concepts and creative ideas to expand their brand. Decks offer a structured format to outline and communicate these ideas effectively, from album launches to immersive experiences.

4. Brand Development: A comprehensive brand is the cornerstone of a successful music artist. Decks help articulate the essence of the artist's brand, encompassing their values, image, and unique selling points.

5. Showcasing Nuances: In the multifaceted world of music, an artist's evolution is marked by unique nuances. Decks act as a canvas to paint these details vividly, capturing the essence of the artist's journey, from humble beginnings to meteoric rises.

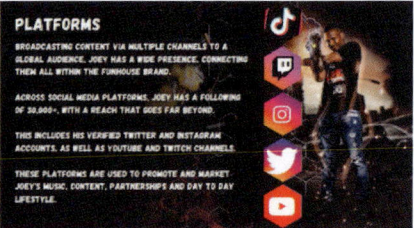

As artists navigate the dynamic terrain of their careers, growth and diversification often become integral parts of their journey. Take Joey, for instance, a recording artist and content creator hailing from South London. An essential member of the renowned SN1 movement, Joey has seamlessly transitioned from the music scene to a new venture – "joey's Funhouse." In this exciting new chapter, he immerses himself in the realms of gaming and tech, producing captivating content for both Millennials and newcomers to these worlds.

Joey's journey exemplifies how artists evolving into different spheres can leverage EPKs/decks to encapsulate these changes. These versatile tools enable artists to present their multifaceted identities comprehensively, segmenting the diverse areas they're exploring under their overarching brand. Just as Joey masterfully bridges the worlds of music, gaming, and tech, EPKs/decks empower artists to tell compelling stories that resonate with their audience, regardless of the creative avenues they traverse.

Radio Promotion In The UK

Radio promotion plays a pivotal role, serving as an influential and effective tool to promote music and reach diverse audiences. One of the primary aspects of radio promotion is securing airplay, which involves having songs featured on radio stations' playlists. By getting their music played on the radio, artists and labels significantly increase the visibility and reach of their music, connecting with potential fans in the mainstream and expand on their fanbases.

In addition to airplay, interviews and live performances are essential components of radio promotion. Artists and labels can participate in interviews on radio shows, providing an opportunity to share their stories, experiences, and insights with a wider audience. Such interviews allow listeners to gain a deeper understanding of the artist and their music, fostering a stronger connection between the artist and the audience. Furthermore, live performances on the radio offer a unique and intimate experience for listeners, providing them with a chance to hear the artist's music in a raw and authentic setting.

Radio advertising is another valuable avenue for music promotion. Purchasing advertising time on radio stations, can customize a message to effectively reach a large audience and promote their music to new listeners.

One significant advantage of radio promotion is the role of radio personalities as tastemakers. These radio hosts have a considerable influence on the preferences and tastes of their audience. Networking with these personalities can provide artists with a sense of validation, as being featured on their shows signals recognition and approval within the industry. Additionally, radio personalities often welcome new music and are open to featuring emerging artists, presenting a valuable opportunity for exposure to a broader audience.

DJs are vital figures in musical conversations and regularly seek new music for their shows and performances. Their constant need for fresh tracks creates an opportunity for artists to submit their music and potentially get featured, exposing them to a larger audience on prominent platforms managed by reputable figures in music.

Radio promotion is not only relevant for established artists; emerging talents can also benefit immensely from radio exposure. As leaders in the music scene, radio stations are eager to discover new and exciting music, making it easier for emerging artists to receive airplay and gain visibility. This exposure can act as a launching pad for their careers and propel them into the spotlight.

Radio promotion holds significant importance in the industry and historically has played a major role in UK music for decades, whether that be mainstream or pirate. Utilizing airplay, interviews, live performances, and radio advertising, artists and labels can effectively promote their music and connect with a diverse and expansive audience. The role of radio personalities as tastemakers and the constant need for new music by DJs create ample opportunities for artists to gain exposure and enhance their presence in the business. Whether established or emerging, artists can leverage radio promotion to forge meaningful connections with their audience, cultivate a dedicated fanbase, and achieve long-term success in the dynamic and competitive music landscape.

Industry Insights: DJ Limelight, Radio Pioneer & National Icon

In this industry insight interview with DJ Limelight, a long term pioneer of UK culture, having worked at the BBC for over a decade, spearheading the BBC Asian network.

In this analysis, we will delve into his advice on his mental approach, business strategies, and routines, building credibility, adapting to change, and connecting with artists. Additionally, we will explore his tips on the booking process, artist affiliation, and making music submissions to radio.

Mental Approach: DJ Limelight stated that the business aspect of the industry can be a major influence on your mind. Building a structure to your time should be at the forefront of your mind, noting that when you have your own way of making money, it can be demotivating to lack a routine. It can be the simple things that help, as he continued to discuss his own way of building a routine early in his career; having weekly appearances or appearing on a regular radio show an give you a routine to keep you motivated. For individuals pursuing a career in music, it's important to establish these routines, find ways to stay motivated and prioritize building an infrastructure that supports their day to day lives.

Building Credibility: According to DJ Limelight, it's crucial to create credibility by finding your formula to service your community at a high-quality level. He stated that,

> "The game isn't a 9-5 job, you need to build some value and the biggest thing is artist affiliation"

He looked back at his interview with Young Dolph, and how connecting a young AJ Tracey, who just happened to be passing by, eventually lead to a Key Glock feature. Providing opportunities, building core relationships, and doing things for the right reasons by thinking beyond your current desires and needs leads to more value for you and your community. Through connecting and playing your role, it may pay off later down the line. Limelight's emphasis on doing things for the right reasons is a reminder that authenticity and passion are crucial in the industry and by focusing on the artist and audience, you can lead yourself on a path with more meaningful and fulfilling work. It's crucial to know what DJ you are and what you represent, preparing the right mixes for the audiences you're performing to is the same as having the right tools for the job.

Radio Submissions: For music submissions to radio, Limelight recommends DJ's having a separate email, to make responding to as many people that hit you up possible easier, and interact even with unknown artists. He suggested keeping it natural and not forcing it to fit into a certain realm noting that the purpose of radio has changed over the years, with premier plays no longer being the main thing. Platforms have changed the way people consume music, and they now tune into radio to listen to the DJ and hear what they're doing. With the rise of social media, DJs can connect with unknown, new artists and their fans, creating new opportunities for collaboration and networking. DJs should be leverage various platforms, including streaming services, to showcase their skills and reach a wider audience.

Artist Connecting With Culture: Limelight suggests finding ways to be unique and different from what's already out there when making music. DJs should aim to differentiate themselves with their unique style, sound, or personality to stand out in the competitive music industry. He emphasizes that it's a business at the end of the day but cautions against running away from who you are, recommending keeping it as close to yourself as possible. For artist he emphasized to Keep it natural,

> *"Don't force it to fit in a certain realm. The purpose of radio has changed over the years, premier plays aren't the main thing. Platforms have changed the way people consume music. The line between underground and mainstream is very thin, so just make tunes that bang."*

DJ Limelight provided valuable insights into the music industry. From navigating the submission process for radio play to staying true to one's unique style when making music, there is much to consider for aspiring artists.

Pro Tip: Create At Least 5 Version Of Your Releases

Musicians often create various versions of a song for good reasons. These versions can include the full version, a clean version, a PA (Public Address) version, a remix, and even an acoustic version. There's no set rule for how many versions an artist should make, but having these different versions serves specific purposes.

The first version is the full version, which serves as the original and complete rendition of the song. This version is typically released on streaming services and physical formats like CDs and vinyl. It includes all the lyrics, instrumental sections, and production elements, allowing listeners to experience the song as the artist intended.

The second version is the clean version, which is crucial for radio airplay and platforms with content restrictions. In this version, any explicit or potentially offensive language is removed or replaced with suitable alternatives. Some radio stations will clean tracks for you, but don't rely on this. Take things into your own hands a get creative during your mixing of clean records. By providing a clean version, artists can ensure that their music can be played on radio stations and platforms with strict content guidelines, broadening their reach to a wider audience.

The third version is the PA (Public Address) version, specially tailored for live performances. Performing a song live requires adjustments to optimize the audio experience for the audience in different settings and sound systems. The PA version allows artists to adapt their music for various live performance scenarios, ensuring that their songs sound great on stage and resonate with the audience.

The fourth version is the remix, a dynamic and creative take on the original track. Remixes are often designed for specific audiences or settings, such as clubs or dancefloors. DJs and producers may collaborate with artists to create remixes that feature different beats, tempo changes, or alternative arrangements, providing a fresh perspective on the original song and appealing to a broader range of music enthusiasts.

Finally, the fifth version is the acoustic version, which showcases a stripped-down and intimate arrangement of the song. This version focuses on the vocals and lyrics, highlighting the raw emotion and song writing prowess of the artist. Acoustic versions can create a more personal and emotional connection with listeners, providing a unique listening experience.

Beyond these key versions, artists may also consider creating other variations, such as an instrumental version for licensing purposes, a radio edit for shorter playtime on radio, an extended version for DJ sets, or an alternative mix to experiment with different sounds and arrangements. Having multiple versions of a song opens up various promotional opportunities for artists. Each version can be strategically marketed and promoted to target specific audiences and platforms. For instance, the full version can be promoted on streaming services, the clean version for radio airplay, the remix for club playlists, and the acoustic version for social media platforms or intimate live sessions.

This approach to music promotion maximizes the potential reach of an artist's music and allows them to connect with a diverse range of listeners. Creating versions that cater to different preferences and platforms can lead to increased exposure, fan engagement, and ultimately, a more successful and sustainable music career.

Music Public Relations And Media Relations

Music public relations (PR) and media relations serve as the bedrock of the promotional efforts. These strategies encompass a broad spectrum of activities, ranging from traditional practices such as press releases and media interviews to harnessing the potential of digital platforms and social media. It's significance cannot be overstated. These PR and media relations tactics are linchpins in enhancing an artist or label's public visibility. This organic growth is indispensable for creating excitement around new releases, tour schedules, and pivotal moments, ultimately shaping the audience's perception of the artist or label.

In the fiercely competitive landscape of the music market, mastering the art of public and media relations is an imperative. Success requires a proactive approach. Artists and labels must build and cultivate relationships with influential journalists and media outlets. They must craft engaging content and adeptly employ a blend of traditional and digital methods to advocate for their cause effectively.

At its core, Music PR aims to generate positive exposure and expand the reach of the artist or project. It encompasses various essential roles and services:

- **Media Outreach:** The establishment of robust connections with music journalists, bloggers, and radio stations to secure media coverage.
- **Press Releases:** The creation and distribution of press releases to announce album launches, tour dates, and other significant updates.
- **Media Monitoring:** The vigilant tracking of media coverage and swift responses to rectify any negative or inaccurate narratives.
- **Social Media Management:** The strategic cultivation and maintenance of a compelling online presence across platforms like Instagram, Twitter, and Facebook.
- **Event Promotion:** The diligent promotion of live events, including album releases, tours, and festival appearances.

These tactics collectively orchestrate an artist's ascent in the music industry, directing them towards recognition and success. In the ever-evolving sphere of music, adeptly manoeuvring through the corridors of PR and media relations is the key to striking the right chords with the audience and industry alike.

Pro Tip: How To Write A Music Press Release

To garner media attention and blog coverage for your music, crafting an excellent press release is key. However, knowing what to write, feature, and link to in your press release can be daunting. Fortunately, we are here to help you create the perfect press release to get your music discovered in 2023.

It is essential to recognize that do-it-yourself PR is not easy, and experienced music PR executives are in high demand for various reasons. One of the main reasons is contacts. The best PR professionals have developed strong relationships with influencers and tastemakers over years or decades in the industry, becoming a trusted source of new music and fresh talent, which takes time, patience, and dedication. Nonetheless, if you do not have the budget to hire professionals, do-it-yourself PR is the next best thing. With great music, there is no reason why your music won't get picked up.

To write a press release that bloggers cannot resist, you must make it easy for the recipient. Understand that music bloggers receive hundreds of emails and press releases every day, and you need to get to the point quickly. Ensure that all your essential information is easy to read, recognize and access with one or two clicks. Remember, some busy music bloggers may copy and paste chunks of your press release into a new post without even contacting you if they are interested in your news.

The subject line is crucial in grabbing their attention. An exciting, interesting, and irresistible subject line can make a significant difference in whether your email gets opened or ignored. A subject line like "Awesome Band Releases New Single" is not compelling, but you can make it interesting by adapting your pitch. For instance, you can indicate if you're heading out on tour, supporting a well-known band, tackling a thought-provoking issue, or collaborating with famous artists or producers.

It is risky to send attachments from someone you do not know, and your email might get deleted if any files are attached. Instead, copy your press release into the body of the email and include links to your tracks on a well-known streaming platform like Soundcloud, YouTube, Bandcamp, or Spotify.

If your music is not officially out yet, create a private Soundcloud link or an unlisted YouTube video to share it with a select number of people in advance of your release date. Include direct links to your social media pages, website, and a folder of press shots to make it easy for bloggers. That way, bloggers do not need to spend their time searching for you online to tag you in posts or find a decent picture of you for their featured image. You can also set up a Dropbox or Google Drive link with all your essential assets such as pictures, logos, and a longer artist bio.

Finally, adding a brief, personal message to the email above your press release can be a nice way to engage and build a potential relationship with the recipient. A quick hello, including their name and the title of their blog, shows that you are genuinely aware of who you are emailing.

Pro Tip: Press Training

The advice for press training is simple and straightforward. The key takeaway is to be mindful of your words and actions during an interview. It's important to be sober and polite during an interview, as well as to avoid saying anything that could be considered rude or disrespectful.

One effective tip is to stop speaking after answering a question. The silence will prompt the interviewer to ask a follow-up question or move on to another topic. However, be aware that journalists may ask sensitive questions, and you should avoid going into detail or saying too much in response if you are unaware of the consequences of speaking out of turn in precarious situations.

In the case of a controversial topic being brought up, such as a disagreement with another artist, it's best to stay silent or give a brief and neutral answer. The interviewer may try to press for more information, but you can politely redirect the conversation by saying "I've given my answer to that, let's move on." By avoiding further discussion on sensitive topics, you can prevent yourself from being quoted in a negative light on multiple platforms.

Approvals

As an artist, it is important to maintain control over the image and message portrayed to the public. Approving cover images and interviews can help prevent any misquoting or misrepresentation of your words. However, it is important to consider the size and reach of the publication before requesting approval. Major publications may not allow for approval, while smaller outlets may be more accommodating.

It is also important to remain honest in interviews, avoiding whitewashed or uninteresting content. Instead, focus on highlighting your positive achievements and projects, as this can also reflect well on the industry as a whole. Consider reaching out to international press, as global exposure can be valuable. However, it is recommended to not conduct interviews simply for the sake of it, but rather time them to align with a specific promotional purpose and ensure that you have something meaningful to contribute. Ultimately, let your music and reviews speak for themselves.

Sing When You're winning

It is important to refrain from conducting interviews that focus on unachieved goals or future aspirations. This can be perceived as overhype and may result in a lack of interest from your audience. Instead, wait until you have achieved your goals before conducting an interview. This provides a compelling story of success, overcoming challenges, and achieving success, which is often well-received and respected. It is important to avoid being perceived as boastful or arrogant and to maintain a level of humility and gratitude towards your success. By intentionally waiting until you have achieved your goals, you can provide a story of inspiration and perseverance, which will be more engaging to your audience.

Industry Insights: Millie May, Freelance Music Publicist

In this industry insight, we spoke with Millie May, a music publicist. Millie has worked with a range of artists and has built her career by creating organic connections with publications and securing quality coverage for her clients.

In our interview, Millie shared valuable insights on topics such as finding a publicist, the average cost for PR, and the importance of EPK and press packs.

PR: Millie is an accomplished DJ, so she understand the artist perspective better than most. according to Millie, music PR provides a lot of freedom in how to speak and operate. For emerging artists, landing a big piece of coverage in a magazine can help build their profile. However, it's important for people to understand where an artist has come from and the way they see the world. Millie emphasizes that quality coverage is not just views or those that generate the most streams. Instead, organic connections are important to build up. Talking to the writer and being genuine can help establish those connections.

> *"I like the old fashion way of press...you can change the narrative"*

Finding A Publicist: There's not one set way to find a publicist, Millie shared that social media is a common way for people to reach out to her regarding potential work. She continued to state that the agency's reputation is important, and building rapport with a publicist can have a big impact as it can be difficult for some people to spend money on a publicist when they don't know what they'll get in return.

> *"Publicists need to manage expectations with artist, they need to know exactly what their money spend is getting in return from the publicist."*

Artist may have high expectations and demands but also not understand how the coverage helps with their SEO and algorithms. A number of artists that Millie works with are independent, with some of them having only one song and aiming to build up their platform. While they may not expect big things at this stage, they understand the importance of building up their profile.

For others, it's a chance to springboard into a new identity or change the narrative around their name. Millie emphasizes that artists can tap into PR at any stage of their career, and some even use campaigns purely to find new collaborators. However, it's crucial for artists to know who they are and what narrative they want to push or take. While they may have an image and make music, without a clear understanding of their desired narrative, their efforts may not pay off. Pinpointing the goals of the artist is crucial, but you can't put a price on their timeline. Touring is important to place yourself in new territories. Some artists purely do these campaigns to find people to collaborate with.

Average Cost: Millie points out that the cost for all 4 services can range from £8 - £10K. If it's just press coverage, it can be £1.5 - £3K. There are many costs involved, and it's important to put yourself in the artist's shoes. Multiple campaigns are often needed to build engagement. There's no set price that will work for every artist. Good music is essential, and there needs to be a build-up over time.

EPK + Press Packs: Millie emphasizes the importance of EPK and press packs for artists. The way the artist looks and how engaging they are is important. She uses Adobe Express to create press packs, and good press shots are important. It doesn't have to be the utmost professional, but needs some quality to it. Nicely curated and selected press packs are more engaging. Usually, a private SoundCloud link is used, and mp3 or wavs are not attached as most people are on corporate systems and won't want to have anything downloaded.

Millie May, advises to keep plugging away in the industry despite experiencing knockbacks. She emphasizes that everything happens for a reason and that setbacks should be seen as opportunities for growth and evaluation. Millie also reflects on how her redundancy led her to rethink and evaluate her career path. She believes that sometimes, it takes a difficult situation to push oneself out of their comfort zone and find a role that is a better fit for their skills and goals.

"Keep plugging away."
Millie May

CHAPTER 7
TOURING AND LIVE EVENTS

How To Book And Promote Shows

Booking and promoting shows is a multifaceted endeavour that demands careful planning and effective strategies. To successfully navigate this process, key steps need to be undertaken.

The initial step in booking and promoting a show is identifying potential venues that align with the artist or band's vision. This entails conducting comprehensive research on various venues, considering factors such as capacity, amenities, and location. The selection of venues should be tailored to the artist's style and target audience. Creating a lead file of pre-existing list of venues can expedite the search process for future events. Building relationships and gathering information beforehand facilitates smoother event bookings, allowing ample time for promotion.

Once potential venues have been identified, the next crucial step is to establish contact and negotiate a contract for the show. Communication with the venue involves discussions on various contract terms, such as the date and time of the performance, ticket pricing, and revenue sharing arrangements. Agreeing on these details solidifies the foundation for a successful show.

Subsequently, the spotlight turns to promoting the show and capturing the attention of audiences. A wide array of promotional activities comes into play, including advertising, public relations, and social media marketing. Crafting a compelling and strategic promotional campaign generates buzz and excitement around the event. Word of mouth remains a significant promotional channel, as garnering trust from potential attendees is pivotal in driving event attendance. Having reputable brand ambassadors spreading the word on social media platforms is a crucial aspect of any effective promotional strategy.

The sale of tickets constitutes an integral component of show promotion and serves as a revenue-generating avenue. Employing diverse channels and strategies to reach potential audiences is key. This includes ticket sales through online platforms, box offices, and mobile apps, providing convenience and accessibility for ticket buyers.

Undeniably, content creation plays an often overlooked yet vital role in the event promotion process. Capturing content at events, such as photos and videos, is an invaluable resource for future promotions. By offering visual takeaways to fans and attendees, they are left with lasting impressions, fostering brand loyalty, and building anticipation for future events.

Booking and promoting shows in the music industry require a well-structured approach and a combination of strategies. Identifying suitable venues, negotiating contracts, and devising compelling promotional campaigns are the foundational steps to a successful show. Additionally, the art of selling tickets and capturing event content play critical roles in generating revenue and fostering continued success. Embracing meticulous planning and leveraging effective marketing tactics enable artists and bands to showcase their talent, connect with their audiences, and leave an indelible mark in the dynamic world of live music events.

Touring And Live Events

Touring and live events play a pivotal role in a artists career, offering a powerful platform to promote their music and engage with their fans. To embark on a successful tour or live event, a series of critical activities must be undertaken.

The first step involves gathering data on your key cities. Understanding what the best locations are for your shows, who and where your audiences are, will allow you to maximise your tours. This is closely followed by actually booking shows at the various venues. This requires adept negotiation skills and involves securing dates and times for performances, all while coordinating with other artists and industry professionals. The process of booking shows can be time-consuming, but it forms the foundation of a well-structured tour or event.

Once the shows have been booked, the logistical aspects of the tour or event come into play. Managing logistics includes arranging transportation for the artists and their team, booking accommodations to ensure everyone is well-rested and ready to perform, and liaising with local promoters and other industry professionals to ensure smooth coordination and execution.

To ensure a successful tour or live event, effective promotion is crucial. Utilizing a mix of traditional marketing methods, such as print and broadcast advertising, alongside digital marketing strategies like social media marketing and email campaigns, helps generate interest and ticket sales. Engaging fans through online platforms and building anticipation can contribute significantly to the success of the tour.

Ultimately, the heart of a tour or live event lies in delivering an exceptional performance. This involves meticulous rehearsals to perfect the setlist, sound checks to ensure audio quality, and attention to technical details to ensure a flawless show. Delivering a captivating performance that resonates with the audience is the ultimate goal of any tour or live event.

For emerging artists, embarking on their first tour can be a daunting prospect. However, understanding and identifying their target audience is crucial in making the journey smoother. Engaging in open mic nights, exploring local performance circuits, and connecting with event coordinators in their community can all help build a dedicated fan base.

In different regions of the UK, there are local promoters and organizations curating line-ups of multiple artists to foster a thriving live music community. These organizers deeply immerse themselves in their local communities, allowing artists without extensive resources or event planning skills to access the same opportunities and platforms. Supporting headline acts on tours can serve as a significant stepping stone for new artists, granting them exposure to new audiences at every tour stop.

Touring and live events are essential components of the music industry in the UK. With careful planning, execution, and a keen focus on the core community of fans, artists and labels can expand the visibility and reach of their music, generate revenue, and create memorable experiences for their audiences.

Touring Budgets And Financial Management

Touring budgets and financial management ensure the success and profitability of touring and live events. At the core of this process lies a detailed financial plan, outlining the costs and revenues associated with the tour, serving as a comprehensive tool to track and manage its financial performance.

The foremost step in creating a touring budget is identifying all the costs associated with the tour or live event. These costs encompass a wide range of elements, including transportation expenses for the artists and crew, accommodation costs, equipment rentals, and personnel expenses. By diligently identifying and accounting for each cost, an accurate and comprehensive budget can be constructed, laying the foundation for financial prudence.

Estimating revenues is equally vital in financial planning. Beyond just identifying costs, projecting revenues generated by the tour or live event is paramount to assess its overall profitability. This entails considering revenues from various sources, such as ticket sales, merchandise sales, and other potential income streams. Precise revenue estimations allow for a clear understanding of the financial viability of the tour or event.

Once the touring budget has been carefully crafted, the next crucial step is to meticulously track both expenses and revenues throughout the tour or event. This task involves employing financial software or other appropriate tools to monitor spending and incoming revenue streams. Staying within the budgetary constraints is essential, and diligent tracking enables timely identification of potential financial challenges. By having a clear overview of expenses and revenues, necessary adjustments can be made promptly to maintain financial stability.

Effective financial management also includes anticipating potential risks and devising contingency plans to address unforeseen challenges. While budgets provide a structured financial plan, it is essential to consider potential fluctuations in expenses or revenues and plan accordingly. Having contingency measures in place safeguards the tour or event from financial distress and fosters adaptability.

Collaboration between various stakeholders, such as the tour manager, production team, and financial personnel, is vital for seamless financial management. Transparent communication and shared responsibility ensure that financial goals are aligned with artistic vision and logistical execution.

Maintaining accurate and detailed financial records is integral to financial management. Precise documentation not only facilitates ongoing budget monitoring but also aids in financial analysis post-tour, providing valuable insights for future financial planning.

Touring budgets and financial management form the bedrock of successful and profitable touring and live events. By meticulously identifying costs, estimating revenues, and diligently tracking financial performance, tour organizers can ensure sound financial planning and informed decision-making. The implementation of contingency measures and collaborative efforts among stakeholders further fortify the financial stability of the tour. Through effective financial management, artists and organizers can navigate the complexities of touring with confidence, delivering exceptional live experiences to audiences while achieving financial success.

Logistics For Tours

Logistics serve as the backbone of any successful touring endeavour or live event, orchestrating a complex array of components that encompass transportation, accommodation, and various other necessities crucial for a smooth and efficient tour. The execution of logistics is paramount, liberating musicians and their crew from the burdens of practical concerns, allowing them to channel their focus entirely into delivering outstanding performances.

Transportation stands tall as one of the fundamental pillars of logistics in touring. The seamless movement of musicians, crew, and equipment from one location to another is pivotal in upholding a well-structured and tightly knit tour. Achieving this level of coordination demands seamless liaisons with airlines, bus and train companies, and rental car agencies to secure the most reliable and efficient transportation options available. Moreover, it necessitates unwavering attention to detail in ensuring that all requisite travel documents and visas are meticulously obtained and kept up to date, sparing no effort to avert any potential impediments that may disrupt the meticulously crafted schedule of the tour.

Another indispensable facet of touring logistics is accommodation. The vitality of providing suitable and comfortable lodging for musicians and crew throughout the duration of the tour cannot be overstated. The quality of rest and rejuvenation they receive at their chosen abodes significantly impacts their ability to deliver peak performances. This paramount responsibility calls for the advanced securing of bookings at hotels, motels, or other appropriate accommodations, carefully tailored to meet the specific needs and preferences of the touring party.

Equally crucial is the handling of equipment and supplies. At the heart of live events and tours lies the availability of all necessary equipment and supplies for each performance. The success of this endeavour hinges upon coordination with reputable equipment rental companies, ensuring that the required instruments and technical gear are readily accessible. Additionally, diligent attention must be paid to the proper transportation and setup of this equipment at each venue to guarantee flawless performances that captivate audiences night after night.

Logistics assume an indisputably integral role in the world of touring and live events. From planning, coordination, to the execution of logistics, these factors are non-negotiable prerequisites for ensuring seamless and triumphant operations. Artists and bands must embrace the imperative of employing effective strategies and techniques in managing logistics, as doing so enables them to unleash their artistic brilliance, knowing that a well-organized and efficient system adeptly handles the practical aspects.

With logistics as their unwavering support system, artists and bands can traverse the exhilarating world of touring and live events with unwavering confidence, secure in the knowledge that their vision will be brought to life with perfection and finesse, making an mark on the hearts of their audiences worldwide.

Case Study: Big Narstie's Successful Independent Touring Strategy

Big Narstie, a well-known grime artist and personality in the UK music scene, has gained significant recognition for his unique style and talent. He decided to take charge of his touring career and handle various aspects of his tours himself. This included booking venues, arranging travel and accommodation, designing sets, and putting together his own security team.

Big Narstie realized that he was not getting a fair share of the profits from his shows, as promoters were paying him £15,000 per show, which indicated that they were making double that amount. This prompted him to question the fairness of the arrangement and motivated him to take control of his touring career.

Narstie's solution was to take charge of his tours and handle all the details himself. He used his extensive network in the industry to book venues that aligned with his artistic vision and style, arranged travel and accommodation that suited his preferences, and designed sets that showcased his unique talent. Additionally, he assembled his own security team to ensure that his shows would run smoothly and provide a safe environment for him and his fans.

By taking control of his touring career, Big Narstie was able to increase his profits and retain more control over his image and career. He was able to offer his fans a unique and exciting live experience, which helped to build a loyal following. Moreover, he established strong relationships with venue owners, security companies, and other industry professionals that will benefit him in the future.

Big Narstie's independent approach to touring also helped him build his brand and expand his reach. He created his own unique identity that differentiated him from other artists and allowed him to connect with his fans on a deeper level. This, in turn, helped him to gain exposure and attract more fans to his shows.

The decision to take control of his tours and handle all the details himself was a wise move that allowed him to increase his profits and control over his career. His independent approach to touring not only helped him to build a loyal following but also enabled him to establish strong relationships in the music. This case study highlights the importance of artists taking control of their careers and finding innovative ways to increase their profits and exposure. By doing so, they can build their brand, gain exposure, and create a loyal following that will support them throughout their career.

Navigating Legal And Insurance Issues For Live Music Events

Amidst the excitement and euphoria of touring and live music events in the UK, it is crucial not to overlook the legal and insurance aspects that underpin the industry. Adhering to legal requirements and securing adequate insurance coverage is not only a matter of compliance but also an essential safeguard against potential risks and liabilities.

At the core of legal and insurance considerations for live music events lies the acquisition of appropriate licenses and permits. These legal documents are indispensable for ensuring that the events are conducted lawfully and in accordance with local, national, and international regulations. Acquiring licenses for music performances and permits for the sale of alcohol, among other activities, is crucial to avoid any legal entanglements that could mar the event's reputation and lead to financial consequences.

Another paramount concern is health and safety. Safeguarding the well-being of both the audience and performers is non-negotiable. This entails strict compliance with health and safety regulations, including fire safety protocols and emergency evacuation procedures. Additionally, ensuring that the venue is equipped to handle live music performances safely is a responsibility that should not be taken lightly.

In the realm of touring and live events, insurance coverage plays a vital role in mitigating potential risks and liabilities. Comprehensive insurance policies that encompass equipment, transportation, and personal injuries provide artists and bands with a safety net should any unforeseen accidents or disruptions occur. The peace of mind that comes with being adequately insured allows performers to focus on their craft without unnecessary worry.

To navigate the complex legal landscape of the music business, artists and bands can seek guidance from reputable legal bodies that specialize in music-related matters. Bodies such as the Musicians' Union, The Incorporated Society of Musicians (ISM), and Arts Council England are valuable resources for gaining a deeper understanding of the legal intricacies involved in touring and live events.

Meticulous attention to legal and insurance issues is indispensable for the smooth and secure operation of live music events in the UK. Compliance with legal regulations, prioritization of health and safety measures, and the acquisition of comprehensive insurance coverage collectively contribute to the success and sustainability of the music industry, ensuring that touring and live events remain a fulfilling and rewarding part of every artist and band's career.

Case Study: Tragedy at Brixton Academy

In December 2022, a tragic incident occurred outside the O2 Brixton Academy in London, resulting in the death of a concertgoer, Rebecca Ikumelo and Gaby Hutchinson. The incident serves as a sobering reminder of the importance of crowd control, security, and event management in ensuring the safety of attendees at music venues.

Thousands gathered outside the O2 Brixton Academy to attend a performance by singer Asake. Unfortunately, chaos ensued when a large crowd attempted to gain entry without tickets. The situation quickly escalated, resulting in a crush that left multiple people injured and two fatalities.

Factors Contributing to the Tragedy

1. **Crowd Management:** The incident highlights the critical importance of effective crowd management strategies during large-scale events. Ensuring that the number of attendees does not exceed the venue's capacity is paramount.
2. **Security Measures:** Adequate security measures, including crowd control barriers and trained personnel, are essential to prevent unauthorized entry and maintain order. It's vital that security teams are prepared to respond swiftly to emerging situations.
3. **Emergency Response**: In cases of emergencies or crowd-related incidents, prompt emergency response can make a significant difference. Properly trained medical personnel and readily accessible medical equipment should be on-site to address injuries quickly.
4. **Communication:** Clear and effective communication among event organizers, security teams, and attendees is vital. Providing instructions in case of emergencies and establishing communication channels for attendees can help mitigate risks.

The tragic deaths have deeply affected family, friends, and the larger community. The incident serves as a stark reminder that the consequences of inadequate safety measures can be devastating, and it underscores the need for continuous vigilance in event planning and management.

Asake, made an emotional return to the stage with his debut O2 Arena show on August 20th. This significant performance marked his first in the UK since the tragic crowd crush incident at the Brixton Academy during his previous tour. The tribute deeply resonated with the audience, both at the O2 Arena and those tuning in via the live stream. Concertgoers described the atmosphere as "beautiful," and many commended the poignant moment of remembrance.

However, not all responses were positive. Rebecca Ikumelo's sister, Rachael, expressed her disappointment in the tribute via Twitter, stating that Asake had not reached out to her family since the incident occurred. Asake had previously expressed his condolences following the tragedy on his Instagram, stating his devastation at Rebecca Ikumelo's passing and extending his sincerest condolences to her loved ones.

The tragedy at the Brixton Academy highlights the critical importance of prioritizing safety and security in event planning. Concert venues, event organizers, and security personnel must work together to ensure that such incidents are prevented through stringent crowd management, security measures, and emergency preparedness. While music venues are spaces for joy and celebration, safety should always be the top priority to protect attendees and prevent future tragedies.

Lessons Learned and Positive Changes

The tragic event at the Brixton Academy compels us to prioritize safety and security in event planning. Concert venues, event organizers, and security personnel must collaborate diligently to prevent such incidents. This entails rigorous crowd management, comprehensive security measures, and unwavering preparedness for emergencies. As we reflect on this heart-wrenching incident, here are key positive changes that can be implemented:

1. **Enhanced Crowd Control:** Implement stricter crowd control measures, including rigorous ticket checks, capacity monitoring, and crowd flow management, to prevent overcrowding and chaos.
2. **Security Training:** Invest in comprehensive training for security personnel to ensure they are well-prepared to handle challenging situations effectively and professionally.
3. **Emergency Response Readiness:** Establish well-equipped medical stations and ensure that medical personnel are present and trained to respond swiftly to emergencies.
4. **Effective Communication:** Develop and rehearse clear communication protocols for event organizers, security teams, and attendees to convey instructions and updates during critical situations.
5. **Thorough Risk Assessment**: Prioritize thorough risk assessments during event planning to identify potential vulnerabilities and address them preemptively.
6. **Public Awareness:** Promote awareness among attendees about the importance of following safety protocols and cooperating with security personnel.
7. **Collaborative Planning:** Encourage collaboration between event organizers, local authorities, and security agencies to enhance safety and security measures.
8. **Community Engagement:** Engage with the local community to foster a sense of shared responsibility for event safety.
9. **Continuous Training:** Ensure that event staff, including security, medical personnel, and ushers, receive ongoing training to remain vigilant and proficient in their roles.
10. **Transparency and Accountability:** Establish clear lines of accountability for safety measures and encourage transparency in incident reporting and investigation.
11. **Artist Team Responsibility:** Artist teams must prioritize the safety of their fans by supporting and cooperating with venue and event organizers on security and crowd management strategies.
12. **Collaborative Security Measures:** Encourage artists to collaborate with security teams to ensure the smooth entry and exit of attendees while maintaining safety protocols.

By implementing these positive changes, we can honor the memory of Rebecca Ikumelo and Gaby Hutchinson. We must work collectively to prevent future tragedies, ensuring that music venues remain spaces of joy and celebration while prioritizing the safety and well-being of all attendees.

Pro Tip: The Golden Rules For Ticket Sales

Mastering the art of ticket sales requires adherence to some golden rules that can make or break your event's success. Here are key pro tips to keep in mind:

Age Limit: Be aware of the age limit for purchasing tickets, as it can be disappointing for customers to be unable to buy tickets after the fact. Although it may not be advertised, it is important to be aware of the age limit.

Ticket Allocation: Determine the number of tickets available for each section during the Pre-Sale. The allocation should take into consideration the customer experience and the goal of the Pre-Sale (e.g. providing access to as many customers as possible, creating a hot ticket, etc.). The allocation should be monitored during the Pre-Sale and adjustments can be made if necessary.

Ticket Pricing: It is not advisable to increase ticket prices during the sale, as this can negatively impact customer perception. If necessary, adjustments should be made before the sale begins.

Check Link: Verify the link for the ticket sale as soon as it becomes available. No one likes to click a link that doesn't work and it reflects poorly on your brand.

Social Media Monitoring: Monitor social media for any issues related to the ticket sale and use social media to communicate with customers and provide assistance.

Ticket Group Limits: Determine the limits for the number of tickets that can be purchased by a single individual or group, in order to prevent ticket scalping.

Ticket Site Availability: Once the tour has been announced, all ticket sites that have agreed to stock tickets should have the link available (although not yet functional until the on-sale). It is important to verify that all information and photos are correct on each site.

Venue And Local Promotion: It is important to verify that the venue and local news outlets have promoted the event.

Listing On Portals: It is advisable to list the show on all personal portals and to add a Pre-Sale and On-Sale event for added visibility. The Pre-Sale Code should be added to the event section for a polished appearance.

Cancelling A Show: If a show must be cancelled, handle the situation professionally and respectfully. Coordinate with the promoter on the announcement strategy. Communicate the cancellation via social media and consider geo-targeting for fans in the immediate area or those traveling to the event. Provide clear and prompt responses to fan inquiries and communicate refund policies or rescheduled date plans clearly.

Working with Marketing Agencies

Working with marketing agencies involves understanding their broad spectrum of services and collective expertise, which can be pivotal in scaling marketing efforts. The foundational principle is to align agency capabilities with business objectives, ensuring that the collaboration drives toward mutual goals.

- **Research Agency Track Record:** Look into the agency's past projects and client testimonials to gauge their experience and success rate.
- **Understand Agency Specializations:** Different agencies specialize in various marketing aspects like digital, print, or social media.
- **Flexibility and Scalability:** Evaluate the agency's ability to adapt to changing project scopes and business needs.

Collaborating with Freelancers

Freelancers offer specialized skills and flexibility, making them valuable assets for targeted projects. The key to successful collaboration with freelancers lies in clear communication of your vision and maintaining a balance between creative freedom and strategic alignment. Making sure that both parties understand and agree on the project scope and outcomes is vital. Review the freelancer's previous work and seek feedback from their past clients. Ensure that you establish preferred methods and frequency of communication to ensure consistent updates.
Open communication is vital across any business so be sure to discuss and agree on intellectual property rights and non-disclosure terms.

Pricing Structures, Negotiations and Deliverables

A crucial aspect of any collaboration is understanding and agreeing on pricing models. Effective negotiation is not about minimizing costs but about recognizing and seeking value in the partnership. Learning negotiation tactics and being open to discussions about pricing and value exchange are essential for establishing a mutually beneficial relationship. Setting clear expectations and a mutual understanding of deliverables from the outset saves time and resources. It involves articulating goals, desired outcomes, and the specifics of what is to be delivered, which is crucial in any collaborative endeavour, whether with an agency or a freelancer.

- **Market Rate Comparison:** Compare the proposed rates with market standards to ensure fairness.
- **Value-Based Pricing:** Consider pricing based on the value and results the agency or freelancer can bring to your business.
- **Long-Term Engagement Discounts:** Explore potential discounts or added value for long-term or repeat collaborations.
- **Detailed Project Briefs:** Provide comprehensive briefs detailing every aspect of what you expect from the project.
- **Progress Milestones:** Set periodic milestones for assessing progress and making necessary adjustments.
- **Revision Policies:** Clarify the number of revisions or edits included in the agreed price.

Key Terms in Marketing Collaborations

Familiarity with industry-specific terms aids better communication and ensures that all parties are on the same page. Understanding these terms is fundamental to enhancing the effectiveness of marketing strategies and ensuring clear discussions about strategies, outcomes, and performance metrics.

- **Conversion Rate (CR):** The percentage of users who take a desired action, crucial in evaluating campaign effectiveness.
- **Customer Acquisition Cost (CAC):** The total cost of acquiring a new customer, important in budgeting and ROI calculations.
- **Engagement Rate:** A measure of audience interaction with content, useful in assessing content effectiveness.

Mastering collaborations with marketing agencies and freelancers requires a blend of clear communication, strategic alignment, effective negotiation, and an understanding of the marketing landscape's key terms and concepts. By adopting these principles, businesses can navigate the complexities of marketing collaborations with confidence, leading to successful partnerships and enhanced market presence.

Pro Tip: Marketing Activations

Marketing activations in the music industry are dynamic strategies designed to interactively promote music-related content, enhancing an artist's brand and engaging their audience. These activations are pivotal for driving brand awareness, sales, and fan engagement. Teams should approach these activations with a focus on strategic innovation and audience-centric thinking. Understanding the goals of the artist and how these align with audience expectations is crucial.

Structuring Marketing Activations

1. **In-Depth Objective Setting**: Begin with a deep dive into the specific objectives of the marketing activation. These objectives should align with the broader marketing strategy and specific goals of the artist or record label. Consider aspects like increasing digital presence, boosting physical album sales, or enhancing the artist's brand image.
2. **Comprehensive Audience Analysis**: Conduct a detailed analysis of the target audience. This involves demographic studies, understanding psychographic profiles, and identifying consumer behaviours. Tailor the activation strategy to meet the audience where they are most active and receptive.
3. **Creative Development and Innovation**: Push the boundaries of conventional marketing tactics. Think beyond traditional media, exploring innovative platforms and technologies like augmented reality, immersive experiences, or viral social media challenges.
4. **Detailed Execution Planning**: This phase should cover every aspect of the activation, from logistical arrangements for physical events to digital campaign timelines. Include contingency planning for potential challenges.
5. **Robust Measurement and Evaluation**: Use advanced analytics tools to measure the impact of the activation. Consider a range of metrics from direct sales to social media engagement and sentiment analysis. Post-campaign analysis is crucial for understanding the effectiveness and for learning lessons for future campaigns.
6. **Post-Implementation Review and Adaptation**: After the execution of the marketing activation, conduct a thorough review to identify successes and areas for improvement. Adaptation and learning from each campaign are essential for continuous improvement in future activations.

Brand Partnerships

Brand partnerships in the music industry play a pivotal role in supporting artists' careers. These partnerships often come into play during marketing activations, serving as a crucial intersection where brands and audiences converge. This collaboration not only offers financial backing and exposure for artists but also allows brands to connect authentically with target audiences through music. Such partnerships are mutually beneficial, enhancing brand image and broadening audience reach for both the artist and the brand. By strategically aligning with compatible brands, artists can significantly amplify their marketing efforts and impact.

The first step involves identifying brands that align well with the artist's image and music style. This alignment ensures a natural and coherent partnership. Establish a clear value exchange between the artist and the brand. This might include financial support, access to new audiences, or co-branding opportunities. Focus on creating high-quality deliverables that benefit both the artist and the brand. This could range from co-branded merchandise to exclusive content or collaborative events. Utilize the partnership to maximize benefits for both parties. This includes leveraging each other's marketing channels, audiences, and resources.

Aim for sustained collaborations rather than one-off deals, as long-term partnerships often yield more significant benefits and greater brand loyalty.

Impact of Marketing Activations

Impact of Marketing Activations: Marketing activations are crucial for amplifying an artist's presence, significantly broadening their audience reach and brand awareness. These activations engage fans more deeply, converting casual listeners into dedicated supporters. The direct result of this heightened engagement can translate to an increase in sales and streaming, contributing significantly to the artist's financial success. Importantly, these activations lay the groundwork for long-term industry recognition and growth, extending their influence far beyond the immediate outcomes.

Effective marketing activations require a harmonious alignment between the artist's identity and the brand's ethos, ensuring genuine and coherent messaging. Customizing these activations to appeal to the specific tastes and interests of the target audience is essential. Incorporating innovative and unique strategies makes these campaigns stand out in a competitive landscape. It's also critical to maintain consistent messaging throughout the campaign to reinforce the artist's brand identity and create a unified marketing narrative.

Case Study: Fredo Unfinished Business Album Launch

In the ever-competitive landscape of music promotion, the Fredo Activation campaign stands out as a paragon of innovative marketing. Orchestrated by Fredo's team and BAYY Agency, a trailblazer in the realm of creative marketing, this campaign showcases a strategic blend of experiential engagement and digital outreach.

Overview of BAYY Agency

BAYY Agency, a dynamic and female-led marketing firm based in London, has carved a niche in the creative world with its unique approach to brand development and marketing. Since its inception, BAYY has been at the forefront of blending traditional marketing techniques with contemporary digital strategies. The agency's founding ethos centres around creating immersive experiences that resonate with target audiences, making them a go-to for brands seeking a creative edge in their marketing campaigns.

Unfinished Business Album Launch

The Fredo Activation was more than a marketing campaign; it was a cultural event that tapped into the pulse of the London music scene. Fredo and his management connected with the BAYY Agency, and were presented with 10 ideas initial ideas, that refined to a final 3 before the concept we saw fully took shape. The objective was to create a buzz around Fredo's latest project, leveraging both the artist's popularity and BAYY's innovative marketing tactics. The campaign centred around a store takeover in a prominent London location, transforming a regular retail space into a branded hub for Fredo's project.

Execution and Crowd Engagement

The execution of the campaign was a masterclass in experiential marketing. Fredo was very hands on, scouting and securing the locations first hand before leaving it to the agency to work their magic. The sites were surveyed to endure they had all of the graphics available, the appropriate spaces for flyposting and how they can keep waste to minimum. BAYY Agency meticulously designed the store to reflect Fredo's artistic style and the theme of his project, with additional merchandise and food available for fans coming to the experience. 7 shops were taken over on his local strip, so this immersive environment was not just about promoting an album; it was about creating a memorable experience that fans could associate with Fredo's music. The activation drew in a significant crowd, and their reaction was spread all across social media.

Media Coverage and Impact

The campaign successfully captured the attention of the press, generating coverage that amplified its impact beyond the physical confines of the store. This media attention played a crucial role in extending the campaign's reach, drawing in a wider audience and contributing to the overall buzz around Fredo's project.

Analysing the Campaign's Success

The success of the Fredo Activation campaign by BAYY Agency can be attributed to several key factors:

- **Community Centric Concept:** The idea of a store takeover in an area synonymous with Fredo and easily accessible for his core fan base, provided a fresh and engaging way to interact with his community. They were giving away food, providing free groceries, and beverages across the day, keeping people in the area and paying back the support he recieves.
- **Effective Execution:** The meticulous planning and execution ensured that every aspect of the campaign aligned with the artist's brand and resonated with the target audience.
- **Integrated Approach:** The combination of experiential marketing with digital and social media strategies created a multifaceted campaign that maximized reach and engagement.
- **Media Leverage:** Utilizing UCG to translate their organic buzz, the team was able to maximise press coverage of the album as all components of the creative execution of the roll out, amplifying the campaign's impact.

The Fredo Activation campaign is a testament to BAYY Agency's ability to push the boundaries of traditional marketing. By creating an experience that was both engaging and reflective of the artist's brand, BAYY managed to not only promote Fredo's project but also to create a lasting impression on fans and attendees. This case study serves as an educational example for marketers and brands aiming to create impactful campaigns that seamlessly integrate experiential and digital marketing strategies.

Pro Tip: The Marketing Plan For A Live Show/Tour

Embarking on a live tour is an exciting endeavour, but its success hinges on effective marketing. To ensure your tour aligns seamlessly with your brand image, core values, and music releases, it's vital to plan your marketing meticulously. Here's a 3-part marketing strategy that combines the best practices of major headliners and emerging artists, ensuring that your live show or tour becomes an unforgettable musical spectacle.

1. Generate Anticipation and Buzz:
- **Teaser Campaigns:** Create visually captivating teasers to showcase unique show elements. Release them strategically on social media platforms. Your tour should be a reflection of your music brand, with a cohesive visual identity. Make sure to provide the tour promoter with a complete marketing package that includes recent press shots, tour details, and any relevant branding elements such as logos.
- **Fan Involvement:** Engage fans with interactive Q&A sessions, contests, and polls. Build anticipation by involving them in show-related decisions.
- **Collaborate with Influencers:** Partner with local influencers and opening acts to expand your reach. Encourage them to share the excitement on their platforms.
- **Strategic Email Marketing:** Utilize email marketing to keep fans informed about tour updates, exclusive content, and ticket sales.
- **Event Listings:** List your show on event platforms to ensure fans can easily discover and access ticket information.

2. Cultivate Fan Connections and Hype:
- **Personalized Engagement:** Respond to fan comments and DMs, and send personalized show invites. Make your fans feel heard and valued.
- **Fan Meetups:** Organize pre-show fan meetups or gatherings to foster a sense of community and excitement.
- **Exclusive Merchandise:** Design tour-exclusive merchandise to give fans something special to look forward to.
- **Storytelling:** Share personal stories and emotions through your content to deepen the emotional connection with your audience.
- **Fan-Generated Content**: Encourage fans to create and share content related to the tour, like fan art or cover songs.

3. Drive Ticket Sales Efficiently:
- **Targeted Advertising:** Use targeted ads on social media and other platforms to reach potential attendees based on demographics and interests.
- **Mobile-Friendly Ticketing:** Ensure the ticketing platform is mobile-friendly for easy purchasing, as many fans use mobile devices.
- **Collaborative Promotion:** Collaborate with opening acts and co-headliners for cross-promotion, tapping into each other's fan bases.
- **Frequent Updates:** Continuously update fans on ticket availability and deadlines to create a sense of urgency. Despite clear instructions, some fans may still face confusion. Having multiple pieces of accompanying artwork ready, whether it's elaborative visuals or simple text blocks, will help you address and rectify any uncertainties efficiently

By following these marketing strategies, you'll not only create a buzz around your live show or tour but also ensure that your audience is well-informed, engaged, and excited to be part of your musical journey.

Case Study: Lancey's Immersive Experience

Lancey is a rising UK artist who in 2022, released the album, "LIFE IN HELL". To promote the album, he wanted to create a live experience that would leave a lasting impression on his fans. With the help of his team, he developed a plan to create a unique and immersive live experience that would capture the essence of his new album.

The challenge for Lancey and his team was to create a live experience that would set his latest project apart from other concerts and live shows. They needed to create an experience that would make fans feel like they were a part of the album and that would leave a lasting impression on them.

Lancey and his team decided to create an experience that would take fans on a journey through the themes and emotions of the new album. They started by selecting a unique venue that would fit the vibe of the album, a large cathedral with an industrial and gritty feel. The team then worked on transforming the space into an immersive experience, using lighting, video projections, and live performers to bring the album to life. Fans were greeted by massive visuals inspired by the album's themes, building on the world that Lancey had built sonically and creating a sense of anticipation and excitement for more areas of the experience.

As fans made their way downstairs and through the purple lit space, they encountered live performers who acted out scenes inspired by the album's lyrics. These performers included dancers, actors, and even a spoken word poet who performed some of the album's spoken word interludes. The highlight of the experience was the live performance by Lancey himself. He performed the album in its entirety, backed by a live band and a team of dancers. The performance was enhanced by the immersive lighting and visuals, which changed in response to the music and lyrics. Overall, the live experience was a huge success for Lancey and his team, and helped to elevate his latest project to new heights. It showed that with creativity and planning, it is possible to create a live experience that truly captures the essence of an album and leaves a lasting impression on fans.

Upcoming artists can learn a lot from the success of immersive experiences in creating a unique brand. Here are a few key takeaways:

Embrace Practical Creativity: Immersive experiences allow artists to think outside the box and create a unique world for their fans to immerse themselves in. Keep things practical by finding locations that require minimal structural changes to communicate the world you're creating. By embracing creativity and pushing the boundaries of what's possible, artists can differentiate themselves from the competition and create a truly unique brand.

Connect With Your Audience: Immersive experiences allow artists to connect with their audience in a deeper and more meaningful way. Find the best moments on a project that fans will love and sculpt the experience around them. By creating a world that fans can fully immerse themselves in, artists can foster a sense of community with shared ideals and belonging among their audience.

Use Technology To Your Advantage: Technology has made it easier than ever to create immersive experiences that transport fans to a different world. From VR to AR to interactive installations, there are endless possibilities for creating immersive experiences.

Consistency Is Key: A unique brand is only effective if it's consistent across all touchpoints. Artists should ensure that their immersive experiences align with their overall brand and messaging to create a cohesive and memorable experience for fans. This can be reflected in the colours, styling, visuals and more. Look for the red thread that ties the whole project through to each point a fan may engage with your brand.

Collaborate With Experts: Creating an immersive experience requires expertise in a variety of areas, from technology to design to storytelling. Upcoming artists should look to collaborate or hire experts in these fields to create an experience that truly stands out and captures the attention of fans.

Action Plan For Creating Affordable Immersive Experiences

Determine Your Budget: The first step is to determine how much money you have available to create the immersive experience. This will help you to identify which elements are feasible to include and which are not.

Choose The Right Venue: Select a venue that suits the experience you want to create. It doesn't have to be a huge space, but it should have the right atmosphere and be large enough to accommodate your audience.

Use Technology Creatively: You don't have to break the bank to create a unique immersive experience. Use technology creatively, such as projection mapping, interactive lighting, and soundscapes to create an immersive environment that will transport your audience to another world.

Partner With Other Creatives: Collaborate with other artists, performers, and creatives to bring your vision to life. You can share costs and ideas, and create a more impactful and memorable experience.

Focus On The Details: Attention to detail is key when creating an immersive experience. Consider every element of the experience, including lighting, sound, set design, costumes, and props, and make sure they all work together to create a cohesive and unforgettable experience. It's important to create a believable world that will allow the audience to forget they're in a performance space.

Interactivity: Interactivity is another crucial component of an immersive experience. It allows the audience to become an active participant in the experience, rather than just a passive observer. Interactive experiences allow the audience to feel like they're a part of the world and engage with the performance.

Get Feedback: After the event, ask for feedback from attendees to understand what worked and what could be improved. This will help you to refine and improve future experiences.

Market Creatively: Finally, market your immersive experience creatively. Use social media and other online platforms to create buzz and generate interest. Consider offering early bird tickets or other incentives to encourage people to attend.

Here are a few nuances that can elevate the immersive experience

Narrative: Narrative is an important part of any immersive experience. A well-crafted story will help to immerse the audience in the experience and make it feel more real. It's important to have a clear and engaging narrative that will keep the audience engaged throughout the entire experience.

Multi-Sensory Experience: The use of multiple senses can also enhance the immersive experience. By engaging multiple senses, such as sight, sound, smell, and touch, the audience can feel more connected to the experience.

Personalization: Personalization can help create a unique experience for each individual audience member. Personalization can be achieved through the use of technology, such as virtual and augmented reality, or by creating different pathways and choices for the audience to make throughout the experience.

By focusing on these nuances, upcoming artists can create immersive experiences that are affordable but still highly effective in engaging and captivating audiences. Additionally, it's important to consider the target audience and their interests when creating an immersive experience, as well as utilizing feedback and data from previous events to continually improve the experience.

CHAPTER 8
INNOVATION IN THE INDUSTRY

Blockchain And The Music Business

Emerging technology is changing the game, especially in the music. It has undergone a significant transformation in the past few decades, largely driven by the digital revolution. Nowadays, streaming services like Spotify, Apple Music, and YouTube have made it easier than ever for fans to discover and listen to music from all around the world. However, as with any major change, this transformation has also come with its own set of challenges.

As touched on earlier one of the biggest challenges that artists and music professionals face is the issue of royalties and compensation. Historically, the traditional model has involved a complex web of intermediaries, including record labels, distributors, and music publishers, all taking a cut of an artist's revenue. While this model may have worked in the past, many people now believe that it is outdated and in need of a major overhaul.

This is where blockchain technology comes in. In recent years, there has been a growing interest in the music industry using blockchain to create a more transparent and fair system for compensating artists and other stakeholders.

One of the most promising applications of blockchain in the music business is in the area of crowdfunding. Traditionally, fans have supported artists by buying their records, streaming their music, going to their concerts, and buying their merchandise. However, in most cases, the revenue from these activities ends up going to a record label or other intermediary, rather than directly to the artist.

Blockchain-based crowdfunding platforms offer a potential solution to this problem. These platforms use cryptocurrency to facilitate direct transfers of value between fans and artists, while NFTs and smart contracts ensure that all transactions are accurately recorded and enforceable. One example of such a platform is Decent, which allows fans to directly fund artists' projects in exchange for a share of the revenue generated. Another platform, Audius, uses a token-based system that rewards users for interacting with artists and sharing playlists with other users.
The key benefit of these platforms is that they remove intermediaries and enable artists to receive direct funding from their fans. In addition, they create a more direct and engaged relationship between artists and their audience, which can help to build a stronger and more loyal fan base over time.

NFTS

NFTs, or non-fungible tokens, have been a hot topic in the industry in recent years, with some hailing them as a potential game-changer for artists, while others view them with scepticism. At their core, NFTs are digital assets that use blockchain technology to verify ownership and authenticity. They have been used to sell everything from art to tweets, and now music.

NFTs have the potential to impact the music business by offering a new way for artists to sell unique and exclusive digital merchandise directly to fans. While there are valid concerns about the environmental impact of blockchain technology and the potential for overinflated prices, there is still room for NFTs to benefit the industry as better systems are developed and adopted.

As with any new technology, it will take time to fully understand its potential and limitations, but it is clear that NFTs have already made an impact on the music industry and will continue to do so in the future.

Tickets: An area where blockchain technology is showing promise is ticketing. Fraud and scalping have long been a problem, with many fans falling victim to scams and fraudulent practices. Blockchain-based ticketing systems offer a potential solution to this problem by using NFTs to create unique, verifiable digital tickets. By using NFTs, event organizers can ensure that each ticket is unique and cannot be duplicated or sold multiple times.

Collectibles: Blockchain technology is also being used to create digital collectibles. Memorabilia has long been a major part of the music, with collectors around the world paying top dollar for rare and historic items. With blockchain, it is now possible to create digital representations of these items using NFTs. This allows collectors to own a piece of music history in a digital format, with all the benefits of blockchain, including authenticity and verifiability.

One example of this is the recent auction of Julian Lennon's NFTs based on Beatles memorabilia from his personal collection. Another example is the collaboration between Kings of Leon and Yellow Heart, which created NFT collectibles for their latest album release. By creating digital collectibles, artists and the rights holders can tap into a new market of collectors who are interested in owning rare and unique items but may not have the means to purchase physical memorabilia. In addition, the use of blockchain technology ensures that each item is unique and verifiable, which adds value and authenticity to the collectibles.

THE BEATLES   KINGS OF LEON   AITCH

THE WEEKND   GRIMES

Case Study: Ard Adz And His NFT Release On Opulous

In 2022, Ard Adz, a prominent UK rapper, partnered with Opulous to release an NFT-backed music ownership campaign. The campaign aimed to allow fans to own a portion of the song's copyright revenue, The campaign also came with exclusive perks and collectibles, including generative artwork NFTs.

Ard Adz has been a fiercely independent artist throughout his career, turning down many label offers. He gained recognition for blending the lyrical style of hip-hop's golden age with the sounds and flows of his home city, London's famed Brixton rap scene. His debut album, Adam, dropped in 2018, landing on the Official Indie Album Breakers Chart. In 2019, Ard Adz rocked streaming platforms with his notable singles "Saudi" and "Habibti," which went viral, garnering millions of YouTube views.

In 2022, Ard Adz embraced the potential of NFTs and partnered with Opulous to release an NFT-backed music ownership campaign. Opulous is a platform that allows musicians to offer fans a share of their music ownership via NFTs.

The Release Campaign: Opulous announced Ard Adz's NFT-backed music ownership campaign in March 2022. The campaign featured exclusive new track "Patek Myself" and was set to launch on Thursday, March 31st. Fans who purchased the Music MFT would earn a portion of the song's royalty revenue alongside Ard Adz. The higher the investment amount, the larger the share of music royalties the fans owned.

Opulous also offered exclusive perks and collectibles for the campaign, including generative artwork NFTs. The Ard Adz NFT Collection included 500 pieces. The generative artwork NFTs were a unique feature of the Opulous ecosystem. The NFTs were built on the Algorand blockchain and offered amazing perks and experiences to fans. Perks included tickets to headline shows, customized speakers, one-on-one Zoom calls, and even studio hangout sessions with Ard Adz. Opulous worked with some of the hottest digital art design teams in the world to craft the NFTs, making each artwork unique.

The Ard Adz NFT-backed music ownership campaign was a success. The campaign raised £50,000, and fans who purchased the Music MFT owned a portion of the song's copyright revenue alongside Ard Adz. The higher the investment amount, the larger the share of music royalties the fans owned. Opulous's generative artwork NFTs were also popular, with fans enjoying the exclusive perks and experiences that came with them

The campaign was a win for Ard Adz as well. He had always been a fiercely independent artist, turning down many label offers throughout his career. The campaign allowed him to share ownership with his fans rather than give it over to a label. He also enjoyed working with the NFT buyers to help push his release, which was an exciting part of the campaign for him.

The Ard Adz NFT-backed music ownership campaign on Opulous proved to be a successful venture for both the artist and the platform. Ard Adz's decision to partner with Opulous was an innovative move that allowed him to share ownership of his music with his fans, providing them with a unique opportunity to become co-owners of his intellectual property.

The industry is constantly evolving, and blockchain technology is poised to play an increasingly important role in shaping its future. By creating more direct and transparent systems for funding, ticketing, and collecting, blockchain has the potential to revolutionize the way the industry operates and benefits all stakeholders involved. As with any new technology, there are still many challenges and questions to be addressed. However, the potential benefits of blockchain for the music business are too significant to ignore. It will be exciting to see how this technology continues to develop and transform the industry in the years to come.

AI For Musicians

The use of Artificial Intelligence (AI) is increasingly becoming a part of our everyday lives. AI-powered applications, such as ChatGPT, have become household names due to the vast possibilities of data creation. This technology presents both opportunities and threats to human creators and musicians.

AI's rapid growth has sparked divergent opinions among artists and music professionals. While some condemn the use of technology, others argue that AI fuels creativity and pushes music in new directions.

The Impact Of AI On The Industry

AI is already transforming the way we create and consume music. Streaming companies have been utilizing AI for a few years now to provide personalized recommendations, create custom playlists, and suggest new tracks. For instance, Spotify's algorithmic playlists base their recommendations on user listening history and activity.

However, AI is not just for big streaming companies; musicians are also utilizing AI tools to create their music and accompanying artwork. Google researchers have even created AI that can produce full musical pieces from text prompts, demonstrating the technology's capabilities. One significant advantage of AI is that it removes cost barriers for independent musicians. AI tools offer an inexpensive alternative to traditional music creation, allowing unestablished musicians to compose, produce, and master their music from the comfort of their homes. With AI, it is easier than ever to write and publish music on streaming platforms.

As AI continues to develop, we can expect even more AI involvement, such as the introduction of more virtual reality events and experiences.

How Musicians Can Use AI

The disruption of AI has opened up new avenues of music creation in recent years. AI apps can suggest lyrics, develop album artwork, master tracks, or do anything else required. However, relying on AI in every aspect of music production may take away the art of being an independent musician, replacing individual creativity and talent. As long as musicians apply a healthy amount of personal flair to their projects, AI tools can enhance their raw talents and provide useful inspiration and starting points.

How To Produce Music With AI

As with every introduction of ground-breaking technology, AI provides the latest generation of musicians with a new base to develop their sound. AI-generated music may lack originality, but it can provide artists with a solid composition to work with. AI production tools now enable producers to generate melodies, basslines, and synth sounds all within the context of their creations. AI can identify new melodic or harmonic ideas that the composer might not have thought of, generate new ideas instantly, and create music beyond the musician's skill level.

How To Master Music With AI

AI has significantly advanced the process of music mastering, offering increased efficiency and improved sound quality. Tools like LANDR use AI to automatically master tracks, providing options for different styles and loudness levels. Other tools such as Izotope Ozone 10 offer AI-powered presets and intelligent processing, enhancing the mastering process and providing useful hints for improvement. These AI mastering tools ensure consistency, reliability, and enhanced listening experience, making music production more accessible and cost-effective for a broader range of artists.

How To Write Songs Using AI

AI is increasingly being used to assist in songwriting, helping to overcome creative blocks by suggesting rhymes and providing inspiration. Tools like Orb Producer Suite offer AI MIDI generator plugins for chords, melody, bass, and arpeggio, allowing for both quick pattern randomization and advanced customization. Other AI drum sequencers like Playbeat automatically create drum patterns, offering infinite variations for rhythmic phrases. These tools help artists quickly generate ideas and provide a foundation for further creative exploration.

How To Use AI To Create Album Artwork

AI technology is now capable of generating bespoke designs for album artwork and merch items based on briefed keywords. Adobe's Sensei AI technology, for instance, can create unique designs tailored to artist specifications. Additionally, AI can analyze music to generate visuals that sync with it, offering a unique visual experience for live shows and music videos. This application of AI in visual art creation opens up new possibilities for artists to visually represent their music in innovative ways.

12 AI Tools For Music Production

1. Amper Music
2. AIVA
3. AI Mastering
4. Amadeus Code
5. Artisto
6. Endel
7. Google Magenta
8. Humtap
9. Jukedeck
10. LANDR
11. Melodrive
12. AI Music Composition

Pro Tip: Custom GPTS

Music-oriented Generative Pretrained Transformers (GPTs) are AI-driven tools designed to assist in various aspects of the music industry. They leverage machine learning to generate creative content, such as lyrics and song ideas, and can also interact with fans or provide music theory insights. These GPTs are trained with extensive music-related data, enabling them to function effectively in tasks like song writing assistance, fan engagement, and educational support for musicians. Their integration into music creation and promotion represents a blend of technology and artistry, offering innovative solutions and support for artists and the music community.

Custom GPT bots for musicians can be designed for a variety of innovative use cases, enhancing the interaction between artists and their audiences and streamlining various aspects of their musical journey:

1. **Fan Interaction and Engagement:** Custom GPT bots can be programmed to interact with fans on social media platforms and websites. They can answer fan queries, provide information about upcoming shows or releases, and even engage in casual conversations, thereby enhancing fan engagement and building a stronger artist-fan relationship.
2. **Lyric and Song writing Assistance:** Musicians can use GPT bots as a creative tool for song writing. These bots can suggest lyrics, rhymes, and even help with song structures based on the artist's style or a given theme. They can be a valuable tool for overcoming writer's block or for brainstorming new ideas.
3. **Personalized Marketing and Promotions:** GPT bots can be tailored to handle marketing campaigns by sending personalized messages, updates about new music or merchandise, and concert announcements to fans. They can analyze user interactions to create more effective and targeted promotional content.
4. **Educational Tool for Aspiring Musicians:** These bots can be educational resources, providing tips on music production, song writing, or even music theory. They can be programmed to answer questions or provide tutorials and resources for learning various aspects of music creation and production.
5. **Managing Bookings and Schedules:** GPT bots can assist in managing an artist's schedule, coordinating bookings for shows or studio sessions. They can interact with event organizers, manage calendar entries, and send reminders to the artist, helping to streamline the logistical aspects of a music career.
6. **Real-Time Performance Assistance:** During live performances, GPT bots can assist with real-time lyrics display, setlist management, or even interact with the audience through screens. They can enhance live shows by providing interactive content or trivia about the artist.
7. **Content Creation for Social Media:** These bots can assist in generating content for social media, such as drafting posts, creating basic graphics, or even suggesting content strategies based on trending topics and fan interactions.
8. **Analytics and Feedback:** Custom GPT bots can analyze streaming data, social media engagement, and other metrics to provide insights to the artist. They can help in understanding fan demographics, popular songs, and regions where the artist is trending, aiding in strategic planning.

The development and implementation of such GPT bots require careful planning to ensure they align with the artist's brand and effectively meet the intended purposes. Collaborating with AI experts and developers is crucial in creating a bot that is both functional and reflective of the artist's unique style and needs.

Pro Tip: Staying Up-To-Date On Industry Trends

Staying up-to-date on industry trends and developments is a crucial aspect of success. The landscape of the music business is constantly evolving, and being aware of these changes is essential for artists and professionals to adapt and thrive. There are various compelling reasons why staying informed is of utmost importance:

The Benefits:
1. Seizing Opportunities: The industry's constant transformation brings forth fresh possibilities and challenges. Staying tuned in equips individuals to anticipate and seize these opportunities, fostering career growth.
2. A Competitive Edge: With countless players vying for the limelight, industry insights provide a competitive advantage. A deep grasp of trends and best practices sets individuals apart in a crowded arena, showcasing their relevance and expertise.
3. Informed Decision-Making: From choosing the right distribution platform to crafting innovative marketing strategies, trend awareness forms the bedrock of informed decision-making. It ensures a solid foundation for plotting one's career trajectory.
4. Strategic Planning: Understanding the industry's current landscape empowers strategic planning. This knowledge enables individuals to position themselves strategically, harnessing emerging trends and navigating potential roadblocks.
5. Remaining Relevant: The music landscape shapes audience preferences, consumption habits, and artist opportunities. Staying attuned ensures that artists and professionals remain relevant, adapting their approaches to resonate with their target audience.
6. A Well of Inspiration: Learning from the triumphs and innovations of peers can spark creative ideas. Drawing inspiration from others' achievements helps individuals refine their craft and produce fresh, compelling content.

The Consequences of Falling Behind: Not staying updated can lead to missed opportunities, outdated strategies, and a diminished competitive edge. It may result in artists and professionals being out of sync with their audience's preferences and industry shifts, hindering their growth and impact.

Methods to Stay Current:
1. Industry News Outlets: Following trusted industry news outlets, music publications, and online resources provides valuable insights and updates.
2. Networking Events: Participating in conferences, workshops, and networking events fosters knowledge exchange and learning from industry peers and experts.
3. Music and Digital Trends: Understanding how technology impacts music consumption, distribution, and marketing is critical in the digital age. Adapting to these changes optimizes digital presence and audience reach.

Understanding how technology impacts music consumption, distribution, and marketing can help artists and professionals optimize their digital presence and reach a wider audience. By staying engaged and knowledgeable, individuals can better understand the challenges and opportunities in the industry, positioning themselves for sustained success and growth.

Case Study: Tencent Music Entertainment's AI-generated Vocal Tracks

The use of artificial intelligence (AI) in music production has rapidly advanced in recent years, with the technology being used to create not only instrumental music but also vocal tracks that mimic human voices.

In September 2022, Tencent Music Entertainment (TME) announced that it had created and released over 1,000 tracks containing vocals created by its patented voice synthesis technology, the Lingyin Engine. This technology can "quickly and vividly replicate singers' voices to produce original songs of any style and language". TME's use of the Lingyin Engine has involved developing synthetic voices in memory of legendary artists such as Teresa Teng and Anita Mui, and creating an AI singer lineup with the voices of currently active stars such as Yang Chaoyue.

TME aims to create original songs with hyper-realistic and expressive AI-generated vocals that are indistinguishable from those of real humans. The company's use of the Lingyin Engine has allowed it to pay tribute to legendary artists and expand its artist line-up with AI-generated voices.

TME rolled out the Lingyin Engine during the three months to the end of September 2022, creating and releasing over 1,000 tracks with human-style vocals manufactured by the technology. One of those tracks, which appears to be called "Today", has become the first song by an AI singer to be streamed over 100 million times across the internet. TME has also created an AI singer line-up with the voices of trending stars such as Yang Chaoyue.

TME's use of the Lingyin Engine has enabled it to create original songs with AI-generated vocals that are highly popular with audiences. The company's track "Today" has surpassed 100 million streams, indicating a strong demand for music with AI-generated vocals. By developing synthetic voices in memory of legendary artists and creating an AI singer lineup with the voices of currently active stars, TME has also expanded its artist lineup and paid tribute to artists who are no longer alive.

TME's use of the Lingyin Engine has shown the potential for AI-generated music to become a significant part of the music business. As the technology advances, AI-generated music could enable artists to create content without requiring them to record audio live in person, as demonstrated by the example of BTS using Supertone's AI voice-creation platform. Other companies such as ByteDance are also betting big on AI-powered music-making, indicating a growing trend towards the use of AI in music production. As audiences continue to embrace AI-generated music, it will be interesting to see how the technology develops and its impact on the music industry.

Case Study: JME's Alternative Approach To Trends In Music

JME, the grime innovator, has always been a unique presence in the UK music scene. He has built his career by staying true to himself and his musical vision, even when the industry has tried to steer him in different directions.

His 2019 album, 'Grime MC,' is a testament to his independent spirit and his refusal to be influenced by current trends. One of the standout features of 'Grime MC' is that it is a physical-only album. In an age where music is primarily consumed through streaming platforms, JME has opted to release his album on vinyl and CD. He believes that music should be tangible, something that you can hold in your hands and cherish. To accompany the album, JME has also released a limited edition book of photographs, held cinema screenings, and set up a pop-up pirate radio station on London's Carnaby Street. He wants the album to be more than just a collection of songs; he wants it to be an experience for his fans.

This desire to create something unique and special is a hallmark of JME's career. He has always been fiercely independent, rejecting the influence of industry executives and staying true to his roots. This is evident in the music itself, which is a straight-up grime album that rarely strays from 140bpm. The beats come produced by Preditah and JME himself, and his bars are as direct as ever, coming in hard and to-the-point. There are exciting moments of real brilliance too, such as 'Knock Your Block Off,' 'Nang,' and the frenetic 'Dem Man Are Dead,' which already have the potential to join the canon of grime staples.

The album's list of features reads like a who's who of grime and UK rap royalty. P Money, Shakka, Giggs, President T, Wiley, Merky Ace, and Skepta all make appearances, but JME is never overshadowed. It's a testament to his influence that he's able to pull in such heavy hitters, but it's also a testament to his talents on the mic that he can hold his own. It's yet another reminder of JME's resistance to change. At a time when others are looking to get the next big thing on a track in order to benefit from the association, JME looks to his left and right, working with grime's veterans instead.

JME's message is clear: he is making music for himself and his community. He is not interested in chasing trends or pleasing industry executives. He is making the music he loves, and he hopes that his fans will love it too. 'Grime MC' is a celebration of grime music and its culture, and it's a reminder that sometimes the best way to make an impact is to stay true to yourself. His most recent collaboration with the UK Alt hip hop pioneers, House of Pharaohs, indicates his continued relevance and influence in the UK music scene. His work remains a testament to his staying power and the enduring response to his projects.

CHAPTER 9
SOCIAL AND POLITICAL AWARNESS

Social And Political Awareness

Social and political awareness refers to an understanding of and engagement with social and political issues and their impact on society. In the music industry, social and political awareness can be expressed through the lyrics and themes of music, as well as through the actions and activism of artists.

Music has a long history of being used as a platform for activism and social change, and many artists have used their platform to raise awareness about important issues and inspire action. In the UK, music has played a significant role in social and political movements, from the anti-war movement of the 1960s to the Black Lives Matter protests of recent years. In addition to using their music as a platform for activism, many artists in the UK also use their influence to engage with social and political issues in other ways, such as through their charitable work or by using their social media platforms to raise awareness about important issues.

Social and political awareness plays a significant role in the music sector, and many artists use their platform and influence to promote social and political change and raise awareness about important issues.

Using Music As Platform For Activism

Using music as a platform for activism can be a powerful way for artists to raise awareness about important issues and inspire change. Music has the ability to reach and connect with people in a way that other forms of communication may not, and it can be an effective tool for raising awareness and inspiring action.

There are many ways in which artists can use their platform to make a positive impact, including: Using lyrics to address social and political issues: Artists can use their lyrics to raise awareness about important issues and inspire change. For example, they can write songs about social justice, environmental issues, or human rights and use their music as a means of promoting change. This can be done creatively, mixing the medicine with the meal as the old adage goes.

Engaging With Social Media: Many artists have large followings on social media, and they can use their platforms to raise awareness about important issues and inspire their followers to take action.

Partnering With Organizations: Artists can partner with organizations that are working on social and political issues they care about and use their platform to promote and support the work of these organizations.

Participating In Protests And Other Forms Of Activism: Artists can use their platform to support and participate in protests and other forms of activism, helping to raise awareness about important issues and inspire change.

Using music as a platform for activism is a powerful way for artists to make a positive impact and inspire change. By using their music and platform to address social and political issues, artists can reach and connect with people in a meaningful way and inspire them to take action.

Ethics And Social Responsibility

Ethics refers to the moral principles and values that guide the behaviour of individuals and organizations in the industry, and social responsibility refers to the ways in which the industry can contribute to the well-being and development of society. Some key aspects of ethics and social responsibility in the music industry include:

Ethical Principles And Values: Ethics is grounded in a set of principles and values that guide the behaviour of individuals and organizations in the industry. These principles and values can include respect for the rights and interests of others, fairness and equity, honesty and integrity, and responsibility and accountability.

Ethical Decision-Making: Ethics in the industry also involves the application of ethical principles and values to the decision-making processes of individuals and organizations. This can involve identifying and analysing ethical dilemmas and challenges, and using ethical frameworks and tools to make informed and responsible decisions.

Social Responsibility: The music business also has a responsibility to contribute to the well-being and development of society. This can involve supporting social and environmental causes, promoting diversity and inclusion, and engaging with local communities and stakeholders. By taking a proactive and responsible approach to social responsibility, the industry can make a positive contribution to society.

The Impact Of The Industry On Society And The Environment

The music industry's impact on society and the environment is multifaceted and significant. Positively, music acts as a powerful tool for cultural and social enrichment. It not only offers a platform for artistic expression and creativity but also serves as a medium for communal bonding and shared experiences. Music's capacity to convey messages and emotions transcends language barriers, fostering global connections and understanding. Moreover, it can be a formidable force in supporting social causes and raising awareness about crucial issues, thus playing a role in societal change and advocacy.

In terms of social and cultural aspects, while the industry offers immense opportunities, it can also perpetuate inequalities. Access to resources, platforms, and representation in the business is not always equitable, leading to disparities in who gets to produce and distribute music. This can reflect and reinforce broader social and cultural inequalities.

The industry also faces challenges, particularly in terms of its environmental footprint. The production and distribution of physical music media, along with the energy consumption of digital streaming services, contribute to carbon emissions. Large-scale live events and tours, while culturally significant, often have considerable environmental impacts, including resource consumption and waste generation.

In addressing these challenges, the industry is seeing growing efforts towards sustainability and inclusivity. Initiatives to reduce the environmental impact of music production and events are being implemented, and there is an increasing focus on ensuring diversity and equality within the industry.

Engaging With Social And Political Issues

In the ever-evolving landscape, ethics and social responsibility stand as guiding stars for both artists and organizations. These principles shape behaviour, decisions, and contributions to society. At its core, ethics embodies fundamental values such as respect for others' rights, fairness, integrity, and accountability. It's the moral compass that defines the industry's character.

Ethics isn't a static concept but a dynamic force that influences decision-making. In the music industry, ethical considerations play a vital role in navigating complex challenges. Artists and organizations grapple with dilemmas, and ethical frameworks aid in making principled and responsible choices. It's about applying these moral foundations to real-world scenarios, ensuring that actions align with values.

Social responsibility transcends profit margins, urging the music business to be a positive force in society. Beyond the entertainment it provides, music can champion social and environmental causes, promote diversity and inclusion, and engage with local communities. This proactive stance fosters a symbiotic relationship between the industry and society, enriching both.
Yet, the industry's impact isn't one-dimensional. Music's reach can uplift societies culturally and socially, offering creative outlets for artists and entertainment for audiences. Conversely, it can also have detrimental effects, contributing to environmental degradation and exacerbating social and cultural inequalities. Recognizing these dualities is essential in steering the industry toward responsible practices.

It's important to acknowledge that the industry's actions can also contribute to social and cultural inequality. Certain genres or artists may receive more prominence, and biases may persist. The industry's power to influence societal perceptions and preferences underscores its responsibility to counterbalance inequalities.

Ethics and social responsibility are not abstract ideals but guiding principles that shape the global music scene. They empower stakeholders to make ethical decisions, contribute positively to society, and harness music's potential for good. By navigating the intricate interplay of ethics, social responsibility, and artistic expression, the industry can harmonize its dual role as a creative powerhouse and a responsible global citizen.

Representation

In the UK's music scene, there has been noteworthy progress in enhancing the presence and involvement of Black, Asian, and minority ethnic groups, particularly among younger artists. A survey highlighted that these groups represent a significant percentage of artists in the younger demographic. However, the music sector still faces challenges in ensuring equitable representation, especially in higher-level positions.

One key issue is the disproportionate representation of minority groups in executive roles. Reports have shown that a minimal percentage of senior executive roles are held by individuals from these backgrounds. This imbalance can lead to a gap in understanding the unique challenges faced by minority communities in the music domain.

Furthermore, minority artists often encounter limited opportunities for advancement. Surveys indicate a disparity in the number of senior positions held by minority individuals compared to their white peers, and a lower likelihood of promotion. In response, industry bodies have set ambitious diversity targets for executive bodies and boards, aiming to create a more inclusive environment.

Efforts to address these issues are ongoing. Notable changes in award categories by prominent music awards reflect a shift towards a more diverse and inclusive recognition system, offering more opportunities for minority artists. However, other challenges persist, particularly for older women in the industry, who face obstacles in representation and career progression. The accessibility of certain award categories for female artists also remains a concern.

Artists from minority backgrounds may also struggle with limited access to industry networks and face stereotyping and typecasting, which can restrict their creative expression and career opportunities. Additionally, racial bias and discrimination remain significant barriers.

To foster a more equitable and diverse music landscape, initiatives are underway to increase minority representation in leadership roles. These steps are vital in achieving a music environment where diverse voices and talents are acknowledged and celebrated. The growing audience demand for diverse music serves as a strong incentive for the sector to support and promote a wide range of talents.

Case Study: The Impact Of Childish Gambino's "This Is America"

Donald Glover, popularly known as Childish Gambino, released his music video "This Is America" in May 2018, and it immediately went viral, amassing 10 million views in just 24 hours. The video presents a powerful commentary on American culture, gun violence, and racism.

It features Glover dancing around an escalating riot, all while hiding the real chaos happening behind him. The music video has sparked a national conversation about the state of race relations in America, and its impact is far-reaching.

The music video opens with a choir singing "We Just Wanna Party," which is juxtaposed with the sound of gunfire. This is a powerful reminder that Americans can no longer afford to ignore the gun violence that plagues the country. Glover's use of the choir also highlights the fact that black people are often the ones most affected by gun violence as it is a direct and in-your-face reference to the 2015 Charleston, South Carolina massacre in which white supremacist Dylann Roof opened fire in a black church. .

The video features a series of dances that have become popular on YouTube, such as the "shoot" dance. Glover and his dancers perform these dances as a distraction from the chaos happening in the background. The use of dance as a distraction is a commentary on how Americans often use entertainment as an escape from the harsh realities of their lives. At the same time, the use of dance is also a reminder of how black culture has been appropriated and commercialized by the mainstream entertainment industry.

Glover's use of exaggerated poses and grotesque smiles has been interpreted as a reference to the Jim Crow era minstrel shows, comedic performances of "blackness" by whites in exaggerated costumes and make-up. The use of these images highlights the ongoing impact of racism in America. The line "Grandma told me: get your money, black man" is a commentary on how black people are often expected to perform stereotypical roles to earn money. Glover's decision to gun down the gospel choir is a powerful statement about how black performers are often expected to stay spiritually uplifted in the face of gun violence and racism.

The line "this a celly / that's a tool" has a double meaning. On the one hand, it refers to the case of Stephon Clark, who was shot dead by Sacramento police while holding an iPhone. The line is a commentary on how black men are often seen as a threat by the police. On the other hand, the line could also be interpreted as a call to use phones as a tool for documenting police brutality.

Childish Gambino's "This Is America" is a powerful commentary on American culture, gun violence, and racism. The music video has sparked a national conversation about these issues and has had a far-reaching impact on American culture. It has brought attention to the ongoing struggles of black people in America and has challenged Americans to confront their biases and prejudices. The video is a reminder that music can be a powerful tool for social change, and that artists have a responsibility to use their platforms to effect change in the world.

Case Study: The Met Police And YouTube's Efforts To Monitor And Remove Music Videos Of Rap And Drill Artists

Rap and drill music have been an integral part of the UK music scene, has been a hub for artists creating this genre of music. However, the police have been actively monitoring the music produced by these artists and referring music videos to be taken down from YouTube.

The Metropolitan Police has referred 510 music videos to be removed from YouTube in 2021, marking a significant increase from the previous years. The Met's Focus on Linking Rap Videos and Violent Crime: The police have been linking rap videos and violent crime since 2015, when the Operation Domain team was formed to monitor YouTube for videos *"that incite violence."* The FOI data reveals the Metropolitan Police's continued focus on linking rap music and violence, and their willingness to work with YouTube to take down such videos.

The relationship between the Met and YouTube has been described as a "collaboration" and "enhanced partnership working." Since 2018, when the Met began working directly with YouTube, the number of referrals and removals has increased significantly. YouTube has stated that it is committed to helping music grow and thrive but strictly prohibits videos that promote violence. They work closely with organizations such as the Met Police and National Crime Agency to understand local context. The speed at which videos are removed, often within hours, highlights the close monitoring of online activity by the Met and YouTube's responsiveness to the Met's requests.

The Met Police and YouTube's efforts to monitor and remove music videos of rap and drill artists show the significant increase in police surveillance of online activities and the willingness of platforms like YouTube to cooperate with the police. The increasing number of referrals and removals of music videos suggests the police's continued focus on linking rap music and violence.

RESTRICTED WHEN COMPLETE

PROMOTION EVENT RISK ASSESSMENT FORM 696

The use of this Form is voluntary. However, it is noted that the completion of this Form may be a licence

Please complete this section to enable Clubs and Vice Unit to monitor the use of this Form.	
Is completing Form 696 for Promoted Events a condition on the premises license?	Yes No
PLEASE NOTE - The use of this Form is not primarily intended for a live music event. If you are using this form for a live music event please give your reasons why in the box.	

condition on some premises licence. In that case the completion of this Form is mandatory in accordance with the premises operating licence.

Recommended guidance to music event organisers, management of licence premises or event promoter on when to complete Form 696 is where you hold an event that is –
* Promoted / advertised to the public at any time before the event, and
* predominantly features DJs or MCs performing to a recorded backing track, and
* runs anytime between the hours of 10pm and 4am, and
* is in a nightclub or a large public house.

The recommended guidance does not restrict the use of the Form solely to any specific event. Event managers and promoters may, if they wish, use it for events not strictly covered by the guidance. The Metropolitan Police Service will aim to give appropriate support and advice to ensure a safe event.

Form 696, introduced by the Metropolitan Police in London in 2005, was a risk assessment aimed at promoters and organizers of music events featuring DJs or MCs. However, the form was criticized for its racist tone and the disproportionate impact it had on genres favoured by Black and Asian teenagers, such as grime, rap, drill and bashment, Although filling out the form was described as "voluntary," promoters who did not submit it 14 days in advance of their event found their license refused, and even those who did often found their night shut down or refused a license for inadequate or unexplained reasons. The questions on the form included details of all performers, such as their stage and real names, addresses, and phone numbers, and questions about the ethnicity of the audience.

There were widespread objections to Form 696 from musicians, promoters, bands, and the Equality and Human Rights Commission. Feargal Sharkey, former Undertones singer and head of the organization UK Music, gave evidence to the Department for Culture, Media, and Sport in 2008 on the discriminatory nature of the form. In 2009, the form was revised, and questions regarding telephone numbers, music styles, and audience ethnicity were removed, but the form itself remained in place.

In 2017, London Mayor Sadiq Khan scrapped Form 696 entirely and replaced it with a "voluntary partnership approach" for venues and promoters, with the hope that venues would willingly share information to allow for the safety of attendees. However, it was found that similar forms were being used in other police forces around the country, including Leicestershire, West Yorkshire, and Hertfordshire.

The controversy around Form 696 demonstrates the need for an inclusive and equitable approach to event risk assessment that prioritizes public safety without stifling artistic expression or diversity in the UK's music scene. It is a positive step that the form was finally scrapped and that a new approach was introduced, but it is essential that other police forces follow suit to prevent a similar disproportionate impact on certain genres and communities.

Case Study: The Impact Of Drill Music On Youth Culture: Krept & Konan's Short Film

Krept & Konan, two prominent artists from South London, released a 10-minute short film in 2019 aimed at combating the misconception that drill songs are the root cause of violence in society. The film, directed by Rapman, charts the story of an individual who turns to drill rapping as a way to escape a life of drug dealing and incarceration.

The release of the film was accompanied by a panel debate featuring prominent voices from the drill scene and beyond. Drill music, which originated in Chicago, has become popularized in the UK since 2017. However, the genre has faced criticism and police crackdown, with criminal behaviour orders (CBOs) being used to restrict the performance of certain songs and ban drill-affiliated groups from certain areas. The police have argued that the lyrics in drill music are associated with gang-related violence, leading to the ban on some songs.

Krept & Konan believe that the portrayal of drill music in the media is unjustified, and it is being unfairly vilified. In an opinion piece published in The Guardian, Konan argued that drill music honestly depicts the violence that he, and others, have experienced and doesn't fuel further violent crime. Instead, it has served as a source of empowerment and inspiration for many young people. The pair felt that the only way to combat these misconceptions was by releasing a film that shows the true impact of drill music on the lives of individuals.

Directed by Rapman, the short film charts the story of an individual who, after dealing drugs and going to jail, begins to experience a better life through drill rapping. The film features two endings, one in which the protagonist's song is taken off YouTube, forcing him to return to drug dealing, resulting in his death, and the other in which his YouTube channel becomes a huge success. The film is intended to show the impact that a ban on drill music can have on the lives of individuals and communities. The film launch was accompanied by a panel debate featuring prominent voices from the drill scene and beyond, including George the Poet, Rapman, Krept & Konan, drill artist Headie One, and human rights lawyer, Jude Bunting. The panel discussed the different tactics used by the police to crack down on the genre and the future of the drill scene.

The release of Krept & Konan's short film and accompanying panel debate highlights the impact that drill music has on youth culture and the negative consequences that can result from a ban on the genre. The film serves as a powerful reminder of the importance of representation and the role that music can play in shaping the lives of individuals and communities. Despite the challenges faced by the drill scene, the panellists were steadfast in their belief that the drill scene will continue to prosper and that those who are part of it will continue to shape the future of music and youth culture.

Case Study: Lowkey And The Pro-Israel Campaign

Kareem Dennis, also known as Lowkey, is a British-Iraqi rapper and Palestine solidarity campaigner. He has been a vocal advocate for Palestinian rights and has been critical of Israel's policies towards Palestine.

In 2010, Lowkey released a track titled "Long Live Palestine Part 2," which features artists including Palestinian hip-hop group DAM, British Palestinian artist Shadia Mansour, and Iraqi-Canadian rapper Narcy. The song has been the target of a pro-Israel campaign to have it removed from streaming platforms, with Spotify being the primary target.

In April 2021, a pro-Israel group believed to be affiliated with the Israeli government, called for the removal of Lowkey's music from Spotify. The group is known as the Britain Israel Communications and Research Centre (BICOM) and has worked closely with the Israeli Ministry of Strategic Affairs. Lowkey described the campaign as an "own goal for the apartheid regime" and denounced the attempt to silence him.

Lowkey's campaign has received widespread support from dozens of musicians and celebrities. A letter of support, signed by various high-profile artists including Wretch 32, Ghetts, Anwar Hadid, Michael Malarkey, Roger Waters, and Charlie Sloth, was sent to Spotify and other streaming platforms. The letter calls on the platforms not to bow to pressure from groups seeking to silence Lowkey and defends his right to free expression. The letter also criticizes the coordinated smear campaign against Lowkey, which they claim is an attempt to demonize, defame, and de-platform him. The artists who signed the letter also highlight the important issues that Lowkey raises in his music and his advocacy work for Palestinian rights.

Lowkey's case highlights the ongoing struggle for free expression and the right to advocate for Palestinian rights without facing backlash from pro-Israel groups. The support he has received from other artists and celebrities is an important reminder that solidarity is crucial in the fight for justice and human rights. The letter of support also demonstrates that pressure groups seeking to silence activists will not succeed, and that the voices of those advocating for a just and peaceful resolution to the conflict will continue to be heard.

Mental Health And Music

The industry is a highly demanding and competitive field, and many musicians and industry professionals struggle with mental health issues. With the long hours in the studio and rampant culture of substance use, that is often associated with the industry, we have a recipe for disaster if artist are not taking care of their mental health and their teams around are not protecting them and encouraging healthy habits.

An example of this is the case of Tim Bergling also known as Avicii, a highly successful DJ and music producer, who struggled with mental health issues throughout his career. In an interview with The Hollywood Reporter, Avicii's family stated that he was "an over-achieving perfectionist who travelled, worked, and performed at a pace that led to extreme stress." Avicii had spoken of his mental health struggles in his documentary Avicii: True Stories, only to have them seemingly dismissed by his management. He struggled with anxiety and depression and eventually took his own life in 2018.

Avicii's suicide sparked an industry-wide conversation about the wellbeing of artists, and influential music summit IMS Ibiza announced that its 2018 edition would focus on mental health. It also launched a three-day wellness retreat, Remedy State, which featured lectures from doctors, nature walks, and breathing workshops. "Avicii's death happened in the middle of preparations for Remedy State," says IMS co-founder Ben Turner. "It suddenly felt like everybody was prepared to talk openly about these issues. It's encouraged people to be much more open-minded [about mental health] and understand that even if you're the most successful person on the planet, you can still be the most unhappy."

Musicians and industry professionals may not have access to mental health services or may be hesitant to seek help due to the stigma surrounding mental illness. This can lead to individuals suffering in silence and not getting the help they need. To address the issue of mental health in music, there needs to be more support and resources available for musicians and industry professionals. This can include providing access to mental health services, creating a more supportive and understanding work environment, and raising awareness about the importance of mental health.

One example of this is the Music Support charity, which is a UK-based organization that provides confidential help and support for those in the music sector struggling with mental health issues. It offers a 24-hour helpline, counselling services, and support groups, as well as providing information and resources on mental health and addiction.

UK Artist Ramz, brought his own perspective to the issue of mental health, in particular suicide, with his track "Think twice about Suicide". In this track, Ramz is open about his personal struggles with mental health and encourages others to have conversations about their own battles. The music video, directed by Kirx, features real-life fans who joined Ramz at the video shoot, representing strength, perseverance and healing. The video shoot was an open call on social media and the result was an emotive visual that represents the struggles of mental health and encourages people to open up about their own battles. Through this track and video, Ramz has shown that it is possible to overcome mental health struggles and encourages others to do the same.

Pro Tip: Healthy Habits

Maintaining healthy habits as a music artist is crucial for overall well-being and creativity. Planning ahead by packing healthy snacks and meals for tours and rehearsals can ensure that you have nutritious options even when on the move. Staying hydrated is equally important, as drinking plenty of water throughout the day can keep your body energized and your mind sharp.

Spending time in nature is a valuable practice for music artists. Regular breaks away from stressful environments can positively impact mental and emotional well-being. Taking time to reset and detach from the hustle and bustle of the music industry can help break patterns of stress and tension, allowing for a more regulated and relaxed state of mind.

Mindfulness breaks are essential for combatting the fast-paced nature of the music industry. Engaging in activities like meditation, yoga, or simply focusing on your breath for a few minutes can help you stay grounded and cantered amidst the busyness. These moments of mindfulness foster focus and clarity, enabling you to stay connected to your creative pursuits.

Collaborating with other artists and creatives can be a great source of inspiration and motivation. Setting aside regular time for collaboration, whether through joint projects or idea-sharing sessions, can invigorate your creativity and offer valuable feedback on your work.

Incorporating regular physical exercise into your routine can have a positive impact on both mental health and creativity. Whether it's a morning run, a yoga class, or a gym session, physical activity can help you stay energized, focused, and provide an outlet for stress.

Journaling is a powerful tool for processing thoughts and emotions, as well as staying inspired and motivated. Setting aside time for reflective writing on your life, the pressure you're experiencing, your creative process, brainstorming new ideas, and simply just expressing your thoughts and feelings without judgement can keep you on track with your creative goals and serve as a valuable resource for future projects.

Exploring alternative outlets for creative expression is essential for a well-rounded artistic journey. Experimenting with different forms of art, such as painting, writing, photography, or cooking, can provide a refreshing break from the demands of your music career and reignite your inspiration. Engaging in other forms of art allows you to connect with your emotions, find new perspectives, and develop new skills that can enrich your music.

By incorporating healthy habits into your daily life, you can prevent burnout and maintain a balanced and fulfilling music career. Taking care of your physical and mental well-being, engaging in mindfulness practices, collaborating with others, and exploring alternative outlets for creative expression can lead to increased creativity, productivity, and overall satisfaction in your music journey. Prioritizing your health and well-being as a music artist is not only beneficial for your personal life but also for the quality and longevity of your music career.

Maintaining Work-Life Balance and Avoiding Burnout

Achieving and sustaining a work-life balance is a considerable challenge for musicians and professionals. With unpredictable hours and the relentless pursuit of meeting artistic goals and industry expectations, the risk of burnout looms large. Striking a harmonious equilibrium is essential not only for maintaining creative output but also for safeguarding physical and mental health.

Work-life balance serves as the linchpin for those in the industry. It acts as a protective barrier against the overwhelming pressure that can lead to stress and fatigue. When out of balance, creative minds may find themselves grappling with exhaustion, stress, and a decline in both work quality and overall well-being.

Crafting a structured schedule proves to be an effective strategy for navigating the intricate dance between work and personal life. Freelancers, in particular, benefit from this approach, setting designated work hours, assigning tasks based on priority, and embracing regular breaks for rejuvenation. Leveraging productivity apps and time-tracking tools offers valuable support in maintaining organization and efficiency.

Establishing clear client boundaries and efficient communication channels is paramount in preserving work-life harmony. Channels such as email or messaging platforms are excellent tools for managing client interactions. Clearly defining response times and notifying clients of working hours and planned downtime play a vital role in managing workloads and maintaining boundaries. The importance of a comprehensive contract cannot be overstated, as it solidifies expectations and commitments between freelancers and clients.

Recognizing the early signs of burnout is pivotal for timely intervention. Burnout manifests in various ways, including persistent fatigue, diminished motivation and productivity, detachment, and mood swings. Preventing burnout necessitates prioritizing physical and mental well-being. Adequate rest, regular exercise, and a balanced diet are fundamental components of self-care. Engaging in non-work-related activities that bring joy and relaxation also contributes significantly to overall health.

Achieving a healthy work-life balance calls for a mindful allocation of time between professional and personal realms. Prioritizing tasks in alignment with individual goals and values can facilitate this balance. When feasible, delegating tasks lightens the load, allowing for more personal time. Transparent communication with clients regarding availability and workloads is indispensable in managing expectations and preventing overextension.

Effective time management techniques and tools empower professionals to boost productivity and efficiency without compromising their work-life equilibrium. Striking this balance is not only vital for sustaining quality work but also for nurturing personal growth and fulfilment.

Maintaining a work-life balance stands as a cornerstone of a flourishing and enduring career in the music industry. With a structured schedule, clear client boundaries, early burnout recognition, and a focus on well-being, musicians and industry professionals can sidestep burnout's pitfalls and cultivate both creativity and productivity for the long haul.

Setting Boundaries

Setting boundaries is an essential stress-management strategy that musicians should prioritize in their professional lives. As artists often face demanding schedules and high expectations, it becomes crucial for them to define limits on their workload and create time for activities that nurture their physical and mental well-being.

To set boundaries effectively, musicians can adopt various practices. One significant aspect is learning to say no to unreasonable requests or demands. By recognizing that their time and energy are valuable resources that should be managed wisely, musicians can avoid overcommitting themselves and becoming overwhelmed.

Another vital aspect of setting boundaries is limiting their availability. Musicians need to allocate sufficient time for personal and self-care activities by defining specific hours for work and personal time. Prioritizing mental and physical well-being is essential for sustaining a successful and fulfilling musical career. By understanding that self-care is not a luxury but a necessity, musicians can invest in themselves, ensuring they remain in peak condition to face the challenges of their profession.

Musicians should openly discuss their needs and limitations to foster a supportive and understanding working environment. This open communication can lead to better teamwork and healthier relationships within the industry. Implementing a structured schedule or routine is another effective way to set boundaries. Having a clear framework for activities, allows musicians to manage their time more efficiently, ensuring they have time for both work and personal life.

Social media and technology can be both a boon and a bane for musicians. While these platforms offer valuable promotional opportunities, they can also become sources of stress and distraction. Setting boundaries with social media and technology usage is essential. Musicians should recognize the importance of disconnecting from these platforms when necessary to avoid unnecessary stress and distractions.

In times of stress, seeking emotional support from friends, family, or a therapist can be beneficial. Having someone to confide in can alleviate feelings of loneliness and empower musicians to better handle stress. Additionally, connecting with peers or industry professionals can offer valuable insights, camaraderie, and mentorship throughout their musical journey.

Setting boundaries and practicing stress-management strategies are crucial for musicians to lead fulfilling and sustainable careers in music. By prioritizing their well-being and maintaining healthy boundaries, musicians can navigate the challenges of their profession with resilience and grace.

Public Pressure / Calling Out

With the music industry being so small, professionalism and reputation are major factors in your progression. Artist are the face of their brand, there's no company to hide behind. Your reputation is your currency so make sure you value it. It invariably arrives in the room before you do in the form of recommendations from fans, colleagues and clients. This is a demanding sector to work in, often with long hours and away from home. Don't underestimate how important it is being someone with whom people can get on well.

Bad industry practice used to be a private conversation, the sort of thing shared between professionals over a coffee, with a warning not to work with someone in industry that another has been mistreated by. However, larger companies in particular tend to hide their behaviour behind settlements, non-disclosure agreements and threats. What members of the industry have in their favour now, though, is the internet.

Anything you say on social media, especially public platforms like Twitter, Instagram or public Facebook pages, can and will affect how you are seen publicly with there being a multitude of social post from various scandals we can use a reference. However, if you have been treated badly by a client/collaborator - for instance, if you haven't received payment or have had your intellectual property stolen - and you've exhausted all other legal and professional avenues in order to resolve the situation, the Social Media Call Out can be a powerful tool in trying to bring about justice.

If you do go down this route, be very careful with your language and framing: state facts, not emotions; be clear what resolution you want, what specific amounts of money you're owed and the ways in which you have tried to resolve this situation already; tag in professional bodies that may be able to apply pressure for you.

Even better is to take the issue to a union, as they will be able to offer you access to legal advice and may be able to bring the situation to light more effectively than you can alone. Companies are very quick to claim defamation which can land you in legal trouble, so legal advice can be invaluable. Speaking publicly about a former employer, collaborator or client of course means you are unlikely to work with them again. But on the other hand, what good is a client or company that doesn't pay you, or steals your work?

Case Study: The Closure Of Radar Radio

Radar Radio was a London-based online radio station that was known for its shows highlighting new and established musical talent. The station had a reputation as a breeding ground for the next generation of musicians and broadcasters and had past guests that included Cardi B, M.I.A, and JME. The station was owned by Ollie Ashley and mainly appealed to the youth across different racial devices, and especially people of colour.

In April of 2018, Radar Radio faced accusations of internal exploitation and mistreatment of staff. Local DJ Pxssy Palace accused the station of stealing ideas from people of colour and exploiting marginalized groups for "capitalist purposes." Additionally, accusations of sexual harassment surfaced, with claims of female employees being inappropriately touched while on duty. These accusations were swept under the carpet under the pretext of the confidentiality agreement.

Furthermore, the station was engrossed in accusations of sexual harassment. For instance, a former producer, Ashtart Al-Hurra, published a blog post detailing what she had experienced at Radar Radio. In her post, she claims to have been sexually harassed by DJs at the station and associated events. On top of this, some of her colleagues were rumoured to have slept with some of them. The station also had financial struggles, with its balance sheet indicating that Radar owed its creditors more than £4m, with this sum falling due just within one year of the period that ended in April 2017. Out of this amount, around £3.6m was owed to Mash Holdings, Radar's parent company, and over £400,000 to trade creditors.

In response to the accusations, Radar Radio suspended broadcasting on April 16th, 2018, with the promise to investigate the allegations. However, the station faced backlash from the wider community for its handling of these issues. Many criticized the station for not taking immediate and decisive action to address the accusations and for failing to create a safe and inclusive work environment. The station was also criticized for not adequately addressing accusations of sexual harassment and for not adequately protecting the rights and well-being of its employees.

The suspension of broadcasting led to a loss of revenue and a decline in listener numbers, resulting in a decline in overall profitability. The financial struggles of the company, in addition to the negative publicity caused by the accusations, ultimately led to the failure and closure of the station.

The closure of Radar Radio had a significant impact on the music and broadcasting industry, as it was a platform that provided a space for emerging talent and diverse voices. The accusations and subsequent closure of the station served as a reminder of the need for accountability and transparency in the media industry and the importance of creating safe and inclusive work environments for all employees. The station management did not release any official communication about the reopening or resolution of the mentioned issues

AFTERWORD

Conclusion

The music industry is a dynamic and challenging field that requires individuals to possess a unique combination of talent, knowledge, and business acumen. However, success in this industry is not solely determined by one's natural abilities or opportunities, but rather by the mindset and strategies employed in pursuit of one's goals.

Through the knowledge and education provided in this book, individuals are equipped with the tools necessary to overcome the barriers that can prevent a successful career in music. By embracing a growth mindset, focusing on self-improvement, and leveraging the power of technology and digital platforms, individuals can transcend the limitations of traditional roles and become the best version of themselves.

The skills discussed in this book are transferable and applicable to various industries and roles, especially in the digital age where individuals are expected to play multiple roles. The strategies and insights presented in this book can be applied to various contexts, enabling individuals to navigate the complexities of modern-day work environments and achieve their desired outcomes.

At its core, this book is not only about succeeding in the music business but about developing a mindset and approach to business that enables individuals to realize their full potential and understand how to utilize their opportunities to the maximum. It is a call to action to leverage one's unique talents, and to forge a path towards personal and professional growth.

So, let this book serve as a guide to not only navigate the business but to also foster a sense of purpose, direction, and passion in your career and life. Remember that success is not a destination but a journey, and by embracing a growth mindset and pursuing your goals with dedication, perseverance, and innovation, you can achieve greatness in all aspects of your life.

References

Page 2: Uk Music timeline:
https://www.imdb.com/name/nm0891038/
https://eu.dispatch.com/story/entertainment/local/2019/04/02/a-great-debate/5506165007/
https://open.spotify.com/artist/1u7kkVrr14iBvrpYnZILJR
https://www.udiscovermusic.com/news/spice-girls-wannabe25-ep/
https://www.huffingtonpost.co.uk/entry/glastonbury-2019-stormzy-headline-set_uk_5d170b06e4b03d61163bc1db
https://www.rollingstone.com/music/music-news/pinkpantheress-lollapalooza-video-1389011/

Page 3: Central Cee - Euro vision: https://www.youtube.com/watch?v=ZlnLvLDP4Zg&ab_channel=CentralCee

Page 3: Skepta Portfolio graphic designed by VZA

Page 4: Drake - https://people.com/drake-disappointed-to-have-no-bras-thrown-at-him-during-montreal-concert-7562400

Burna boy - https://www.gq.com/story/burna-boy-african-king-profile

Giggs - https://www.complex.com/music/a/james-keith/giggs-now-or-never

Jorja Smith - https://indie-mag.com/2018/09/jorja-smith-interview/

J hus - https://www.thefader.com/2023/06/29/j-hus-announces-new-album-beautiful-and-brutal-yard

Page 6: Central Cee x Dave - Sprinter - https://www.newwavemagazine.com/single-post/dave-central-cee-solidify-their-dominance-in-uk-rap-with-split-decision-review

Page 12: Industry Insight Thor Sutherland: https://www.instagram.com/p/CZfF6p6MZOF/?hl=en

Page 15: G Frsh Chivas campaign: https://www.youtube.com/watch?v=l7LwO5CCe3c

Page 17: Hannah Edmonds: https://www.linkedin.com/in/hannah-edmonds-63a3b8193/?originalSubdomain=uk

Page 19 - https://www.forbes.com/sites/tommywilliams1/2020/10/28/meet-glyn-aikins--riki-bleau-the-duo-behind-the-scenes-driving-the-success-of-the-uk-rap-industry/

Page 31: Kano Press Photo: https://press.atlanticrecords.com/kano

Top Boy soundtrack cover art: https://www.complex.com/music/2019/09/top-boy-soundtrack

Kano in top boy: https://thetab.com/uk/2019/10/01/these-are-all-the-hidden-meanings-you-may-have-missed-on-top-boy-127152

Tower block cover art:https://en.wikipedia.org/wiki/Tower_Block_%28film%29

Page 32: J cole Born sinner:
https://www.reddit.com/r/Jcole/comments/god7iq/born_sinner_cover_in_black/

Page 32: The artist way: https://www.goodreads.com/review/show/198277640

Page 34: Sphero Beatz: https://www.instagram.com/spherobeatz/

Page 36: Steel bangles: https://en.wikipedia.org/wiki/Steel_Banglez

Page 37: Fumez The Engineer https://twitter.com/FumezEngineer/status/1125115386331107328

Page 38: Black box Logo: https://www.instagram.com/blackboxhub/

Page 44: Mikey Joe: https://www.instagram.com/mikeyjoemadethis/?hl=en
Page 51: Ed Sheeran, potter payer, Loyal Carner
https://en.wikipedia.org/wiki/Ed_Sheeran
https://www.theguardian.com/music/2022/jul/19/loyle-carner-coyle-larner-hate-hip-hop
https://www.independent.co.uk/arts-entertainment/music/features/potter-payper-interview-album-b2311114.html
Page 57: Chance the rapper: https://www.theguardian.com/music/2016/nov/21/chance-the-rapper-review-resistance-is-futile-this-is-rap-as-a-religious-experience
Page 62: Kamille: https://marinaandthediamonds.fandom.com/wiki/Kamille
Page 79: Aj Tracey: https://ra.co/dj/ajtracey
Page 82: Craig Evans: https://www.amsterdam-dance-event.nl/en/artists-speakers/craig-evans/14545/
Page 86: Despa Robison: https://nationbillions.com/0121-the-rise-rise-of-birmingham
Page 93: Bugzy Malone: https://www.livenation.co.uk/artist-bugzy-malone-673814
Page 108: Ivorian Doll: https://www.hungertv.com/editorial/bow-down-meet-ivorian-doll-the-queen-of-drill/
Page 117: John Sorzano: https://commons.wikimedia.org/wiki/File:John_O.Sorzano.jpg
Page 121: Chamillionaire: http://t1.gstatic.com/licensed-image?q=tbn:ANd9GcTyHJ12BB-4OKtRO_bsLRJlwoD7PpXz37imnmE9aAsQt89hzNEqURkwhxiFoR5dzMq8PZupKkhySAT8GZU
Page 122: Rihanna: Https://www. washingtonpost.com/ne ws/arts - and- entertainment/wp/20 15/0 7/05/rea sons- we- think- bb hmm-is-about-rihannas-former-accountant-peter-gounis/
Page 124: Sync Licensing
https://by.tribuna.com/tribuna/blogs/football/1407029/
https://traxion.gg/in-depth-speed-race-gameplay-trailer-for-need-for-speed-unbound-released/
https://consequence.net/2018/02/kendrick-lamar-releases-black-panther-soundtrack-stream/
https://www.thissongslaps.com/2012/12/adele-skyfall-wiggz-wonz-young-piff-sandor-trap-remix/
Page 127: Vince staples and Black panther
https://time.com/4420739/black-panther-movie-cast/
https://www.np r.org/2 017/ 04/02/ 522 236 735/vince-staples-we-live-in-a-space-where-your-name-isnt-enough

Page 128: Central cee x Trapstar: https://www.aliexpress.com/item/1005004937018297.html
https://www.instagram.com/centralcee/?hl=en
Page 129: Ephraim Yeboah: https://www.linkedin.com/in/ephraim-yeboah-04a1b7136/
Page 133: Aj tracey x Tottenham:
https://www.spotern.com/en/spot/instagram/ajtracey/323514/the-down-jacket-black-canada-goose-worn-by-aj-tracey-on-his-account-instagram-atajtracey
Page 134: Skepta x havana: https://havana-club.com/en/project/havana-club-x-skepta-2-0/
https://hypebeast.com/2020/7/havana-club-skepta-bottle-collaboration
Page 135: Krept and konan x Puma: https://pausemag.co.uk/2016/05/puma-x-krept-and-konan-exclusive-collaboration/
Page 141: J2K: https://genius.com/artists/J2k
Page 142: Fredo x kick game: https://positiveworldonline.com/category/music/page/3/
Page 144: Krept: https://www.independent.co.uk/topic/krept
Page 148: Marketing and branding: https://www.thepitldn.com/pitnews/tag/Skepta
https://www.bayy.co.uk/central-cee-wild-west-takeover
https://en.wikipedia.org/wiki/No_Thank_You_%28album%29
Page 149: Brand identity:
https://www.pirelli.com/global/en-ww/life/interview-with-pharrel-williams
https://www.cbsnews.com/news/rick-rubin-60-minutes-2023-01-15/
https://www.vogue.com/article/virgil-abloh-biography-career-timeline
Page 150: Shop window
https://fomoblog.com/2018/11/16/some-come-to-complexcon-for-the-music-we-came-for-the-art/
https://www.vogue.co.uk/news/article/rihanna-new-album-vogue-interview
https://www.standard.co.uk/showbiz/ksi-in-real-life-prime-video-louis-theroux-b1055583.html
Page 151: Virgil Abloh Design language: https://www.nssmag.com/en/fashion/28147/virgil-abloh-for-italian-gen-z
Virgil at Qatar museums: Creator: Craig Barritt | Credit: Getty Images for Qatar Museums Copyright: 2021 Getty Images
Page 154: Emma Rose: https://www.bbc.co.uk/programmes/m000vr7q
Page 161: Tik Tok Best Practices PDF - https://www.tiktok.com/
Page 161: AJ Tracey - https://www.dailymail.co.uk/sport/football/article-11100531/British-rapper-AJ-Tracey-drops-cheeky-tease-brand-new-Tottenham-kit-TikTok-feed.html
Page 161: Tia Corine - https://www.tiktok.com/@janellejs/video/7181679566295928110?lang=ar
Page 172: Wikipedia: https://www.pngitem.com/middle/iTRoxJ_wikipedia-logo-logo-wikipedia-png-transparent-png/
Page 181: Stormzy gang sign and prayers:
https://www.theguardian.com/music/2017/feb/26/stormzy-gang-signs-prayer-review
Page 182: Central Cee: https://www.bayy.co.uk/central-cee-wild-west-takeover
Page 184: Adele: https://www.harpersbazaar.com/celebrity/latest/a32387752/adele-black-dress-birthday-instagram-photo/

Page 187: Channel AKA https://www.bbc.com/news/newsbeat-44411966
Stormzy Mel made me do it - https://www.youtube.com/watch?v=2litzsFCwkA&ab_channel=Stormzy

Page 190: J-mal: https://www.instagram.com/itsjmal/

Page 193: Video Treatment examples designed by A-KRST

Page 194: Big Watch EPK Site https://www.instagram.com/bigwatchab/?hl=en

Page 195: Jatz da Kid Press Kit: https://www.instagram.com/jatzdakid/?hl=en
Sorzano Press Kit https://www.instagram.com/sorzano.3xn/?hl=en

Page 197: Joegrind Press kit: https://www.instagram.com/joegrindsn1/?hl=en

Page 199: Dj Limelight:
https://www.bbc.co.uk/programmes/profiles/2nVmmv9L360gqywTgjcfPvl/dj-limelight

Page 205: Millie may:https://www.instagram.com/__milliemay__/

Page 212: Big narstie: https://www.theguardian.com/lifeandstyle/2018/jul/14/big-narstie-scared-of-fish-rapper-tv-host-interview

Page 214: https://www.dailymail.co.uk/news/article-11556109/Heartbroken-partner-pays-tribute-second-Brixton-O2-victim-crushed-death.html
https://www.independent.co.uk/arts-entertainment/music/news/asake-o2-brixton-tribute-b2396487.html

Page 221: Behind The Scenes - Fredo's Unfinished Business Album Launch - https://www.youtube.com/watch?v=wGLSM9DwdMk

Page 224: Lancey Foux: https://www.nme.com/features/music-interviews/lancey-foux-live-evil-kanye-west-3101743

Page 229: The Beatles https://www.thetimes.co.uk/article/julian-lennon-to-sell-beatles-memorabilia-as-nfts-55b080c8q
Kings of leon https://twitter.com/YellowHeartNFT/status/1367870780416004099
Aitch https://blog.cryptoflies.com/rapper-aitch-launches-nft-collection-on-limewire-to-celebrate-the-release-of-his-debut-album-close-to-home/
The Weekend https://www.revolt.tv/article/2021-04-03/56362/the-weeknds-acephalous-nft-features-new-music-and-limited-edition-art/
Grimes https://news.artnet.com/art-world/grimes-sold-nft-art-1948177

Page 226: Ard Ardz https://opulous.medium.com/opulous-announces-patek-myself-s-nft-sale-and-artwork-nft-collection-wi th-ard-adz-c07da6a54746

Page 237: https://www.clashmusic.com/news/yizzy-jme-salute-the-art-on-new-single-grime/

Page 244: Childish Gambino: https://www.newyorker.com/culture/culture-desk/the-carnage-and-chaos-of-childish-gambinos-this-is-america

Page 247: Krept and konan: https://www.complex.com/music/2019/06/krept-and-konan-diane-abbott-ban-drill

Page 248: Lowkey: https://www.vice.com/en/article/597mdn/lowkey-return-interview-uk-rap-2019

Page 254: Radar Radio: https://www.thewire.co.uk/news/50606/allegations-made-against-radar-radio

About The Authors

Kieran Trestain

Kieran Trestain is a highly accomplished Transformational Business Leader, known behind the scenes for his expertise in music industry through breaking new artists and creating cultural moments. With over a decade of experience negotiating recording deals, Kieran has amassed an impressive track record of securing contracts for his clients. In addition to his work in the music industry, Kieran has also established successful businesses across a range of industries.

Kieran Trestain's personal journey is a testament to the power of self-belief and resourcefulness. Despite leaving school without any qualifications and struggling with basic literacy, Kieran's unwavering determination and entrepreneurial spirit propelled him to achieve remarkable success in the music industry and beyond. Leveraging his expertise in business development, he has helped numerous companies achieve new levels of growth and success. Kieran's broad skillset and diverse experience make him a unique asset to any organization seeking to innovate and expand.

Kieran's personal story serves as a powerful reminder that success is not solely defined by formal qualifications or credentials, but by the willingness to learn, adapt, and persevere in the face of challenges. His journey is an inspiration to anyone seeking to overcome adversity and achieve their goals.

K. Trestain

"Success isn't just about winning or losing, but how you react to outcomes. A bad reaction to a win causes long-term loss; a good reaction to a loss results in eventual victory."

Kieran Trestain

Ricardo Sorzano

Ricardo Sorzano's journey is a testament to the power of determination and a willingness to learn. While pursuing an international business degree, Ricardo started managing artist and organizing events overseas, inadvertently bringing a new style of events to the south of France. After returning to Manchester, he established a creative agency and platform to provide a professional image and storytelling aspect for emerging artists in the UK.

Ricardo went on to collaborate with cultural institutions on short films, direct campaigns for major department stores and record labels, and produce multiple musical works. His work in the creative industry led him to broker high-value partnerships for international music acts during their world tours, generating over six figures in additional revenue with brand partners.

Ricardo takes pride in his ability to communicate and be the bridge between generations. He believes in the power of self-improvement and resourcefulness, making it his mission to impact as many lives as possible with the tools and knowledge they need to achieve success. Through his journey, Ricardo connected with Kieran, and together they have ventured into the world of business, collaborating with industries such as commercial space, sustainability, and entertainment to create innovative partnerships and collaborations. Their work has broken new ground and set new standards for success in these industries.

Ricardo's personal journey is an inspiration to anyone looking to overcome challenges and make a positive impact in their community.

"Be intentional, with the impact you seek to have on the world. Strive to positively effect as many lives as possible, to create a domino effect of change.
-
Ricardo Sorzano

Printed in Great Britain
by Amazon